T0402370

Arabic and Persian Manuscripts in the Birnbaum Collection, Toronto

Islamic Manuscripts and Books

Christoph Rauch (*Staatsbibliothek zu Berlin*)
Karin Scheper (*Leiden University*)
Arnoud Vrolijk (*Leiden University*)

Invited editor for this volume

Jan Just Witkam (*Leiden University*)

VOLUME 18

The titles published in this series are listed at *brill.com/imb*

Arabic and Persian Manuscripts in the Birnbaum Collection, Toronto

A Brief Catalogue

By

Eleazar Birnbaum

TUTA SUB AEGIDE PALLAS · 1683 ·

BRILL

LEIDEN | BOSTON

Cover illustration: [*Kitāb al-khayl*], ca. 5–6/11–12th century; f. 80ᵃ: see Arabic catalogue, no. 11, p. 25–27.

Library of Congress Cataloging-in-Publication Data

Birnbaum, Eleazar, 1929- compiler.
Title: Arabic and Persian manuscripts in the Birnbaum Collection, Toronto : a brief catalogue / by Eleazar Birnbaum.
Description: Leiden ; Boston : Brill, [2019] | Series: Islamic manuscripts and books, ISSN 1877-9964 ; volume 18 | Includes bibliographical references and indexes.
Identifiers: LCCN 2019011691 (print) | LCCN 2019016614 (ebook) | ISBN 9789004389670 (ebook) | ISBN 9789004388215 (hardback : alk. paper)
Subjects: LCSH: Birnbaum, Eleazar, 1929—Library–Manuscripts–Catalogs. | Manuscripts, Arabic–Ontario–Toronto–Catalogs. | Manuscripts, Persian–Ontario–Toronto–Catalogs.
Classification: LCC Z6605.A6 (ebook) | LCC Z6605.A6 B57 2019 (print) | DDC 011/.30973541–dc23
LC record available at https://lccn.loc.gov/2019011691

Typeface for the Latin, Greek, and Cyrillic scripts: “Brill”. See and download: brill.com/brill-typeface.

ISSN 1877-9964
ISBN 978-90-04-38821-5 (hardback)
ISBN 978-90-04-38967-0 (e-book)

Copyright 2019 by Koninklijke Brill NV, Leiden, The Netherlands.
Koninklijke Brill NV incorporates the imprints Brill, Brill Hes & De Graaf, Brill Nijhoff, Brill Rodopi, Brill Sense, Hotei Publishing, mentis Verlag, Verlag Ferdinand Schöningh and Wilhelm Fink Verlag.
All rights reserved. No part of this publication may be reproduced, translated, stored in a retrieval system, or transmitted in any form or by any means, electronic, mechanical, photocopying, recording or otherwise, without prior written permission from the publisher.
Authorization to photocopy items for internal or personal use is granted by Koninklijke Brill NV provided that the appropriate fees are paid directly to The Copyright Clearance Center, 222 Rosewood Drive, Suite 910, Danvers, MA 01923, USA. Fees are subject to change.

This book is printed on acid-free paper and produced in a sustainable manner.

Contents

List of Illustrations VII

Catalogue

Arabic Manuscripts

Introduction to the Arabic Manuscripts 5

A Geography 10

B Language and Lexicography 13

C Literature: Poetry 41

D Literature: Prose 45

E Qur'ān 53

F Tafsīr 63

G Islām: Other (*Ḥadīth, ʿAqāʾid, Fiqh, Fatwā,* Eschatology, Prayer, etc.) 69

H Sufism 104

I Druze 107

J Ethics 109

K Encyclopedic; Sciences and Pseudosciences; Medicine; Mixed 112

L Ijāza 120

M Calligraphy 125

N Persian Philology 126

Persian Manuscripts

Introduction to the Persian Manuscripts 133

A History 137

B Literature 147

C Islam; Religion 171

D Ethics 175

E Language, Lexicography, and Prosody 180

F Encyclopedia 202

G Astrology 208

H Document 211

I Addendum: [*Majmūʿa*] 212

Bibliography and Sigla 215
Arabic Manuscripts: Author Index 220
Arabic Manuscripts: Title Index 221
Concordance of Arabic Manuscripts 222
Persian Manuscripts: Author Index 224
Persian Manuscripts: Title Index 225
Concordance of Persian Manuscripts 226

Illustrations

Arabic Manuscripts

1 No. 1 (A36). al-Bākūhī, ʿAbd al-Rashīd b. Ṣāliḥ, fl. 8/14th century, *Talkhīṣ al-āthar*. Copied 987/1579; f. 48^{b}–49^{a} 11

2 No. 3 (A33/I). al-Mubarrad, Muḥammad, d. 285/898, *Rasāʾil*. Copied 646/1248; 35^{b}–36^{a} 15

3 No. 4 (A33/II). al-Ḥarīrī, d. 516/1122, *Mulḥāt al-iʿrāb*. Owner's date 660/1262; f. 49^{b}–50^{a} 17

4 No. 8 (A21). ʿUthmān b. ʿUmar al-Mālikī, *Muqaddimatā al-taṣrīf wa al-khaṭṭ*. Ownership date 8/14th century 23

5 No. 11 (A10/I). [*Kitāb al-khayl*], ca. 5–6/11–12th century; f. 80^{a} 26

6 No. 22 (A20). al-Suyūṭī, Jalāl al-Dīn, d. 911/1505, *Maqāmāt*. Copied ca. 1031/1612; f. 1^{b}–2^{a} 46

7 No. 25 (P9). *Qurʾān*, parts of Sūras 9 and 10; with interlinear Persian translation. Copied 6–7/11–12th century; f. 2^{b}; 1^{a} 54

8 No. 31 (A18). al-Bayḍāwī, ʿAbdullāh b. ʿUmar, d. ca. 685/1286, *Anwār al-tanzīl*. [*Tafsīr*]. Copied ca. 8/14th century; f. 1b 64

9 No. 31 (A18). al-Bayḍāwī, ʿAbdullāh b. ʿUmar, d. ca. 685/1286, *Anwār al-tanzīl*. [*Tafsīr*]. Copied ca. 8/14th century; f. 1^{b}. Part of Mamlūk binding doublure, inscribed *alʿizz al-dāʾim wa al-iqbāl* 65

10 No. 35 (A26). [*Masāʾil wa ajwiba: ḥāshiya ʿalā kitāb fī uṣūl al-fiqh*]. Copied ca. 7/13th century; f. 1a 72

11 No. 36 (A27). [*Masāʾil wa ajwiba fī uṣūl al-fiqh al-Ḥanafī*]. Copied ca. 7/13th century; f. 4^{b} 75

12 No. 41 (A16). "al-Imām Shaykh al-Islām", *al-Jawāhir fī uṣūl al-dīn*, composed 570/1174/75. Copied [7]93/[13]91; f. 57^{b}–58^{a} 81

13 No. 42 (A24/I). [*Risāla fī yawm al-Qiyāma*]. An eschatological and apocalyptic historical work in rhymed prose and poetry, about events ranging from antiquity to the early 10/16th century; f. 40^{b}–41^{a} 83

14 No. 47 (A15). al-Kisāʾī, Muḥammad b. ʿAbdullāh, 5/11th century. *Kitāb al-malakūt*. Copied apparently in the author's lifetime; f. 1^{b}–2^{a} 92

15 No. 48 (A23a). al-Ṣaghānī, d. 650/1252. *Mashāriq al-anwār*. Copied 756/1355; f. 120^{b}–121^{a} 94

16 No. 48 (A23b). al-Ṣaghānī, d. 650/1252. *Mashāriq al-anwār*. Copied 756/1355. Fine Mamlūk flap binding, with repeat pattern of 6-pointed star within a hexagram 95

17 No. 49 (A29). ʿIyāḍ al-Yaḥṣubī, d. 544/1149. *al-Shifāʾ bi-taʿrīf ḥuqūq al-Muṣṭafā*. Copied 757/1356; f. 1^{b}–2^{a} 97

18 No. 50 (A25/I). al-Bābilī, Aḥmad, fl. 964/1557. *Muqaddima fī al-basmala wa al-ḥamdala*. Copied 964/1557; f. 32ᵇ–33ᵃ 100
19 No. 57 (A19). al-ʿĪshī, Muḥammad, d. 1016/1607. *Rawḍat al-ʿulamāʾ*. Copied 1031/1622; f. 1ᵇ 110

Persian Manuscripts

20 No. 1 (P1). Idrīs Bidlīsī, d. 926/1520. *Hasht bihisht*, f. 322ᵇ–323ᵃ. Copied early 10/16th century 138
21 No. 2 (P3). Shīrāzī, Sayyid Muḥammad, d. 1065/1655. *Tarkhānnāma*. f. 1ᵇ–2ᵃ. Copied 1097/1686 143
22 No. 4 (M4/III). Rashīd al-Dīn Vaṭvāṭ, d. 573 or 578/1177–1182. *Ḥadāʾiq al-siḥr fī daqāʾiq al-shiʿr*. f. 1ᵇ–2ᵃ. Copied late 6th or 7th/12–13th century 148
23 No. 12 (P4). Muʿammāʾī, Mīr Ḥusayn, d. 904/1499. *Risāla-i muʿammā*. f. 38ᵇ–39ᵃ. Copied ca. 905/1500 163
24 No. 13 (P5). Ṣāʾib Tabrīzī, d. 1087/1676. *Dīvān*. f. 1ᵃ. Copied 1092/1681 166
25 No. 16 (P9). Qurʾān with interlinear Persian translation; parts of Sūras 9 and 10. f. 2ᵇ; 1ᵃ. Copied ca. 6–7/12–13th century 172
26 No. 19 (P11). [*Akhlāqnāma*]. An unidentified old compendium of moral and religious advice. f. 30ᵇ–31ᵃ. Copied ca. 8–9/14–15th century 177
27 No. 20 (P7/I). Farāhī, d. 640/1242–1243. *Niṣāb al-ṣibyān*. f. 1ᵇ–2ᵃ. Copied ca. 10/16th century 181
28 No. 30 (P8). "Jahānnamā" [?]. An unidentified old encyclopedic work, f. 17ᵇ–18ᵃ. Copied ca. 7/13th century 203
29 No. 31 (P6). Kūshyār b. Labbān, fl. 4/10th century. f. 2ᵃ [left page]. *Tuḥfat al-ikhtiyārāt*. Copied ca. 7/13th century 209

Catalogue

Arabic Manuscripts

Introduction to the Arabic Manuscripts

Languages and classical travel literature were among my main interests as a high school student in England, especially books about the Middle East.* As for languages, I spent many happy childhood hours reveling in such works as *The Book of a Thousand Tongues*. My father Dr. Solomon A. Birnbaum was a multilingual philologist and a paleographer, and before I reached my teen years I persuaded him to teach me how to write my name in the Arabic script. At the age of 17 I enrolled in the BA course in Arabic at SOAS (the School of Oriental and African Studies) in the University of London (1947–1950). The Arabic material consisted entirely of classical Arabic texts, much of it poetry from the pre-Islamic period to Mutanabbī, and only from printed books—never from manuscripts. In my second year at SOAS, I also took the Diploma course in Hebrew Paleography, taught by my father, which consisted entirely of the study and analysis of photographs of the script in a wide range of old Hebrew manuscripts. On completing my degree in Arabic, and having become aware of the importance of the Ottoman Empire in Middle Eastern and European history, I took another degree at SOAS (1950–1953)—this one in Turkish (with Çaĝatay, and Persian, 1950–1953). One of my teachers, Cyril Mundy, would lend us (his students) original Turkish manuscripts of the 16th and 17th centuries from his own collection, to prepare passages to be analyzed and translated for his classes. This nourished my passion for manuscripts, which has continued to the present time as I approach my 90th birthday.

---

* I have published short descriptions of all the Islamic manuscripts in my collection, in three parts:

1. *Ottoman Turkish and Çaĝatay Manuscripts in Canada: a Union Catalogue of the Four Collections*. Leiden, Brill, 2015 (i-xxx-521 pages), describes 206 items in the Birnbaum collection, followed by the total of 71 MSS in the libraries of the University of Toronto, McGill University of Montreal, and the Royal Ontario Museum of Ontario.
2. "Persian Manuscripts in the Birnbaum Collection, Toronto: a Brief Catalogue" (in *Journal of Islamic Manuscripts*, vol. 8, 2017, pp. 144–217). Reprinted with the addition of several MSS, in the present volume, pages 212–214.
3. "Arabic Manuscripts in the Birnbaum Collection, Toronto: a Brief Catalogue" [The present catalogue].

I would like to record my sincere thanks to the Islamic Manuscript Association for a grant for typing of this catalogue; to Professors Arnoud Vrolijk, Jan Just Witkam and academic publisher Brill for accepting this work in the series "Islamic Manuscripts and Books"; to Dr. Halil Şimşek for his skillful multilingual typing, and to Stephen Batiuk for his excellent photography of a selection of pages from the manuscripts. Words do not suffice to express my gratitude to my wife Rebecca for letting me share with my manuscripts some of the time and affection due to her.

© KONINKLIJKE BRILL NV, LEIDEN, 2019 | DOI:10.1163/9789004389670_002

As a cash-starved student, the only books which I bought were printed texts for my studies. After my appointment in 1953 as Assistant Librarian in the then recently established Oriental Section of Durham University Library in England, I used some of the my incredibly modest salary to buy my first manuscript, in April 1955. It was an account in Ottoman Turkish, by a contemporary witness, of a battle between two sons of the Ottoman Sultan Sulayman the Magnificent in 966/1559, actually written down immediately after the battle. I found it at Luzac's "oriental" bookstore in London. It had previously belonged, like some of my later manuscript purchases there, to the late A.G. Ellis, a learned manuscript cataloguer formerly at the British Musuem and later at the India Office Library. Eleven years later I purchased my first *Arabic* manuscript, also at Luzac's: the first quarter of *Rasāʾil Ikhwān al-ṣafāʾ* [MS 58, A2, described below].

When I was Near Eastern Bibliographer at the University of Michigan in Ann Arbor some years later (1960–1964) I travelled to Turkey, Iran and Israel to buy books, in order to develop the research collections of Islamic books in the University of Michigan Library. Although my mission was strictly limited to the purchase of printed books, I noticed that some manuscripts were for sale in some bookshops, although I did not buy any. The situation changed after my appointment as Professor of Turkish at the University of Toronto in Canada in 1964. In subsequent years I was sometimes able to spend summer months and sabbatical time in the Middle East doing my own manuscript-based research in some of the wonderful collections of Islamic manuscripts—mainly in Turkey, and particularly in the amazingly rich collections already gathered at the Süleymaniye library in Istanbul. The research libraries in Turkey at that time were so poorly funded that the reading rooms for manuscripts were open on weekdays only, and staffed mainly by ignorant men and women who were incredibly badly paid. The manuscript reading rooms were open from 9 a.m. to 5 p.m., and sometimes closed also for an hour at noon. At 4:30 p.m. the bored staff would already start coming to the readers' desk to urge them the return of the manuscripts and encourage the scholars to leave.

After being ejected from the manuscript libraries between 4:30 and 5 p.m., I would often visit the nearby *Sahhaflar Çarşısı*, the booksellers' shops near the Bayezid mosque complex to examine the latest publications. There I would also drink tea with the store owners and some of their regular clients: teachers, university professors, graduate students, imams, etc., and listen to their discussions, which ranged from literature, history, religion, and sometimes to impassioned evaluations of recent books. After some of these sessions the bookseller might show me a few MSS in Turkish or Arabic or Persian brought from his *anbar* ("warehouse")—items often lacking the beginning or the end or both. If the text seemed interesting to me, I would sometimes buy the MS even without knowing its author or title, and would work on identification later. Many of the MSS offered to me were 18th and 19th century copies of well-known standard in *madrasa* textbooks in Arabic, which were of no interest to me. I noticed however that such MSS were being bought in quantity by visiting Saudi Arabian "clerics" and shipped to Arabia.

1 The Present Catalogue

The present catalogue describes the works in my collection of Arabic MSS, the copies ranging in age from the 5th or 6th to early 14th centuries A.H./11th–12th to early 20th centuries C.E. A minority are copies made in the Balkan territories of the Ottoman Empire, but most were copied in the Middle East, some of them before the rise of the Ottomans. Quite a number of the old copies dating from pre-Ottoman times now bear later marginal or interlinear notes in Ottoman Turkish, added by later Turkish readers long after the MSS were originally copied.

A few of the MSS in my collection were acquired in London, starting in 1955; the majority in Istanbul at various times between the 1970s and the early 1990s. The last was bought in 1994. A more precise purchase date is included at the end of each manuscript description.

2 Classification

The MSS cover a wide range of topics. For practical purposes, in the present catalogue they have been grouped in the following broad subject categories: A. Geography; B. Language and Lexicography; C. Literature: Poetry; D. Literature: Prose; E. *Qur'ān*; F. *Tafsīr*; G. Islam: Other; H. Sufism; I. Druze; J. Ethics; K. Encyclopedic; Sciences; Pseudosciences; Medicine; Mixed; L. *Ijāza*; M. Calligraphy; N. Persian Philology.

3 Information Sequence in Each Catalogue Entry

Each manuscript description contains the following elements, where applicable:

1. Running number (i.e., sequence in this catalogue).
2. Original accession group and number in the Birnbaum manuscript collections: A= Arabic collection; P= Persian collection; T= Turkish collection; M= Mixed collection.

3. Author's name in both Latin and Arabic scripts, with his death date, and folio number in the manuscript where his name appears.
4. Title of the work in both scripts, and alternative titles, if any, and the folio numbers where the title appears.
5. Beginning and ending phrases of the MS (*incipit* and *explicit*).
6. Colophon with date of copy, if given, or as estimated.
7. Description of the subject and contents of the work, and basic information on its author.
8. Physical description of the manuscript, including the following details, if applicable:
    a. Type of script (*naskh*; *nastaʿliq*; Turkish *taʿlīq*; etc.).
    b. Vocalization, if any.
    c. Number of folios, or pages if paginated.
    d. Dimensions in centimeters of the page, and of its written area.
    e. Number of lines per page.
    f. Paper, with description of any watermarks (*filigrain*) in the paper (useful to confirm copy date or to provide approximate time of undated MSS).
    g. Decoration, such as *ʿunwān* (ornamental headpiece), the use of gold and colored ink, rubrics, and framing of written areas.
    h. Previous owners, as indicated by handwritten statements or seal impressions.
    i. Other notes added by previous owners or readers.
    j. Binding: material and ornamentation.
    k. "Other MSS": Brief references to copies cited in some reference works, mainly C. Brockelmann, *Geschichte der arabischen Litteratur*, and R. Mach, *Catalogue of Arabic manuscripts* (*Yahuda section*) *in the Garrett Collection, Princeton University Library.*

4 Some Important Arabic Manuscripts in the Birnbaum Collection: a Selection

- 1, A36. al-Bākūhī, ʿAbd al-Rashīd, fl. 8th/14th century. *Talkhīṣ al-āthār*. Rare geographical work about the places and peoples of the "Seven Climes". Copied in 987/1579.
- 2, A33. [3 works bound together]: al-Mubarrad, d. 298/898, *Rasāʾil*; al-Ḥarīrī, d. 516/1122, *Mulḥat al-iʿrāb*; al-Anbārī, d. 577/1181, *Bast al-maqbūḍ*. These classics on Arabic language and prosody were all copied between 646 and 660/1248–1262.

- 8, A21. ʿUthmān b. ʿUmar. *Muqaddimatā al-taṣrīf wa al-khaṭṭ*. Rare treatise on Arabic philology, in Yamanī script. Later owner's note of 8/14th century.
- 11, A10/I. [On horses]. An old fragment of the genre *Kitāb al-khayl*; [author and title not identified]. Copied ca. 5–6/11–12th centuries.
- 25, P9. *Qurʾān* [fragment] with interlinear translation in medieval Persian; ca. 6–7/12–13th centuries.
- 31, A18. al-Bayḍāwī, d. 685/1286. *Anwār al-tanzīl* [*Tafsīr*]. A rather early copy, ca. 8/14th century, in Mamluk binding.
- 39, A16/II. al-Nasafī, Najm al-Dīn ʿUmar, d. 537/1142. *al-ʿAqīda al-Nasafīya*. On the Muslim creed. Copied probably 793/1391.
- 41, A16/IV. "al-Imām Shaykh al-Islām". *al-Jawāhir fī uṣūl al-dīn*. A very rare treatise on the Ḥanafi creed, entirely in verse, composed in 570/1174–1175. Copied "9 Shaʿbān 93", probably 793/1391.
- 42, A24/I. [*Risāla fī Yawm al-Qiyāma*]. An old eschatological work in rhymed prose and verse, partly updated in the early 16th century; copied on 16th century paper.
- 47, A15. al-Kisāʾī, 5/11th century, *Kitāb al-Malakūt*. Sermon on the doctrines of Creation; rare; apparently copied in the author's lifetime.
- 48, A23. al-Ṣaghānī, d. 620/1252. *Mashāriq al-anwār al-nabawīya*. An unusual arrangement of *ḥadiths*. Early copy, dated 756/1355; in a fine Mamluk binding.
- 49, A29. ʿIyāḍ al-Yaḥṣubī, d. 544/1149. *al-Shifāʾ*. A classic of popular piety. Copied 757/1356.
- 50, A25/I. al-Bābilī, Aḥmad, fl. 964/1557. *Muqaddima fī al-basmala wa al-ḥamdala*. Composed in Shaʿbān 964/1557; this MS was copied one month later, and seems unique.
- 57, A19. al-ʿĪshī, Muḥammad al-Tīrawī, d. 1016/1607 (?). *Rawḍat al-ʿulamāʾ*. Rare treatise on ethics. Copied 1031/1622.
- 59, T77/V. al-Barmakī, Yaḥyā, 3rd/9th century (reputed author). *Sirāj al-ẓulma wa al-raḥma*. A rare treatise on alchemy, with diagrams. Copied ca. 11/18th century.

A. Geography

[1] A36

al-Bākūhī, ʿAbd al-Rashīd b. Ṣāliḥ, fl. 8/14th century (f. 1^{b})

الباكوهى ، عبد الرشيد بن صالح

Talkhīṣ al-āthār jamīʿ mā waṣal ilayya min laṭāʾif ṣunʿ Allāh (f. 1^{b})

تلخيص الاثار جميع ما وصل اليّ من لطائف صنع الله

[***Talkhīṣ al-āthār fī ʿajāʾib al-aqṭār***]

[تلخيص الاثار فى عجائب الاقطار]

Begins (f. 1^{b})

الحمد لله ذى العظمة و الكبرياء و القدرة و البقاء و العزة و العلا

Ends (f. 51^{b})

و يذهبون اليها بالمراكب فيجمعون عليها و يقطعون من لحمها و اذا لم يلق فى البحر من تلك السيوف لم تخرج لهم السمكة لجاوا لان قوتهم من هذه و الله اعلم بما ورآء ذلك تمت [sic] الكتاب يوم الاثنين السبع عشر من شوّال المبارك سنه سبع و ثمانين و تسعمايه تم

A survey of the various places and peoples in each of the "Seven Climes" (*aqālīm*) of the world, attempting to briefly describe in each section where applicable—under alpahabetically arranged place names—the peoples, geography, rulers, moral character of their wise men, arts and crafts, mines, agricultural products, animals, etc.

After a brief introduction explaining the intended scope of the work (f. 1^{b}–2^{b}), Clime 1 begins on f. 2^{b}; headings for Clime 2 and 3 are apparently on lost folios or were omitted; Clime 4 begins on f. 23^{b}; Clime 5 on f. 36^{a}; Clime 6 on f. 44^{b}; Clime 7 on f. 49^{b}.

© KONINKLIJKE BRILL NV, LEIDEN, 2019 | DOI:10.1163/9789004389670_003

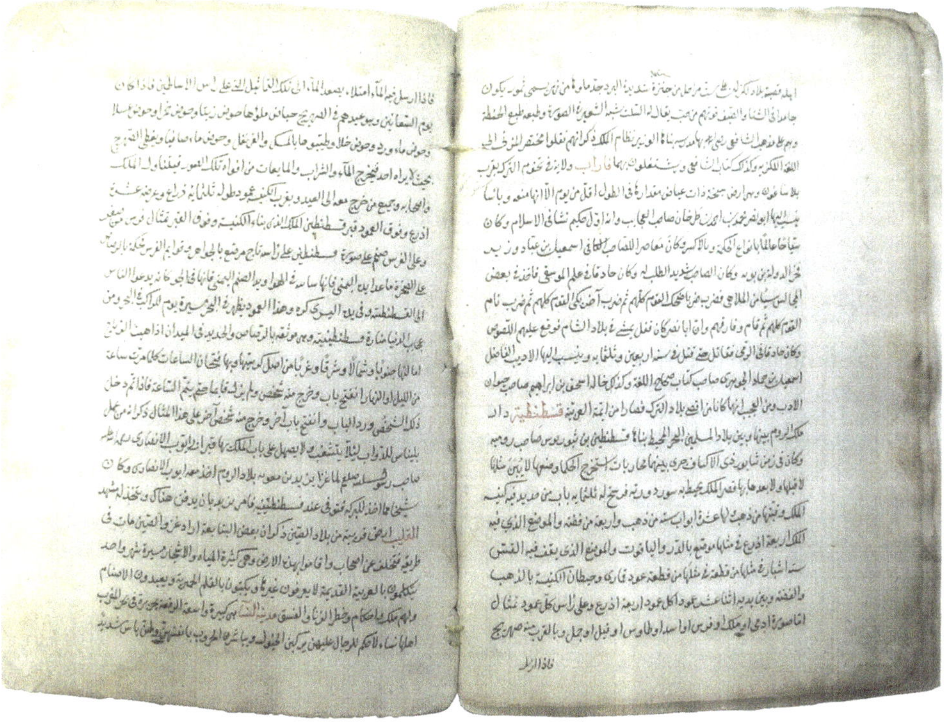

FIGURE 1 No. 1 (A36). al-Bākūhī, ʿAbd al-Rashīd b. Ṣāliḥ, fl. 8/14th century, *Talkhīṣ al-āthar*. Copied 987/1579. Copied 987/1579; f. 48^{b}–49^{a}

The author notes the death of his father Ṣāliḥ b. Nūrī in 705/1305 in Bākū (f. 38^{b}).

Crabbed small *naskh*, occasionally vocalized, mainly for place names; f. 1^{a}–51^{b} (1 folio missing between f. 10 and 11). Several marginal comments in Turkish noted an omission in the text at the entry for Yemen (f. 7^{b}); and, in the entry for Baṣra (at 12^{b}–13^{a}), that a page had been skipped in error; 21 × 15.5 (16 × 10) cm; 21 lines; Copyist's colophon (f. 51^{b}) 17 Shawwāl 987/December 1579. (A 19th century note on f. 1^{a} stated that the MS had 54 folios).

Paper: Watermarked: Anchor suspended from a Ring, within a Circle, and topped by a 6-armed Star.

Binding: None. Original binding probably removed; folios roughly resewn in mid-20th century.

The 17th century bibliographer Kātib Chalabī recorded the title as *Talkhīṣ al-āthār fī ʿajāʾib al-aqṭār* (*Kashf al-Ẓunūn*, Istanbul 1941, col. 471–472). Brockelmann (G I, p. 633, S I, p. 983) considered it as derived from the *ʿAjāʾib al-makhlūqāt* of al-Qazwīnī (Zakarīyā b. Muḥammad, who died about 682/1283), citing MSS in Munich and Paris.

Ownership: (1) A 19th century owner noted on f. 1^{a}, a passage on "The island of women" (now on f. 5^{a}). He did not note another passage on f. 49^{a-b}, near the end of the MS, describing a different "city of women" (*madīnat al-nisāʾ*) in the 6th Clime on an island in the Western Sea (*Baḥr al-maġrib*); (2) Bought by E. Birnbaum in Istanbul in July 1991.

B. Language and Lexicography

[2] A33

[*Majmūʿa: 3 Kutub ʿan al-lugha al-ʿArabīya, wa al-iʿrāb wa al-ʿarūḍ*]

[مجموعة ٣ كتب عن اللغة العربية و الاعراب و العروض]

A collection of 3 separate MSS on Arabic language and prosody, all copied about the middle of the 7/13th century and later bound together in one volume. From old notes on f. 68ª, which previously acted a "title page" to the bound volume, we deduce that the original sequence of copying was probably:

1. al-Anbārī, ʿAbd al-Raḥmān b. Muḥammad, d. 577/1181. *Basṭ al-maqbūḍ fī ʿilm al-ʿarūḍ* (see **MS 5, A 33/III**, f. 68ª–116ª), MS dated *sitta miʿa* ... [remainder illegible, f. 68ª, i.e. 7/13th century];
2. al-Mubarrad, d. 285/898. [*"Rasāʾil al-Mubarrad"*] (see **MS 3, A33/I**, now f. 1ª–43ᵇ) under the general title *al-Muqniʿ* (perhaps for *al-Maʿnā* ?) and dated 646/1248;
3. al-Ḥarīrī, d. 516/1122. *Mulḥat al-iʿrāb wa subḥat al-ādāb* (see **MS 4, A33/II**, f. 49ᵇ–66ª) copied before 660/1262, which is the date of a "reading certificate" on f. 66ª.

For a full description of each work see **MSS 5, A33/III; 4, A33/II; 3, A33/I.**

Old *naskh*; different copyist for each work; total f. 1–118 (including f. 117–118 added ca. late 17th or 18th century at a rebinding, and containing some notes) **MS 3, A33/I**, 17×12.5 (13.5×9.5) cm: 15 lines; **MS 4, A33/II**, 17×12.5 (12×9) cm; 11 lines; **MS 5, A33/III**, 17×12.5 (13.5×9.5) cm; 15 lines.

Paper: "Oriental", without watermarks.

Binding: Leather edged paperboard, covered with paper; front cover lost; leather backstrip; a rebinding ca. late 17th–18th century.

Ownership: All three works bound in this volume have marginal notes of varying but considerable age, mostly in Arabic, some attributed to named Turkish scholars (e.g. Dede Efendi, f. 31ᵇ–32ª); some notes in Turkish language and in

© KONINKLIJKE BRILL NV, LEIDEN, 2019 | DOI:10.1163/9789004389670_004

"Turkish *taʿlīq*" script, some datable to the 17th century onwards (e.g. f. 13^b; 15^b; 90^a). Occasional marginal additions reference standard Arabic linguistic works (e.g. *min al-Ṣiḥāḥ*, f. 116^b). Two ink seal impressions inscribed in Arabic, but in Turkish style *taʿlīq*, "*wa mā tawfīqī illā biʾllāh ʿalā ʿabdih*", possibly 18th century. Bought by E. Birnbaum, Istanbul, July 1991.

Additional notes to **MSS 3–5, A33/I–III**: On blank pages between the three main works in this volume previous readers have added various items in different old but inelegant hands:

1. f. 44^{a-b}, "*Khuṭba khaṭabahā Abū Bakr b. Qurayʿa fī dār Abī Isḥāq al-Ṣābī.*"
2. f. 44^b, "*Khuṭba min khuṭab Ibn Nubāta.*"
3. f. 45^a–46^b, "*mimmā akhtarnāhu min al-juzʾ al-thālith min al-Ashbāh wa al-naẓāʾir*" [of Tāj al-Dīn al-Subkī, d. 771/1370].
4. f. 46^{a-b}, *min al-Ṣiḥāḥ.*
5. f. 46^b, *Duʿā ʿallamahu Jibrāʾīl li-Yūsuf ...*
6. f. 47^{a-b}, *al-Asmā allatī nuzilat ʿalā Ādam ʿalā ḥurūf al-muʿjam.*
7. f. 66^b–67^b, *min al-Ṣiḥāḥ.*

[3] A33/I

al-Mubarrad, Muḥammad, [f. 43^b Aḥmad], d. 285/898 (or 286/900)

المبرد ، ابو العباس محمد

[***Rasāʾil al-Mubarrad wa ghayrihi***]

[رسائل المبرّد و غيره]

A collection of grammatical, linguistic and other works by the famous philologist and litterateur al-Mubarrad of Basra.

First page(s) missing; now begins (f. 1^a)

بفكره معانى ما تضمنته الكتب الكبار و نظمته العلل الطوال و كُفِى معناه الحفّظ ... و من ذلك مختصر الاعراب و ثم مختصر المذكّر و المؤنث ...

FIGURE 2 No. 3 (A33/I). al-Mubarrad, Muḥammad, d. 285/898, *Rasāʾil*. Copied 646/1248; f. 35^{b}–36^{a}

Ends at end of section *Mukhtaṣar khalq al-faras* (f. 43^{b})

الصدف عوج فى الحافر على السى اليد

تم الكتاب المقنع [sic] لابى العباس احمد المبرّد و الحمد لله رب العالمين ... وافق الفراغ منه

يوم الخميس ثانى عشر حمدى [= جمادى] الاول سنة ست و اربعين و ستمايه

Sections which may also be considered individual treatises, and listed, starting on f. 1^{a}:

Mukhtaṣar al-iʿrāb; *Mukhtaṣar al-mudhakkar wa al-muʾannath*; *Mukhtaṣar laḥn al-ʿāmma*; *Mukhtaṣar al-maqṣūr wa al-mamdūd*; *Mukhtaṣar al-hijāʾ*; *Mukhtaṣar khalq al-insān*; *Mukhtaṣar khalq al-faras wa lawnuh wa shiyatuh*; the last of these begins on f. 41^{a}.

The copyist's colophon (f. 43[b]), which is dated Thursday 12 Jumāda I 646 [= October 3, 1248], refers to the whole collection as *Kitāb al-Muqniʿ*, a title not attested for al-Mubarrad in the literature that I have seen. However, Ibn al-Nadīm, in his famous bibliography *al-Fihrist* mentions a *Kitāb al-maʿnā* attributed to al-Mubarrad (see F. Sezgin, *Geschichte des arabischen schriftkunst*, Bd. 9, p. 80). Many medieval copyists often omitted diacritics, so a copyist may have misinterpreted المعنى of his Vorlage as المقنى or vice versa.

Old *naskh*, fully vocalized. For details of collation, paper, binding and ownership see **MS 2, A33**.

[4] **A33/II**

al-Ḥarīrī, al-Qāsim b. ʿAlī, d. 516/1122

الحريرى ، القاسم بن على

Mulḥāt al-iʿrāb wa subḥat al-ādāb (f. 49[a]; 66[a])

ملحة الاعراب و سبحة الاداب

Begins (f. 49[b], after *basmala*)

قال الشيخ الامام ابو محمد القاسم الحريرى اقول من بعد افتتاح القول محمد ذى الطول الشديد الحول

Ends (f. 66[a])

و قد نقضّت ملحه الاعراب مؤدعةً بدايع الاعراب فانظر اليها نظر المستحسن و حسّن الظن بها و احسن و ان تجد عيباً فسد الخلالاً فجلّ من لا عيب فيه و علا و الحمد لله على ما اولى فنعم ما اولى و نعم المولى ثم الصلاة بعد حمد الصمد على النبي المصطفى محمد ... نجزت بحمد الله و عونه و حسن توفيقه

A grammatical work in verse by the famous literary stylist al-Ḥarīrī, author of the *Maqāmāt al-Ḥarīrī*.

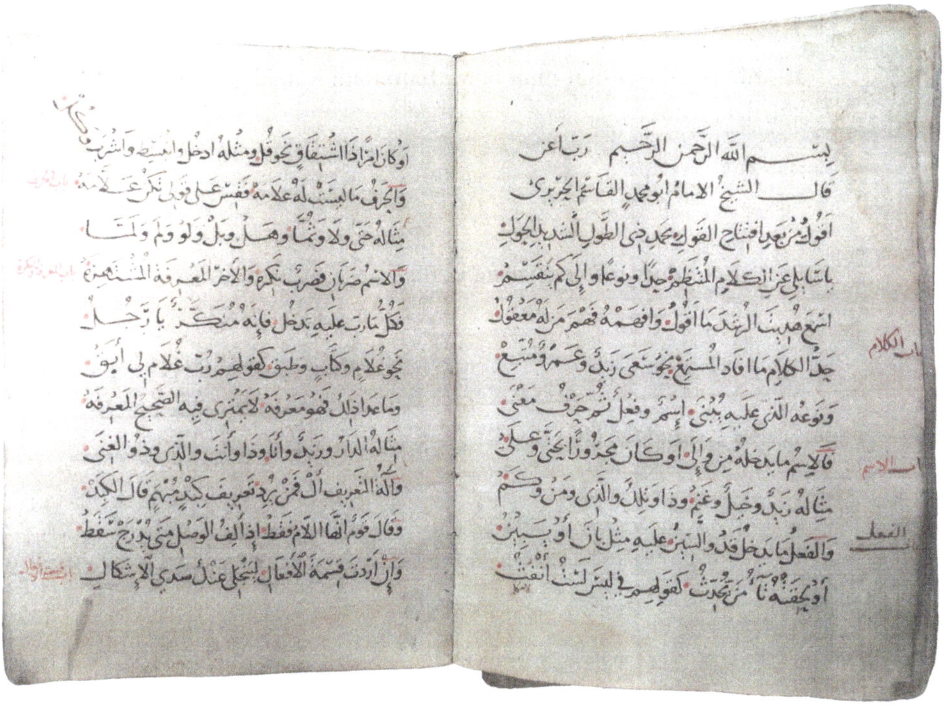

FIGURE 3 No. 4 (A33/II). al-Ḥarīrī, d. 516/1122, *Mulḥāt al-iʿrāb*. Owner's date 660/1262; f. 49b–50a

See GAL I, 328.

After the text, at the bottom of f. 66a, a certificate of reading this work in the presence of "the great man, chief of the litterateurs … Muḥammad ʿUthmān al-Bulghārī", followed by a chain of authorities back to al-Ḥarīrī; this followed by a statement in a different and unpractised ugly hand, dating this reading to "the month of God's mercy 660"/1262.

For collation, paper, binding, and ownership, see **MS 2, A33**.

[5] A33/III

al-Anbārī, ʿAbd al-Raḥmān b. Muḥammad, Kamāl al-Dīn Abū al-Barakāt, d. 577/1181

الانباری ، عبد الرحمن بن محمد ، ابو البرکات

Basṭ al-maqbūḍ fī ʿilm al-ʿarūḍ (f. 68[b])

بسط المقبوض فی علم العروض

Begins (after *basmala*, f. 68[b])

الحمد لله الواحد القديم و الصلاة على محمد عبده و نبيه الكريم و على آله و صحبه و أُولى النهج
القديم و بعد فانك سألتنى ايدك الله ان ابسط لك مختصرنا المقبوض فى علم العروض

Ends (f. 116[a])

و هذا البحر لم يذكره الخليل بن احمد و انما ذكره غيره و الذى عليه الجمهور و المذهب المشهور ما
ذكره الخليل بن احمد رحمة الله عليه تم الكتاب ...

The author was a member of a family of philologists in Baghdad. This is a detailed manual on the system of Arabic prosody, with many examples. It is illustrated by *dāʾiras* (circular diagrams) of poetic meters (f. 80[a], 89[b], 112[b], 115[b]).

This text is very rare; it is not recorded by Brockelmann, Mach, etc.

The precise copy date of this MS is not given, but a note on f. 68[a] mentions a date beginning "*sitta miʾah* ..." [remainder illegible]. Paleographically the MS may be dated to approximately the same period as the copy of MS of Mubarrad's work (**MS 3, A33/I**) with which it is bound, which was completed 12 Jumādā I 646/December 3, 1248.

For details of collation, dimensions, paper, binding, and ownership, see **MS 2, A33**.

Note: f. 118[b]: *Later addition to this manuscript.*

A list of Ottoman Turkish books, with names (authors, donors, owners ?). They include the following:

Emīn Efendi *Şafaḳnāma ve Siyer-i Veysī*	Ḫalīl Āġā *Ḥadā'iḳ üs-su'adā*	'Abdül—(?) Efendi *Dīvān-i Nef'ī*	Ḫayr Efendi —[obliterated]
Sa'dullāh Efendizāde *'Arūsī*	Ḥalīm (?) Aḥmed Çelebi *Risāle-i—(?)*	Mektūb Efendi	*Ḫamse-i Nergisī*
Ḥadīḳa-i Ḫalīl Efendi	[Verses about] *Eflāk* (Wallachia) by Nābī Efendi		
Ḫoca Efendi *Ḥadīs̱-i erba'īn*	*Ḥadīḳa* Ḫalīl Efendi		

[6] **A22**

al-Isfarā'īnī, Muḥammad b. Muḥammad, d. 684/1285

الإسفرايني ، محمد بن محمد

al-Ḍaw' (f. 1b) [***'alā al-Miṣbāḥ***]

الضوء [على المصباح]

Begins (f. 1b)

امّا بعد حمد الله امّا كلمة فيها معنى الشرط و ذلك كانت الفاء لازمة (فيها) قال سيبويه قولهم

Ends (f. 105b, last lines partly rubbed out)

فاقتصرتُ على هذا القدر [----] عن التمشاق (؟) و الله اعلم بالصواب و اليه المرجع و الماب
تم الكتاب بعون الله ...

Commentary on *Miṣbāḥ fī al-naḥw*, a grammatical work by 'Abd al-Sayyid al-Muṭarrizī (d. 610/1213), which was widely studied in traditional *madrasas* for centuries.

Old fashioned *naskh*, partly vocalized; f. 1–105; in several different hands of the same period, ca. 8/14th century, some sharing the same page; 5 later supply leaves (f. 2–4; 31; 41) on different paper, these sharing the same 16th century watermark (Anchor in Circle, topped by Maltese Cross); 26 × 17 (17 × 10.5) cm; 17 lines; occasional headings in red ink; copious interlinear and marginal notes; instead of catchwords, the last two words at the end of a folio are repeated as first words on the next folio.

Paper: "Oriental", except for 5 watermarked supply leaves noted above.

Binding: Missing, but the MS is still sewn to its original backstrip.

Ownership: Bought by E. Birnbaum in Istanbul, July 1981.

Other MSS: GAL I 351; S I 514; Mach 3490.

[7] A3

al-Taftāzānī, Saʿd al-Dīn Masʿūd b. ʿUmar, d. 793/1390 (f. 1[a])

التفتازانی ، سعد الدين مسعود بن عمر

Sharḥ Talkhīṣ al-Miftāḥ

شرح تلخيص المفتاح

or

al-Sharḥ al-Muṭawwal

الشرح المطول

Begins (f. 1[b]; after *basmala*)

الحمد لله الذى الهمنا حقايق المعانى و دقايق البيان

Part I ends, f. 116[a]

Part II begins, (f. 116^{b})

الفن الثانى علم البيان

Ends (f. 186^{a})

... الفراغ من السواد الى البياض ... سنه ثمان و اربعون و سبعمايه بمحروسة هراة ... تمت هذا
الكتاب ... فى شهر شوال ... من شهور سنه ست و سبعين بعد الف

al-Taftāzānī is noted for his commentaries and supercommentaries on standard texts studied in *madrasa*s from the 14th to the 19th century. They became *madrasa* text books themselves which were studied for centuries. The present work is a supercommentary on the *Talkhīṣ al-Miftāḥ* (also called *al-Sharḥ al-Muṭawwal*) by al-Khaṭīb al-Qazwīnī (d. 739/1338) which was itself a commentary on *Miftāḥ al-ʿulūm* by al-Sakkākī (d. 626/1229), a standard composition on Arabic rhetoric.

Although al-Taftāzānī's works were composed in Central Asia, they were copied and studied throughout the Islamic lands. The composition of the present commentary was completed in Herat in 748/1347, and our manuscript copy was finished in Shawwāl 1076/April 1666 (colophon, f. 186^{a}), probably in Central Asia. The wide margins of this MS are mostly filled with extensive notes, comments, and references in the hands of several generations of *madrasa* students, who sometimes even inserted them in the main text. Many are citations from named standard works.

Good small *naskh* (main text in centre of the page); small *nastaʿliq* (marginal comments and annotations throughout); f. 1^{a}–186^{b}; 25.5×15.5 (16.5×8.5) cm; 26 lines; headings overlined in black or red ink; text block in centre of pages framed in red rules.

Paper: Thin beige "oriental" paper, without watermark designs.

Binding: Brown leather flap binding; repaired several centuries ago, but now in bad condition: front cover loose; front doublure and flyleaf replaced with old European paper bearing the watermark of 3 Anvils (ca. 17th century); back flyleaf doublure replaced by paper bearing the serifed letters $\frac{\text{AS}}{\text{G}}$; the flap binding is covered with old marbled (*ebru*) paper, attached with a ribbon of striped cloth.

Ownership: (f. 119[a]) oval seal (1.4×1 cm) inscribed "*yā Fattāḥ* 1068" [= 1648], showing that this seal was engraved 8 years before this MS was completed in 1076/1666; (2) (f. 1[a]) round seal (1.4×1.4 cm), defaced and nearly illegible, accompanied by a defaced note beginning "*taraka*" (legacy), which indicates that its previous owner had died; (3) (f. 1[a]) remnant of an old rectangular seal (illegible) accompanied by a partly cut-off note about some deceased owner and "his son Abū Ṭālib ʿAbd al-Muṭṭalib ..."; (4) an early anonymous reader wrote on f. 1[a] the scatological proverb "*Qāl al-ḥukamāʾ: al-ʿilm madhbūḥ fī furūj al-nisā*'"; (5) Bought by E. Birnbaum, Istanbul, 1973.

Other MSS: GAL I 354 (commentary 4A), S I, 516; Mach 3883.

[8] **A21**

ʿUthmān b. ʿUmar b. Abī Bakr al-Mālikī al-Nāṣirī, Abū ʿAmr, (f. 1[a])

عثمان بن عمر بن ابی بکر المالکی الناصری ، ابو عَمرو

Muqaddimatā al-taṣrīf wa al-khaṭṭ (f. 1[a])

مقدمتا التصریف و الخط

Begins (f. 1[b] after *basmala*)

التصریف علم باصول یُعْرَف بها احوال

Ends (incomplete, f. 32[a])

لازم فی نحو میقات و غاز و قیام و حیاض و شاد فی نحو و صیم و صبیة //

A rare treatise on Arabic philology. Fully vocalized in several Yemeni hands. ff. 33–38, originally blank, are now annotated with Arabic grammatical notes, verses and citations also in old Yemeni hands. Ownership dated 8th/14th century.

On f. 33[a]: a satirical old Turkish couplet written in an old Ottoman hand:

Ḥusayn didi bize kāfir ∗ *biz diyelüm oña müslümān*
Diyelüm ḥużūr-i Ḥaḳḳda ∗ *ikimizde ola yalan*

FIGURE 4 No. 8 (A21). ʿUthmān b. ʿUmar al-Mālikī, *Muqaddimatā al-taṣrīf wa al-khaṭṭ*. Ownership date 8/14th century

Ḥusayn called me an infidel * Let me call him Muslim.
Let us say that in God's presence * both of us are liars!

On f. 34[b] Persian poetry: 2 couplets in an old hand and in old Persian orthography (using *dhāl* instead of *dāl*):

اكر نآلم روا باشذ * اكر سوزم سزا باشذ
هر كِرا دفتر نباشذ * در بغَل او نبايذ . لذّت عِلمٍ عُمَل

f. 35[a]: verses headed:

هذه ابيات من مشكلات الاعراب

Old Yemeni *naskh*, fully vocalized; main work f. 1[a]–32[b]; preceded by f. 0[b], a flyleaf of similar age and script containing verses and citations; followed by f. 33–38, originally blank, but now containing various notes in Arabic, largely grammatical, some in verse, in old Yemeni hands; 17×12.5 (13×9) cm; 13 lines; headings in red ink; interlinear and marginal notes.

Paper: Thick "oriental", without watermarks.

Binding: Rebound many centuries ago, as shown by cropped marginal notes; present binding, several centuries old, has leather spine and edges, on worn pasteboard covers.

Ownership: (1) Old note on f. 1[a]: "Fī nawbat ʿAbdullāh b. Aḥmad b. ʿAbd al-Raḥmān al-Yamanī, thumma al-Jabartī ... sana 773" [/1371–1372]; (2) Rāʾif Yelkenci (Istanbul bookseller, 1894–1974); on his death bought by (3) an Istanbul bookseller who sold it to (4) E. Birnbaum, Istanbul, June 1981.

Note: This MS was probably in Turkey for many centuries, judging by (1) the citation in Persian, in antique Persian orthography (consistent use of *dhāl* rather than *dāl* at a time when Persian was still current as a prestige language at the Ottoman court); and (2) the satirical couplet in Turkish noted above, f. 33[a].

[9] **M1/I**

See MS 67 below.

[10] **A10**

[*Majmūʿa rasāʾil mutanawwiʿa*]

[مجموعة رسائل متنوعة]

A collection of some 15 main items, written on many different papers and later bound together. They were copied at various times ranging from the 5th or 6th centuries AH/11th or 12th centuries CE to the 11th century AH/early 18th century CE. The majority were copied at various times in the 10th/16th century.

The present physical volume consists largely of short items in Arabic of special interest to *ʿulamāʾ* and *madrasa* students of the Ottoman Empire, with many references to standard Arabic linguistic, grammatical, religious and legal works. On some previously blank pages several Ottoman *fatwā*s in Arabic and Turkish were added later.

As it now stands, this volume includes parts of a variety of separate notebooks bound together, perhaps in the late 16th century, and then again rebound later, perhaps in the 18th century, at which time some edges containing marginal notes were partly trimmed off.

Native speakers of Turkish apparently predominated among the several generations of copyists, *ʿulamāʾ* and *madrasa* students who penned most of the Arabic texts. Some also wrote brief passages in Turkish in this volume. In the descriptions below, entries which include portions written in Turkish are marked by a bold **T** in the margins and parts in Persian are indicated by a bold **P** in the margins.

Paper: Each group of watermarked papers included within the present covers of the bound volume is indicated below by a Roman number (I–XV). Where examples of the same paper now occur in different parts of the volume, the Roman number is followed by a lower case letter in parentheses, e.g. II (a); II (b).

[11] A10/I

f. 80; 89[***Kitāb al-khayl***]

[كتاب الخيل]

This fragment, the oldest MS bound within the covers of this *majmūʿa*, consists of a 4-page bifolio (now numbered f. 80 and 89) describing the desirable characteristics of horses. It belongs to the late classical Arabic genre of *Kitāb al-khayl* or *firās* or *furūsīya*. On these pages, horses of the following color are described:

(f. 80^{a-b}) *al-aṣfar*; *al-aghbar*; *al-ashhab*; *al-aḍḥā*; (f. 89^{a-b}) *al-taḥjīl*.

f. 80^{a} Fragment begins [see Figure 5 on page 26, below]

وفوق الفضحة . ثم الاصفر . وهو الذى شملته كله الصفرة

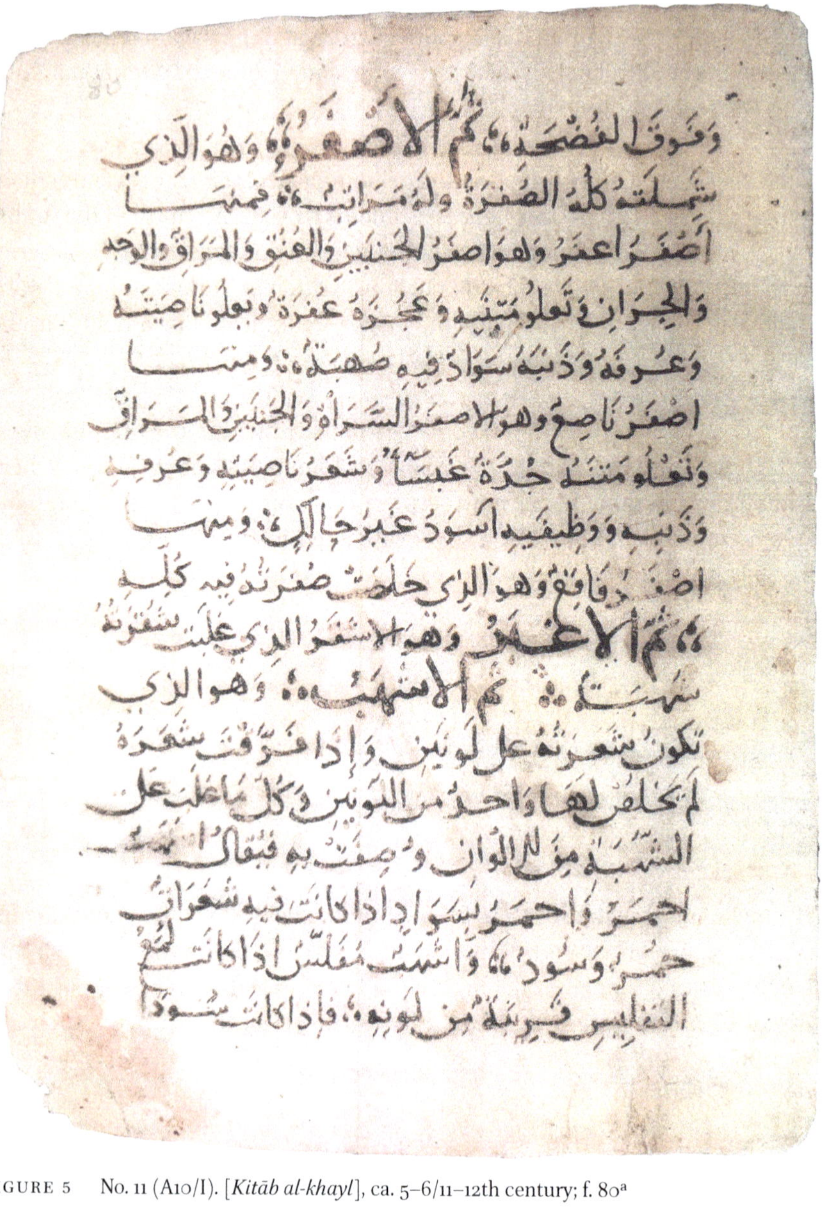

FIGURE 5 No. 11 (A10/I). [*Kitāb al-khayl*], ca. 5–6/11–12th century; f. 80[a]

Ends (f. 89^{b})

ذكر ذلك ابو عبيده و قاسم بن ثابت فى كتاب الدلايل له ء و لا [؟] يقال ابيض ء و البهايم من
الخيل و المصمت هو //

As noted above, the author cited the early philologists Abū 'Ubayda (d. 209/824), compiler of a *Kitāb al-khayl* about famous Arab horses, and *Kitāb al-dalā'il* [*fī al-ḥadīth*] by his later follower Qāsim b. Thābit (d. 302/914).

Clear old *naskh*; fully vocalized; 17.5×13.5 (14.5×10) cm; 17 lines; undated but paleographically ca. 5–6 century AH/11–12th century CE. The paper is not watermarked. (For a general overview of early Arabic treatises on horses, see EI^{2} articles Firās and Furūsīya).

The other main contents of MS A10 are described below in their present sequence, but only a selection of the details are noted.

[12] A10/II(a) T

Front cover board, f. 01^{a}–02^{b}+; back cover board, f. 03^{a}–04^{b}+.

Fragments of a prose work in fully vocalized simple Old Ottoman Turkish, containing dialogues between God and Moses (*Mūsā*). These pages were probably copied in the 14–15th century judging from the paleography and antiquated Turkish vocabulary (e.g. *yoḳsullar*; *baylar*; *yarlıġaram*; *ḳaḳısa*). They were later stuck together, with other pages of the same MS, to form the binding cover boards of **MS 10**, A10. The paper is buff colored and seems to be without watermarks.

Sample passage A (f. 01^{b}, lines 1–2):

موسى ايتدى الهى سعيد كمدر حق تعالى ايتدى اول كم كوز اَجُب يومشنجه عاصى اولمز

Sample passage B (f. 02^{a}): *Mūsā eyitdi: İlāhī, ḳangı ḳuluñ ḫayırludur? Ḥaḳ te'ālā eyitdī: Ol kişikim ġażab vaḳtinde yavaş ola ve koñşınuñ cefāsına ḳatlana ...*

T

A10/III

f. 04^{b}: Inner doublure of the binding, covered with notes of different ages in several hands.

T f. 1–11

A10/IV

f. 1^{a}: Originally a blank quire, it contains notes in different hands in Arabic and Turkish, written over several centuries. Among them, in Arabic, one noting that 4719 *ḥadīth*s are cited in *al-Maṣābīḥ* [*al-Sunna*, by al-Baghawī, d. 516/1122] and bringing citations from *Mafātīḥ sharḥ al-Maṣābīḥ* [by al-Khalkhālī, d. 745/1344], and from Najm al-Dīn ʿUmar al-Nasafī (d. 537/1142).

In different hands on the same page are 2 chronograms in Turkish, one recording the *hijrī* date of the Ottoman conquest of Istanbul in 857/1453, and the other the death of Sultan Muḥammad the Conqueror of that city in "986" (a scribal slip for 886, probably an indication that its copyist lived in the 10th/16th century).

f. 1^{b}: Includes a long note in Arabic about the time when "*Mawlānā Aḥmad b. Sulaymān Ibn Kamāl al-wazīr, raḥimahu Allāh*" (i.e. Ibn Kamāl Pāshā/Kamāl Pashazāda, d. 940/1534) composed his great history of the Ottoman dynasty, "completing it on Friday 19 Ṣafar 926"/February 1520.

f. 2^{a}: Includes notes on the ritual for preparing the dead for burial, taken from *al-*
T *Miṣbāḥ*, and sayings attributed to ʿAlī and Fāṭima; and detailed prescriptions in Turkish to cure *tuzlı belġam* ("salty phlegm") and *ṣoġulcān* (intestinal worms).

T f. 2^{b}: Text of a *fatwā* in Turkish by the Shaykh al-Islām Abū al-Suʿūd [Ebū 's-Suʿūd, d. 982/1574] on the doctrinal differences between "our" *madhhab/mez̲heb* and others. As the copyist did not add *marḥūm* or an equivalent, this transcript might have been written in Abū al-Suʿūd's lifetime.

f. 3^{a}–4^{a}: Notes on Arabic grammar in various hands, most written in Arabic, but some in Turkish, many citing standard *madrasa* texts such as "*Sharḥ al-Miftāḥ*" [probably on *Miftāḥ al-ʿulūm* of al-Sakkākī (d. 626/1229)]; *Ṣiḥāḥ*; *Talwīḥ* [of Taftāzānī, d. 791/1389]; *Mirqāt al-uṣūl* [of Mullā Khusraw, d. 885/1480]; *Ḥasan Chalabī*, etc. etc.

T f. 4^{b}–6^{a}: Grammatical notes in Turkish and Arabic.

f. 11^{a}: Citation in Turkish on the meaning of *ṣalāt*, sourced to *Şerḥ-i Gülistān*; a quotation in Old Ottoman from a work by Yūsuf Efendizāde. T

f. 12^{a}: Several items in Persian. A fragment headed "*Dar Kitāb-i Būstān*" with citations in poetry. P

Further on the same page a heading *Hijv-i malīḥ-i Ṣubḥī barā-yi Shāmī*: satirical bilingual Persian and Turkish verses. (The target may have been the historian P, T
Niẓām al-Dīn Shāmī, the author of *Ẓafarnāma*, a contemporary history in Persian of Timur, composed early in the 9/15th century). In the margin, a Persian P
verse by the historian Ḥasan Kāshī (d. 708/1308), author of the Persian *Tārīkh-i Rashīdī*.

A10/V

f. 12^{b}–16^{b}

Taʿrīfāt wa iṣtilāḥat

تعريفات و اصطلاحات

A fragment of an anonymous alphabetical vocabulary of literary terms.

Begins (f. 12^{b})

ال اله الا الا [sic]حق صمده ... و بعد فهذه تعريفات جمعتها و اصطلاحات اخذتها من
كتب القوم على حروف الهيجاء [sic] من الالف و اليا

This fragment, in *nastaʿliq* script, does not get beyond the middle of *alif*: The last entry is *al-istiʿāra* (f. 16^{b}), followed by a catchword. The margins are heavily annotated with linguistic notes in contemporary [16th century?] *nastaʿliq*, with named references; headings in red ink.

A10/VI

f. 17^{a}–18^{a}: Two linguistic discussions on *al-mufrad*, one by Ḥusām Kātī, the other by Bardaʿī.

18^{b}: A 6-*bayt* poem on calligraphy, attributed to Abū Ḥāmid al-Ghazālī (d. 505/1111); begins:

عشر حرف هنّ نور فى الغطط * خمس ها ات و خط بعد خط

T Turkish notes in margins.

f. 19^{b}–20^{b}: Linguistic notes in many different hands. Among sources cited are *Hindī*; *Sharḥ al-Miftāḥ*; *Kashf al-asrār*; *Durar ghurar*; *sharḥ Maṭāliʿ*; *sharḥ Shirʿat al-Islām li-Ibn Sayyid*; *Tātār Khān*; *Tafsīr al-Qāḍī*, *Mishkāt al-anwār*; *Ramaḍān*; *Sayyid Sharīf*.

A10/VII

f. 21^{a}–31^{b}. (A quire of paper watermarked with a Crown surmounted by a Star topped by a recumbent Crescent and the letters A and L on either side of a triple Clover Leaf's stem. This watermark was used in 17th century papers).

f. 21^{a-b}. Fragment of an Arabic grammatical work with commentary, and a marginal reference to *Baḥr al-afkār*, presumably Ḥasan b. Ḥusayn's 10/16th century supergloss to a work by Khayālī.

f. 22^{a}–31^{b}. Originally blank, but now containing notes and comments including:

f. 25^{b}. Various Arabic measurements with their Turkish equivalents.

f. 25^{b}. An explanation in Arabic by the Ottoman Shaykh al-Islām Saʿd al-Dīn of the difference between a *bāb* and a *faṣl*.

f. 26^{b}–31^{b}. Linguistic/grammatical notes in Arabic in various hands, attributed to *Ḥājjī Bābā*; *Kashf al-qulūb*; *al-Ṣiḥāḥ*; *Taʿammul*; *Sayyid ʿAbdullāh*; *Ashkāl sharḥ al-Miftāḥ*; *shaykhunā Ibrāhīm Efendi al-Adranavī al-marḥūm*; *Mughnī al-labīb*; *ʿAwāmil Ḥājjī Bābā*; *Abū al-Suʿūd*; [*Ibn*] *Kamāl Pasha Aḥmad*; *Ḥasan Chalabī*; *Sharḥ al-Minhāj*.

A10/VIII

f. 32ᵃ–32ᵇ. On different paper, trimmed during an old rebinding, cutting off part of the old marginalia.

f. 32ᵃ. *Fatwā* of Ibn Kamāl Pasha (d. 940/1533) about *Fuṣūṣ ḥikamīya wa Futūḥāt Makkīya* [of Ibn al-ʿArabī]. T

f. 32ᵃ. Discussion of the linguistic differences between *maṣdar* and *ism al-maṣdar*, cited from the *Kashshāf* [of al-Zamakhsharī, d. 533/1144]; and between the uses of *ghayr* and *illā*.

A10/IX

f. 33–42. On different paper, watermarked: Anchor suspended from a Ring, both within a Circle topped by a 3-leaf Clover. This watermark is found in many 16th century papers.

f. 33ᵃ. "*Risāla-i Durr-i manqūd dar suʾālāt-i kitāb-i Maqṣūd li-Jār Allāh*" [i.e. al-Zamakhsharī, d. 538/1144]. This "title" is in Persian, but the work is in Arabic. The rest of the page, originally otherwise blank, now contains 2 couplets about marriage, followed by another 4 in rhyme by al-Shāfiʿī, and 3 other sets attributed to him. These are followed by verses in Turkish by Veysī (969–1037/1561–1628); and a satirical comment in Arabic on marriage by Shams al-Dīn al-Kurdī. T

f. 33ᵇ–42ᵇ. A linguistic *risāla* in Arabic (written in Turkish style *taʿlīq* script), dated 991/1583.

Begins (f. 33ᵇ)

الحمد لله الذى جعلنا ما صدق عليه الانسان

Ends (f. 42ᵇ)

احد الساكنين و هو غير جائز. تمت ٩٩١

f. 43–51 **A10/X**

On paper similar to A10/IX, but with smaller version of the same watermark.

f. 43^{a-b} مباحث التصغير On dimunitives, in vocalized Arabic.

f. 43^{b}. Three *ḥādīths* and a citation on marriage from *Majmaʿ al-fatāwā*.

f. 44^{a}. Short grammatical notes, citing Ḥājjī Bābā; *Sharḥ al-Maṣābīḥ*, *Iṣbāḥ*; *Sharḥ al-Lāmīyah*; *Sharḥ al-Miftāḥ*; Surūrī Chalabī (d. 897/969).

T f. 44^{a} (margin): A Turkish *rubāʿī*, on syntax (*naḥv ü ṣarf*) and linguistic "opposition" (*taqābul*).

f. 45^{a}–45^{b}. Grammatical analyses of verses in Arabic, with a marginal *fāʾida* attributed to Ḥājjī Bābā, *al-Miṣbāḥ*.

f. 45^{a} [In a different hand] Several Arabic verses with interlinear grammatical
P anaylysis, and a verse in Arabic with a related verse in Persian.

f. 45^{b}. *Bāb dukhūl ḥurūf al-maʿānī fī makān baʿḍ* with interlinear notes in Arabic and references to Ḥājjī Bābā, *Miftāḥ*, *Kashf* ...

f. 46^{a-b}. Notes referencing *madrasa* classics, including some by named Ottoman *ʿulamā*: Saʿd al-Dīn, Mawlānā [Ibn] Kamāl Pāshā, Hindī, *Kashf*, *Daqāʾiq*, *Shujāʿ* ...

f. 47^{a-b}. Heading: *Iṣṭilāḥāt ahl al-ʿuqūl*. Citations, mainly grammatical, by 16th century Ottoman scholars: Ḥasan Chalabī, *Sharḥ ʿAbdullāh*, Kamāl Pāshāzāda, Mawlānā Saʿd al-Dīn, Surūrī Chalabī.

f. 47^{a}. In margin, in a different hand, the names of months in an unidentified language, and the corresponding Islamic month below.

اسامئ ماهاستى

مؤتمر ناجز حوّلن ابصاره حين زكى منفل الانسله عاذل
محرم صفر ربيع الاول ربيع الاخر جمادى الاول جمادى الاخر رجب شعبان

وَعلْ   ورنجيه   برك
شوّال   ذو القعده   ذى الحجه

f. 48^{a-b}. Linguistic notes, including Turkish translations of Arabic terms. T

f. 49^{a}. "Questions and Answers" in Arabic. In margin, names of days of the week in an unidentified language: beneath each name the translation in Persian:

شيار   اول   آهُون   جَبَار   دُكَار   مُونَس   عروبه   … P
شنبه   يكشنبه   دوشنبه   سه شنبه   چهارشنبه   پنجشنبه   ازينه ما   …

f. 49^{b}–50^{b}. List of body parts which are feminine in Arabic, some translated into Turkish. T

f. 51–60 A10/XI

Watermark: Anchor suspended from a Ring, within a Circle.

Linguistic and other notes in Arabic, mostly in the same hands, citing mainly *madrasa* texts, including many by Ottoman *ʿulamāʾ*: Sayyid ʿAlī, *Sharḥ Ḥamdīya, Sharḥ Hindī, Sharḥ Lāmīya*; a Turkish marginal note headed سرّ عجيب; Qāḍī; *Miftāḥ*; Sayyid ʿAlī; Jāmī; Muṣannifak; Khiḍr Beg Chalabī *li'l-Muṭawwal*; Ḥusām al-Dīn al-Dūqādī; Ibn Ḥājib *fī al-Kāfiya*; al-Churlawī; al-Marʿashī; *Talwīḥ*; Sayyid ʿAbdullāh; Sayyid ʿAlīzāda; Ḥasan Chalabī *li'l-Muṭawwal*; Raḍī al-Dīn; *al-Qisṭās*; *Qāmūs*; *Maqāmāt* al-Ḥarīrī; *Sharḥ Mughnī*; *Mukhtār*; *Sharḥ Kashshāf*; *Ṣiḥāḥ al-Mukhtār*. T

f. 56^{a}. Names of weights and measures, and their equivalents in *dirhams*, e.g. وسق 62400 *dirham*; قفيز 12400 *dirham*; صاع 1040 *dirham*; رطل 130 *dirham*; قراط بش اربه اغرى [Compare this list with a previous list on f. 25^{b}].

f. 56^{a}. The difference between an *ʿārif* and an *ʿālim*: the *ʿālim* does not know anything for certain: he says "God knows" (الله عالم [sic]) but the *ʿārif* is sure (*bi'l-taḥaqquq*).

f. 59^{a}. Two *masʾala*s and *jawāb*s in Turkish, about the legal situation arising from the case of two men who marry each other's mothers and have sons: what are their relationships? T

f. 61–62 A10/XII(a)

[Some watermark in papers as f. 21–26; 70–71; 81–88]

T Originally blank; contains linguistic notes, mostly in Arabic, some in Turkish. Sources cited include ʿAbd al-Laṭīf Shāmī; Ibrāhīm Efendi; Shaykh al-shuyūkh Adranawī (Edirnevī); "Abūnā al-Maʿānī wa shaykhunā al-Ṣūrī."

f. 63–68 A10/XIII

[Different paper; in a rather old-fashioned hand]

Linguistic notes, citing *Sharḥ al-Muqaddima*; Khwājazāda; İmād Kāshifī; Ḥasan Chalabī; Jāmī; *İftitāḥ* [of Ḥasan Pasha b. ʿAlā al-Dīn Aswad, d. ca. 800/1397]; *Ḍawʾ*; Ramaḍān; *Kashshāf* [of al-Zamakhsharī]; *Ḥayāt al-ḥayawān* [of al-Dāmirī, d. 808/1405]; *Tafsīr Ibn ʿĀdil* [d. 880/1475].

f. 69–79 A10/XII(b)

(Same paper as A10/XII(a))

Mostly Arabic linguistic notes.

T f. 77[b]. On a blank page: note in Turkish dated 14 Shawwāl 1195/November 1781.

T f. 78[b]–79[a]. A *risāla* dated 26 Jumādā II, 1113/November 1701, refuting charges of heresy, partly in Turkish.

Begins (f. 78[b])

الحمد لله و سلام على عباده الذين اصطفى . اعلم ان بعض الناس زعم ان قول قال قائل اكر
بندن كفر صادر اولديسه توبه اتدم دين اسلامه كردم يوجب الشق فى الايمان

Ends (f. 79[a])

بتعليقها بالشرط كالنكاح و البيع و الله سبحانه هو اعلم و احكم و اليه ينتهى السبيل الاقوم ...

f. 80; f. 89 [A10/I]

This single bifold is a remnant of a very old MS on horses. It has been fully described in section I of this **MS 10**, **A10**, above, p. 25–27.

f. 81–88 **A10/XIII**

f. 81b–88a [***Risāla fī al-kuḥl***]

[رسالة فى الكحل]

Begins (f. 81b, after *basmala*)

و بعد فلما انتهت مباحثاتى معى اصحاب الذين لحم درّيه لتحقيق المعانى ... الى مسئله الكحل من الكافيه اردت ان كتب لهم

Ends (f. 88a)

البارى سار منصوب بوقى و قيل حال من ضمير اجوف و قيل الخير منه . تمت الكتاب ...

An anonymous treatise on *kuḥl*, an eye salve and cosmetic. Undated; perhaps copied in the 17th century. Paper watermarked with an unususal Crown topped by 3-leaf Clover; countermark 3-leaf Clover and letter E.

f. 90 **A10/XII(c)**

[Originally the blank last folio of quire **A10/XII**, following the present f. 79]

f. 90a. Letter of thanks in Turkish, about the writer's journey from Gegbüze ككبوزه [modern Gebze in Kocaeli] to Istanbul; sent by "*Aḥmed el-ʿIlmī el-Müderris bi-Gegbüze*". Written on an originally blank quire which now also contains another note dated 1113/1701; on f. 90a, note dated 1114/1702. T

f. 91–96 **A10/XIV**

f. 91ᵇ–96ᵇ

[*Risāla fī al-iʿjāz*]

[رساله فى الاعجاز]

A short treatise on *iʿjāz*, lacking beginning and end. Paper watermarked (f. 91/96) with Anchor in Circle, surmounted by a three-leafed Clover, common in 16th century papers.

f. 97–106 **A10/XV**

f. 97ᵃ. Fragment of a grammatical work in Arabic. MS dated 1 Muḥarram 930/1523.

Now begins (f. 97ᵃ)

وسى فى هذه الوجوه اسم لا و خبرها محذوف

f. 102ᵇ on *iʿrāb*:

الباب الخامس بل جوزيهاء كظهر الحجفت آقول اوّله داراً

Ends (f. 106ᵃ)

و الاستشهاد على ان رب يكون مضمداً بعد بل نحو بل بلد الخ
تم بعون و حسن توفيق فى غرة محرم الحرام سنه تاريخ ۹۳۰

f. 106ᵇ. In a different hand, a note dated *awāʾil Rajab* 937/1531.

T f. 107ᵃ (which is the doublure of the back cover): An anecdote in Turkish, probably written in the late 16th or early 17th century, beginning: *Laṭīfe: Bir cemāʿat ṭālib ül-ʿilm bir imāmuñ evine ḳonuḳ olmuşlar. İmām onlara bir ḳaz boġazlayub* ...

f. 107ᵇ. The back cover of the volume, like the front cover, consists of paperboard made of pages recycled from an Old Ottoman prose text and glued together. The details are given in section II(a) above.

Binding: Both front and back covers are old leather. The middle of each bears a small blind-stamped medallion with a floral motif. The leather backstrip is very worn. The inner surface of the leather binding is covered with old penmanship exercises. Many of the quires within the present binding were trimmed at their edges when they were (re)assembled and rebound in this volume several centuries ago, as indicated by truncated words of some of the marginal texts.

Ownership: Bought by E. Birnbaum in Istanbul, August 1980.

[13] **M1**

[*Rasā'il fī al-lugha al-Fārsīya*]

[رسائل فى اللغة الفارسية]

Five separate tracts on the Persian language. Three of them, **MS 67, M1/I**; **MS 68, M1/IV**; and **MS 69, M1/V**, are in Arabic, and were composed by Ibn Kamāl Pasha (though anonymous in this manuscript). See the descriptions in this catalogue, nos. 67, 68, 69 (below).

The other two tracts, **M1/II** and **M1/III**, were composed by Jāmī in Persian. See the descriptions in the catalogue of my Persian MSS (below), entries 33 and 34.

Turkish *ta'līq*; f. 1–55; 20×13 (17×7.5) cm; 19 lines.

Paper: Watermarks (1) Hunters' Horn; (2) Anchor suspended from a Ring, within a Circle and topped by a 6-armed Star; (3) Single headed Eagle within a circle, topped by a 6-armed Star.

Date of Copy: **MS 67**, M1/I dated 11 Rabī' "108", either 1108 or 1008/1696 or 1599. For details, see entry 67, M1/II–IV, not dated but about the same age.

Binding: 19th century (rebinding) cardboard, covered with paper; cloth spine, now loose.

Ownership: Bought by E. Birnbaum in Istanbul in August 1980.

[14] M1/I

See MS 68 below.

[15] M1/IV

See MS 69 below.

[16] A34/I–II

[*Ḥawāshī ʿalā sharḥ Mukhtaṣar al-maʿānī Talkhīṣ Miftāḥ al-ʿulūm li-Khaṭīb Dimashq ʿalā Miftāḥ al-ʿulūm liʾl-Sakkākī*]

[حواشى على شرح مختصر المعانى تلخيص مفتاح العلوم لخطيب دمشق على مفتاح العلوم للسكاكى]

[Two supercommentaries on the *Talkhīṣ al-Miftāḥ* of Khaṭīb Dimashq Muḥammad ʿAbd al-Raḥmān, (d. 739/1338), itself a commentary on the *Miftāḥ al-ʿulūm*, on Arabic rhetoric by Abū Bakr al-Sakkākī (d. 626/1229)]. These works were widely studied in *madrasas* for centuries. This double MS was made in 1093/1682, presumably as a student textbook.

[17] A34/I

al-Khiṭāʾī, ʿUthmān, Mullāzāda, d. 901/1495 (f. 1[a])

الخطائى [عثمان ، ملا زاده]

[*Ḥāshiya ʿalā sharḥ Mukhtaṣar al-maʿānī*]

[حاشية على شرح مختصر المعانى]

Begins (f. 1[b], after *basmala*)

نحمدك اللهم على ما اعطيتنا من سوابغ النعم و بوالغ الحكم

Ends (f. 52[a])

و هو ان يتعلق قوله مع معيّن بيكون لا بالخطاب و كلامه رحمة [sic] الله لا يحتمل ذلك هذا
و الاولى ان يتقابل المترك بالمتروك اليه فيقال يترك المعيّن الى غير المعيّن او بالخطاب تم تم سنه
١٠٩٣

Small Turkish *ta'līq*, unvocalized; f. 1–52; 20×13 (14×6.5) cm; 23 lines; old marginal and interlinear notes; f. 1[a] has heading: *Ti'dād 'alāqāt al-majāz*, listing 25 categories.

Paper: Watermark: Cross within an oval surmounted by small Crown; MS dated 1093/1682 (f. 52[a]).

Binding: Flap binding with leather spine and edges on pasteboards which are covered by old marbled paper; different old marbled paper on inner doublure.

Ownership: (1) Hexagonal seal, diameter 1 cm, difficult to decipher (f. 1[a]); (2–3) Notes by 2 different booksellers in Turkish, ca. late 17th–18th century: *"Khaṭā'ī ve digar 'alā dībāja-i ma'ānī: fi'ātı 10"* (= price 10 [*ghurūsh*]]; f. 1[a]); (ii) *qiymat thaman 14* (f. 2[a]); (4) Ḥasan Bōsnavī Nehirbenli (?), 1227/[1812], (f. 1[a]); (5) Bought by E. Birnbaum, Istanbul, July 1991.

References: Mach 3906; GAL I 355, commentary 4B, gloss a; S I 518.

[18] A34/II

[**Ḥafīd al-Taftāzānī, Aḥmad b. Yaḥyā**, d. 916/1510]

[حفيد التفتازانى ، احمد بن يحيى]

[*Ḥāshiya 'alā sharḥ Mukhtaṣar al-ma'ānī*]

[حاشيه على شرح مختصر المعانى]

Begins (after *basmala*, f. 53[b])

قوله نحمدك انما اختار الحمد على الشكر مع ان المتبادر من الابارة

Ends (f. 82[a])

متكلما او مخاطبا او غائبا او مشار اليه مثلا و قد حقق ذلك فى موضعه تمت

Supercommentary on Khaṭīb Dimashq (d. 739/1338)'s commentary (see preceding entry **MS 17, A34/I**).

Small Turkish *taʿlīq* in the same hand as al-Khiṭāʾī's work which precedes it in this manuscript volume but script is slightly narrower, and unlike it, *without any students' marginal or interlinear notes*. (This indicates that this supercommentary was not much studied, if at all, by the owners of the MS); f. 53[b]–82[a]; 20 × 13 (13.5 × 6) cm; 23 lines.

Paper: Several watermarks including (1) Cross within oval, surmounted by a small Crown; (2) large Crown, surmounted by 6-armed Star; (3) unidentified different watermarks. While this MS is not dated, the fact that it shares the first watermark with Khiṭāʾī's work which precedes it in this volume, as well as the same copyist, would date this copy to the same period, about 1093/1682.

Binding and ownership: see **MS 17, A34/I** above.

References: Mach 3909; GAL I 355, comm. 4B, gloss b; S I 518.

C. Literature: Poetry

[19] M1/II

Jāmī, ʿAbd al-Raḥmān, d. 898/1492

جامی ، عبد الرحمن

[*Risāla fī al-ʿarūḍ*]

[رسالة فى العروض]

Begins (f. 20^{b})

سپاس وافر قادری را که حرکات سریع دوائر افلاك را سبب ازدواج اصول

Ends (f. 34^{b})

مسدس مجنون کدرم همه بر دست چکنم دل من برست فعلن فعلن فعلن مقطوع هر دم ایم
سوبت باشد بینم رویت فعلن فعلن فعلن تم

A treatise in Persian by the Persian poet and mystic on the Islamic *ʿarūḍ* metrical system of poetry, illustrated with 5 circular diagrams of the poetic meters (f. 24^{a}–29^{a}).

Other MSS: Storey, PL, vol. 3, pt. 1, pp. 183–185; Topkapı Sarayı Kütüphanesi Farsça Kataloğu, no. 318; 322/II.

[20] M1/III

Jāmī, ʿAbd al-Raḥmān, d. 898/1492

جامی ، عبد الرحمن

© KONINKLIJKE BRILL NV, LEIDEN, 2019 | DOI:10.1163/9789004389670_005

[al-]Wāfī bi-qawāʿid ʿilm al-qawāfī

[ال]وافى بقواعد علم القوافى

Begins (f. 35ᵇ)

... بعد همين بموزون ترين كلامى را كه قافيه

Ends (f. 39ᵇ)

و آن كوكشايدش دل خون كشته كاردست .
تمت القوافى من تصنيف مولانا عبد الرحمن الجامى

A treatise in Persian on rhyme.

Other MSS: Storey, PL, vol. III, pt. 1, pp. 184–185, no. 288; Topkapı Sarayı Kütüphanesi Farsça Kat., 678 XX.

Part of the collection of 5 *risālas*, two of them by Jāmī in Persian, and three "anonymous" in Arabic and Turkish by [Ibn Kamāl Pāshā (d. 940/1534)], including a Persian-Turkish glossary of infinitives (*muḍāriʿ*) with an introduction and some text in Arabic. For further details of these *risālas* by Ibn Kamāl Pāshā, see nos. 67–69 below.

[21] T15/I

Niyāzī Mıṣrī, d. 1105/1694

نيازى مصرى

Tasbīʿ al-Qaṣīda al-Burda (f. 3ᵇ)

تسبيع القصيده البردة

Alternative titles:

Sharḥ al-Tasbīʿ al-Qaṣīdat [sic] *al-Burda* (f. 1ᵇ)

شرح التسبيع القصيدة [sic] البردة لمحمد المصرى

Tesbīʿ ül-Ḳaṣīdet ül-Bürde [sic]

تسبيع القصيدة البردة

Preface begins (f. 1ᵇ)

قال رسول الله ... الرؤيا الصادقة جزء من ستّة و اربعين جزء

Main text of the *Tasbīʿ* begins (f. 3ᵇ)

محمد جاء بالآيات و الحكم * مبشراً و نذيراً جملة الامم

Ends (f. 25ᵃ)

على الرسول اجلّ السادة النقبا * ما رَنّحت عذبان آلبان ريح صبا واطرب العيس حادى العيس و النغم [sic]

Colophon (f. 73ᵇ): Copyist: "al-Ḥājjī Aḥmad Efendi fī wārōsh jazīra Limnī, 9 Dhū al-Ḥijja 1120"/February 1701

Note: This work is followed by *Dīvān-i Niyāzī* in Turkish by the same copyist [See E. Birnbaum, *Ottoman Turkish and Çağatay MSS in Canada*, pp. 107–109].

Niyāzī, founder of the Egyptian branch of the Khalwatīya sufi order, expanded the famous Arabic *qaṣīda* titled *al-Burda*, in praise of Muḥammad, which had been composed by al-Būṣīrī (d. 694/1294) by adding 5 hemistitches (*miṣra*) to every original verse (*bayt*), thus constituting a group of 7 hemisititches (*tasbīʿ*). He added commentary in Turkish prose to each *tasbīʿ*. The contemporary Ottoman authorities considered Niyāzī a troublesome personality and exiled him to the Aegean island of Limni/Lemnos, where he died in 1105/1694. This MS was copied there on Dhū al-Ḥijja 1120/February 1709, 15 years after his death.

Professional *naskh*; f. 16–25^{a}; 20×14 (15×8.5) cm; 15 lines.

Decoration: Good floral *ʿunwān* in gold, red, green, and blue (f. 3^{b}); opening f. 3^{b}–4^{a} framed in thick gold rules; all other pages framed in red rules; al-Būṣīrī's original verses and the name Muḥammad in red ink throughout.

Binding: 18th century brown leather over pasteboards, which are framed in gold-painted rules and edged with gold *zanjīrak*: central lozenge-shaped medallion blind-stamped and outlined in gold paint on both covers; Turkish marbled paper (*ebru*) doublures.

Ownership: Bought by E. Birnbaum in Istanbul in April 1973 from a bookseller who had acquired it from the collection of the late scholarly bookseller Raif Yelkenci: it still contains Raif's stock number label T208 on the spine.

Other MSS and references: İstanbul Üniv. Ktp. MS 502/2 (See *Türk Yazmalar Divanlar Kataloĝu*, pp. 489–490), and THSS, Tl. 2, 413, both following Niyāzī's Turkish *Dīvān*. See also Kenan Erdoĝan, *Niyāzī-i Misrī hayatı, edebî kişiliĝi, eserleri*. Ankara, 1998.

D. Literature: Prose

[22] **A20**

al-Suyūṭī, Jalāl al-Dīn, d. 911/1505

السيوطى ، جلال الدين

[***Maqāmāt***]

[مقامات]

[1. On fruits, flowers and vegetables]

Begins (f. 1b, after *basmala*)

سالت طايفة فاقها عن مناقب الفاكهه ... الرمان و ما ادراك ما الرمان

Chapter ends (f. 12a)

تقول فى الطب حقا * على لجين و عسجاله
و هذا اخر ما قصدت ايراده * و الحمد لله وحده. و صلى الله ...

[2. On nuts]

Begins (f. 13a, after *basmala*)

مرت من النقول طايفه * على النقول عايفه

Incomplete (ending lost in the description of pine nuts حب الصنوبر)

Ends (f. 15b)

و الرطوبات العقنه و البلاغم قالع ينقى // الكلا [catchword]

© KONINKLIJKE BRILL NV, LEIDEN, 2019 | DOI:10.1163/9789004389670_006

FIGURE 6 No. 22 (A20). al-Suyūṭī, Jalāl al-Dīn, d. 911/1505, *Maqāmāt*. Copied ca. 1031/1612; f. 1ᵇ–2ᵃ

[3. On precious stones]

Begins (f. 16ᵇ, after *basmala*)

اجتمع سبعة من اليواقيت فى بضعه من المواقيت

Ends (f. 22ᵇ)

فكانه قضب للزبرجد اخضر * قد قعوا اطرافه فيروزجا

تمت المقامه بحمد الله و عونه و حسن توفيقه

Among al-Suyūṭī's prodigious output of works is a series of *maqāmāt* in a high-flown literary style of rhymed prose studded with verse. Each *maqāma* consists of "disputations" within different sub-groups, each asserting its own superiority over the others in that group.

The present MS contains 3 such disputations: between (1) a variety of fruits, flowers and vegetables; (2) nuts of various kinds; and (3) different kinds of precious stones.

Good professional old *naskh*; f. 1–22; 18.5×12 (13×8) cm; 17 lines.

Paper: Watermarked: Crossbow [similar to one in Birnbaum **MS 57**, **A 19**, *Rawḍat al-ʿulamāʾ*, which is dated 1031/1622].

Binding; Rebound ca. 19th century, (i.e. sewn onto a Turkish marbled paper (*ebru*) front cover). The present MS was clearly extracted from a larger MS volume, very likely containing al-Suyūṭī's complete *maqāmāt*. The three chapters here are not in their original sequence, as the blank page (now f. 13[a]) preceding the section on "Nuts" bears an old heading in Arabic احدى و عشرين [i.e. section 21] while that on "Precious stones" (now f. 16[a]) is preceded by a blank page numbered "16".

Decoration: All pages double-framed in red ink, which is also used for headings and for separating rhyming phrases and poetic verses.

Ownership: (1) Round seal stamp (f. 1[a] and 21[b]) "Ṣabrī Muṣṭafā, 1307" [1889–1890]; (2) "Laʿlīzāda waqfdur"; (3) bought by E. Birnbaum in Istanbul, June 1981.

Other MSS: Cf. GAL S II, p. 187, 197–198 (no. 332); Mach 4342; ed. Cairo 1276.

[23] A25/II

[*Nawādir wa maḥāsin min shuʿarāʾ wa udabāʾ ahl al-Jibāl wa Fars …*]

[نوادر و محاسن من شعراء و ادباء اهل الجبال و فارس ...]

A two leaf fragment of a 10th/16th century collection of extracts from Arabic works, placed at the end of an unrelated manuscript: [**MS 51**, **A25/I**, al-Bābilī's *Muqaddima fī al-basmala wa al-ḥamdala*]

Beginning missing; now begins (f. 34[a])

و نوادرهم و فصوص فصول المترسلين منهم و القسم الثالث فى محاسن اشعار اهل الجبال و فارس و جرجان و طبرستان من وزراء الدولة الديلميه و كتابها و فضائلها و شعرايها و ساير فضايلها ... و القسم الرابع فى محاسن اشعار اهل خراسان و ما وراء النهر ما انشاء الدولة السامانية و الغزية ...

f. 34[a] (middle)

... كان ابو بكر الخوارزمى فى اَيْقان ... بلاد شام و حصل من حضرة سيف الدوله بحلب فى مجمع الرواة و الشعراء ...

و نقلته من كتاب يتيمة الدهر فى محاسن اهل العصر للاديب العلامة عبد الملك بن محمد بن اسمعيل الثعالبى رحمه الله و نقلت فى كتاب النايم الغمر على مراسم القمر للعلامة الحافظ ابى الفرج ابن الجوزى رحمه الله

f. 34b

فايده من كتاب عيون الحقايق

f. 35[b], Extract from the introduction of an unnamed work "on the virtues of the science of history":

و قال ايضا فى مقدمة كتابه المذكور فى فضل علم التاريخ و بيان ما عرض للمورخين من الغلط و الوهم اعلم ان فن التاريخ فن عزيز المذهب ...

Small Turkish *taʿlīq*; f. 34–35 (inserted after **MS 51, A25/I**); 21×15.5 (16×12) cm; ± 25 lines [varies].

Paper: Watermarked: Anchor suspended from Ring within Circle, surmounted by six-armed Star (common in mid-10/16th century); margins bookwormed.

Binding and ownership: see **MS 51, A25/I.**

[24] T108(A)

Faṣīḥ, Aḥmad Dede, d. 1111/1699

فصيح ، احمد دده

[*Majmūʿā munshaʾāt*]

[مجموعة منشئآت]

This MS is a rich collection of letters, documents, poetry and other items in Turkish, Persian and Arabic, mostly composed in very florid language in what was considered elegant style in the 11/17th century. **This MS, Faṣīḥ's autograph**, constitutes a sort of preliminary selection or draft, copied by Faṣīḥ, himself a famous stylist, from many sources over a period of nearly eight years: between 1079/1668 (f. 1^{a}) and 1087/1677 [f. 138^{b}]). Faṣīḥ later compiled a final and more formal *munshaʿāt* collection, of which several MSS are extant in libraries.

The present MS consists of a very large number of items selected by Faṣīḥ, composed by a great variety of authors, including some items composed by Faṣīḥ himself. The majority are in Ottoman Turkish while many other items are in Persian. Only a minority are in Arabic, and these are noted below. Most of Faṣīḥ's selections are in verse. Many of the quotations are written at an angle of 45 degrees: this is a common convention used by authors to indicate that the text is a draft (*musawwada/müsvedde*) and not in final form.

The compiler, Faṣīḥ, had a thorough education in *al-alsina al-thalātha*, the "three languages" of classical Islam, (Arabic, Persian and Turkish). After serving for many years in the Ottoman imperial administration at the Sublime Porte in Istanbul, he spent the last quarter of his life leading the Mawlawī dervish center in the Galata district of Istanbul.

Faṣīḥ's selection of items in both verse and prose testifies to the breadth of his reading and his linguistic sensitivity—a random collection reflecting his own tastes. The Arabic material, which in this MS is interspersed among the Turkish and Persian items, consists mainly of *inshāʾ*, both prose and verse, by many different authors, as indicated below.

f. 1[b]. "*Waqfīyat al-Wāʿiẓ Ḥusayn Efendī*", composed by "Muḥammad [Nargisī] when he was *qāḍī* in Bānā Lūqa" (in Bosnia), is headed by a note that it was transcribed from [Nargisī's] own handwriting (*khaṭṭ*). (Muḥammad b. Aḥmad Nargisī [d. 1044/1635] was famous as an Ottoman literary stylist [*munshī*]).

f. 74[b]–75[a]. On points of Arabic grammar: on the feminine, etc. "transcribed from Nargisīzāda's handwriting".

f. 75[a]. On the feminine in Arabic, by "Muḥammad b. Muḥammad al-Khwārizmī" [in verse].

f. 75[b]–76[a]. Marginal citations from: *al-Miṣbāḥ*; *al-Ṣiḥāḥ*; al-Muṭarrizī; *Tadhkirat Ṣalāḥ al-Dīn al-Ṣafadī*; *Fāʾiq al-lugha*, and others; "*Nāṭiq al-lugha*; *Tadhkirat Ṣalāḥ al-Dīn al-Ṣafadī*, min khaṭṭ Quṭb al-Dīn Makkī, min khaṭṭ al-Mawlānā [*sic*] Waysī Efendi".

f. 120[a–b]. A composition in Arabic by "Khinālīzāda" [Qinālīzāda]. After a brief introduction in verse, beginning:

لك الحمد يا من اكرم الانس بعد ما

it continues in rhymed prose:

و بعد فان الموصوفين بالبراعه ...

Ends (f. 120[b])

ثم بخلق اللوح و القلم و لم يعلم الان ما لم يعلم . صلى الله ... و على آله و صحبه و سلم . ١٤ ش سنه ٨٧

In the margin the source is cited:

الكواكب ويكتب السحايب بامطار

Faṣīḥ copied it on 14 Shawwāl [10]87/ December 1676.

f. 124[a]. Unsī Chalabī. Arabic introduction to a letter.

f. 126^{b}–127^{a}. A series of documents composed in Arabic *inshā'* by the Ottoman Empire's Ra'īs al-Kuttāb Madḥī Efendi. The first is a *bar'āt* bearing a transcription of the *imḍā'* (formal signature) of Akhīzāda ʿAbd al-Ḥalīm Efendi. Another *bar'āt*, also composed by Madḥī follows. It was sent to Mecca. Two more documents in Arabic *inshā* follow, also the work of Madḥī when he was Ra'īs al-Kuttāb.

f. 127^{a-b}. "*al-Risāla al-ṣayfīya*" composed by "Imāmzāda Aḥmad al-Sarā'ī". Faṣīḥ dated his transcription Ṣafar 1085/1674.

f. 128^{a}. Document composed by the "Ra'īs al-Kuttāb Madḥī Efendi" for ʿAbd al-Karīm, former *qāḍī* in Yeñishehir "[transcribed] in Ṣafar 1085 [1674] from the copy made by Nargisīzāda"

f. 128^{b}–129^{a}. Letter "from Madḥī Efendi to Akhīzāda Efendi, copied from the autograph of the composer [i.e. Madḥī Efendi], long may he live".

f. 135^{b}. A full page of citations of Arabic poetry, mostly from unnamed authors, some recording the name of the person being praised. Several are introduced by rubrics beginning ... قال مخاطبا ل ;

e.g., قال مخاطبا لمولانا قاضى القضاة ناصر الدين التنسى رحمة الله عليه. Various verses are cited in praise of Shihāb al-Dīn al-Fāriqī; Burhān al-Dīn al-Qirāṭī; "Muhājir"; Ṣāyigh; Uṣūlī; Burhān al-Dīn al-Mikhlātī (?).

f. 136^{a}. Includes verses by Shihāb al-Jafājī.

f. 138^{b}. [last folio of this MS, in the right margin]. A poetic challenge in the form of 2 couplets in Arabic verse addressed by the last Mamlūk ruler of Egypt [Qanṣwah/Qanṣūh al-] "Ghawrī/Ghūrī" to the invading Ottoman "Sulṭān Selīm" [I] and the latter's response (*jawāb*), also in 2 Arabic couplets; presumably both were composed in 922/1516.

Ottoman *taʿlīq* of various sizes, often lacking some diatritics; written at many different dates between 1079/1668 (f. 1^{a}) and 1087/1676 (f. 138^{b}), and all in the distinctive hand of Faṣīḥ; f. 1^{b}–138^{b} [f. 138^{b} now loose, and placed between f. 136 and 137]; 28.5 × 17.5 cm; writing on leaves varies in width, length and number of columns; headings in red ink.

Paper: Several different watermarks, difficult to identify because of the density of the writing on the pages.

Ownership: 5 seal/stamps, all on f. 1[a]; (a) small round, 1.4 diameter, faded but may include "Aḥmad" (the personal name of Faṣīḥ); (b) and (c) identical oval, 2 cm diameter, include the Persian words *bende-i kemter* (the humble servant) *Faṣīḥ* in large *taʿlīq*; (d) 1.7 × 1.5 cm includes the words "Faṣīḥ Aḥmad"; (e) oval, 2 cm, impression incomplete but seems to include *kemterīn* ("the most humble" in Persian); (f) Bought in Istanbul by E. Birnbaum, 1987.

Binding: Disbound: covers have been removed, but the quires are held together by original sewing.

MSS: **This autograph draft by the compiler is unique.** For fuller details of the Turkish and Persian contents of this MSS, see E. Birnbaum, *Ottoman Turkish and Çağatay MSS in Canada: a Union Catalogue*, pp. 182–191. See also DİA, vol. 12, pp. 213–214, which mentions 4 MSS of Faṣīḥ's formal *Munshaʾāt* in Turkish libraries, not cited as autographs.

E. Qur'ān

[25] P9

Qur'ān (fragment) **with interlinear translation in Persian**

[القران مع ترجمته بالفارسی]

Begins (f. 1a) [Sūra 9: 100–101]

يُرَدّون الی عذاب عظیم وآخرون
بار [—]ند ایشان را بعذابی بزرك و دیکران

Ends (f. 2b) [Sūra 10: 2]

ان اوحینا الی رجل منهم ان انذر الناس وبشر الذين
کی وحی کردیم بمردی از ایشان که بیم کن مردمان را و مردکان ده آنکس هارا

Fragment of an elegant illuminated manuscript of the Qur'ān in Arabic, with a word-by-word interlinear translation in medieval Persian in small script, angled downwards at 45 degrees.

This fragment is a single bifold sheet: f. 1a–b contains Sūra 9: 101–110; and on f. 2a–b Sūra 9: 124-Sūra 10: 2. Between the end of Sūra 9 and the beginning of Sūra 10, a conventional account in Arabic in small *naskh* script of the circumstances of revelation of Sūra 10, and a tally of the numbers of words and letters in it, and finally, the reward awaiting those who recite it.

In addition to this bifold, I obtained photocopies of the two adjacent bifolds of the original manuscript, so that the Quranic text with this medieval Persian translation covering Sūra 9: 34–40; 64–69, 101–129 [end of Sūra 9] and Sūra 10: 1–2 is available for study here. (These photocopies are kept with this manuscript). The margins contain letters and signs (mostly in gold ink) for *tajwīd*, pauses and subdivisions of various kinds. The recension of this translation remains to be identified.[1]

1 The Istanbul *ṣaḥḥāf* from whom I bought the present fragment was selling this disbound Qur'an with interlinear Persian translation piecemeal, bifold by bifold. When I tried (unsuc-

© KONINKLIJKE BRILL NV, LEIDEN, 2019 DOI:10.1163/9789004389670_007

FIGURE 7 No. 25 (P9). *Qur'ān*, with interlinear Persian translation; copied 6–7/11–12th century; f. 2b; 1a

The MS is not dated, but paleographically is probably 6th or 7th/12th or 13th century. The translation contains much fewer Arabic loanwords than later interlinear translations. In the Persian, the letter ذ (*dhāl*) is widely used rather than د (*dāl*), e.g. خذای ; دهذ ; کویذ ; etc.

Excellent old *naskh* for the Qur'ān text; small clear old naskh for interlinear translation; 19×15.5 (14×10.5) cm; 18 lines (9 Arabic, 9 interlinear Persian).

Paper: Buff colored "oriental"; not watermarked.

Decoration: Marginal decorations in gold and blue on all pages, and in a "wheel" on f. 1b, bearing the "voluntary pause" sign قلى at its center. Title of sūra 10 (*Yūnus*) is outlined in blue ink and filled in gold (f. 2b). Large water stain at top and inner margin does not affect legibility.

cessfully) to persuade him not to break up the MS, he replied: "You speak as a professor, but I am a businessman, and I make much more money selling it page by page than as a single volume!"

Ownership: Bought by E. Birnbaum in Istanbul, July 1991.

References: E. Birnbaum, 'Interlinear translation: the case of the Turkish dictionaries', in *Journal of Turkish Studies*, vol. 26/I = *Essays in honor of Barbara Flemming*, I. Cambridge, MA, 2002, pp. 61–62, and 75 (illustration A). For some dated MSS (not Qur'āns) of similar period, see St. Petersburg, Akad. Nauk, C 652 (of 549/1154–1155 in *Arabskie rukopisi, Inst. Vostok. Akad. Nauk SSSR, Kratkie Katal.* II, 1986, p. 249); St. Petersburg [etc.], B 865 (dated 570/1164), D 345 (dated 595/1199); Paris, Bibl. Nat. Suppl. persan no. 1314 (of 635/1238); Strasbourg, Bibl. Nat. et Univ. 4256 (dated 641/1245).

[26] **A6**

Qur'ān

[القران]

Juz' 12 of a 30-part Qur'ān

Begins (f. 1b)

الجزء الثانى عشره من اجزاء الثلاثين و من دابّة فى الأرض

Ends (f. 29a)

بالغيب و انّ الله لا يهدى كيد الخائنين

A good copy in excellent *thulth* script, fully vocalized; probably 14–15th century Mamluk (Egypt or Syria).

f. 1–29; 20×15 (15×10) cm; 7 lines; marginal *'ushr* marks in red ink.

Paper: "Oriental", without watermarks; bottom left corners stained by many generations of readers' fingers which have turned the pages.

Binding: Original Mamluk dark brown leather flap binding exterior with sophisticated round *shamsa*/medallions, each enclosing seven small hexagons stamped in the middle of both covers, and refined frames around the outer edges of the binding. The binding is now in bad condition, having been roughly repaired with a light red leather on the spine and top and bottom edges. Good Mamluk style light brown leather doublures embossed with leaf pattern, repaired by being glued to the text block with paper some centuries ago.

Ownership: (1) f. 1[b] margin: "waqf Qaraja Pasha." This name is rare and may perhaps refer to either the father-in-law of the Ottoman Sultan Muḥammad I ("Meḥmed Chelebī"), who was killed at the battle for Varna in 847/1443, or to Dayı Qaraja Pasha, who met his death during the Ottoman conquest of Istanbul in 857/1453. (See Meḥmed Ṣüreyyā, *Sicill-i ʿOsmānī*, [İstanbul] 1308–1315/1890–1897, vol. 4); (2) f. 1[a]: "ṣāḥib u mālik ʿAlī"; (3) Flyleaf preceding f. 1[a]: "al-ḥājj ʿAlī المدبندرى" (as part of a 5 line request in Turkish for the recitation of the *Fātiḥa*), dated 1153 [1701–1702]; (4–5, on verso of flyleaf) two old illegible seals, one obliterated with black ink, the other a small square only partly impressed; (6) Bought by E. Birnbaum, Istanbul, May 1974.

[27] **A28**

Qurʾān

[قران]

A fragment consisting of the lower half of a page of an illuminated Qurʾān. The recto contains *āyāt* 1–8 of sūra *al-Nabāʾ* (sūra 78), and the verso *āyāt* 17 to the middle of 27.

Begins (recto)

سورة النبا مكية اربعون ايات بسم الله الرحمن الرحيم عم يتسآلون عن النباء العظيم

Ends (verso)

انهم كانوا لا يرجون

This MS was probably produced in the Mamluk era, about the 8–9/14–15th century in Egypt or Syria. The heading naming the sūra is in gold script on a black blackground, decorated with floral motifs. The text-block is in elegant *muḥaqqaq* script; the verses are separated by gold roundels, to each of which six small blue disks are attached. The text is enclosed in an inner frame of gold and an outer frame of blue. In the margin of the recto are the words *al-juz' al-thalāthūn* in gold ink, and in the outer margin of the verso the division marker *khums*, also in gold ink, surmounted by a stylized flower in blue, black and gold.

Fully vocalized; fragment now 17.5×24 (13×18) cm; 5 lines; [original full-page size was about 36×24 (26×18) cm].

Paper: "Oriental", not watermarked.

Ownership; Prof. Glyn Meredith-Owens, (previously at the British [Museum] Library) who, on his retirement from the University of Toronto, presented it to E. Birnbaum, May 14, 1986.

[28] T10

[**Qurʾān**, with interlinear translation in Turkish]

[القران مع ترجمته بالتركی]

Begins (f. 1[b] [supply leaves, ca. 18th century of Arabic text only, on f. 1[b]–11[b]])

بسم الله الرحمن الرحيم الحمد لله رب العالمين

The interlinear translation on the original folios (after supply leaves) begins on f. 12[a] (sura 2, 167–168)

بخارجينَ من النار يا ايها الناس
چِقِچلَر اُوْدَن اِی اَدَمِلَر

Ends (f. 219[b], end of sura 114)

يوسوس في صدورالناس من الجنة و الناس
وَسْوَسَ اَيْلَرْ اَدَمِلَر كُكُزْلَرِنْدَه پَرِی لَرْدَنْ دَقِ اَدَمِلَرْدَن يعنى شيطان اِكِ دُرلُودُر بِرِی
پَرِیدُر بری اَدَمِيدُرْ

Colophon (f. 219b)

الحمد لله على التمام و لرسوله افضل السلام

A large, generally excellent and carefully written copy of the Qur'ān in Arabic, together with an interlinear translation in rather archaic Old Ottoman, in an inconsistent but generally conservative orthography and with full vocalization. The large format of the manuscript would indicate that it was prepared to be read aloud to an audience. The translation is short phrase by short phrase, and it is written at an angle of 45 degrees below the Arabic text in script much smaller than the Arabic original. For a fuller description of this MS see E. Birnbaum, "On some Turkish interlinear translations of the Koran" [*JTS* vol. 14/*Fahir İz Armağanı* I (1990)], pp. 113–138, especially pp. 115–120, which demonstrates that it belongs to what I have termed the "Recension A" tradition exemplified also by manuscript T40 in the Türk ve İslam Eserleri Müzesi (TİEM) in İstanbul which was copied in Ramaḍān 827/Aug. 1424. (See *XVI. yüzyıl başlarında yapılmış Satır-arası Kur'an Tercumesi*, hazırlayan Ahmet Topaloĝlu. İstanbul, 1976). The Turkish language of both this MS and TİEM no. 40 was already archaic when they were copied; they are both textually very close to one another, though our MS was probably copied at least half a century later, judging by the age of its watermarked paper.

A comparison of this MS and the interlinear translation of our **MS 29, T120** shows the latter to belong to a very different and considerably later translation tradition e.g., in Sura 2, 167–168, **MS 28, T10** translates *çıkıçılar oddan. İy ademiler ...*, whereas **MS 29, T120** renders it *hiç çıkmazlar cehennemden. İy kişiler ...* In Sura 114, 5–6, **MS 28, T10** has *ademiler göğüzlerinde perilerden daḳı ademilerden*, while **MS 29, T120** has *ḫalḳ yüreginde perilerden daḫı ademilerden.*

Many marginal inscriptions by the original copyists explicate in Turkish the meaning of the Arabic text, when the literal Turkish translation is unclear. These interpretations, usually derived (although written without attribution) from standard Arabic commentaries, are often introduced by the word *yaʿnī*. They are also found verbatim in some "Recension A" MSS.

Excellent fully vocalized professional script, *thulth* for Arabic text and *naskh* for interlinear Turkish. Both texts are the work of several different copyists, all late 15th or early 16th century. However fol. 1–11 are supply leaves, probably from the 18th century, containing only the Arabic text, without interlinear Turkish; f. 1b–

219^{b} (one folio missing between f. 165 and 166 must have contained suras 39:70 to 40:38); 35 × 25 (28 × 17) cm; 26 lines (13 Arabic, 13 Turkish).

Paper: Watermarked: Hammer striking an Anvil, common in papers of the first third of the 16th century.

Decoration: Red ink in other hands, used for sura headings, marginal markings for *ʿushr*, *ḥizb*, *sajda*, etc., and for roundels at the end of *āyāt*.

Ownership: (1) *Waqf* written on the last folio, after sura 114; (2) bought by E. Birnbaum, Istanbul, April 1973.

Binding: Reddish brown leather, with very large central medallion with floral motifs and pendants above and below on both front and back covers, each of which is framed in blind-stamped *zanjīrak*.

Other MSS and references: See article by E. Birnbaum, noted above, and references there; DİA, art. Kur'an, kısım 9 "Tercümesi", cilt 26, pp. 405–407; EI^{2}, vol. 5, p. 430, art. "al-Kur'ān" and bibliographical references there.

Other MS in Birnbaum collection: **MS 29, T120**, (different recension).

[29] T120

[*Qurʾān*, with interlinear translation in Turkish]

[قرآن مع ترجمه بالترکی]

Begins (f. 1^{b})

بسم الله **الرحمن** **الرحيم**

بَشْلَدُمْ اَدِيلَه تَكْرِ تَعَالَيْنُكْ كه رِزْق وِرِجدُر و رَحْمَت اِدِجدُر

الحمد **لله رب العالمين** **مالك يوم الدين**

شُكُرْ جميع عَالَملرى يَرَدَنَ تكْرِيَه ... قِيَامَتْ كُونِنُكْ پَادِشَاهِى دُر

Ends (f. 444[b])

يوسوس   فى صدور الناس   من الجنة   و الناس

اُولكم وَسْوَسَه اَيْلَر   خَلْق يُوره كِنْده   پَرِيلَرْدَنْ   دَخِى اَدَه مِيلَرِنْ

Colophon

صدق الله الر[حيم] و صدق رسوله الكريم و نحن بذلك من الشاهدين

The Qur'ān with an Old Ottoman interlinear translation, phrase by phrase. The text of this translation is quite different from that of **MS 28, T10**, the other Old Ottoman interlinear rendering in the Birnbaum collection. For brief samples comparing the texts of these two MSS, see the entry for **MS 28, T10**; the Old Ottoman renderings in the present MS are less archaic than the text of "Recension A", represented by **MS 28, T10** and TİEM no. 40. It does not belong to any of the groups of translations mentioned in E. Birnbaum, "On some interlinear translations of the Koran" (*JTS* 14, 1990, pp. 113–138), but seems similar to Konya Mevlana Müz. 4687 (ca. 16–17th century).

The Arabic text is in fully vocalized *thulth*, the interlinear Turkish in fully vocalized *naskh* in black ink, except for f. 1[b]–f. 29[a], which are in red ink, but in the same copyist's hand; f. 1[b]–444[b]. The occasional old supply leaves (f. 9; 99–106; 227–234, some with watermark Trelune in diminishing size) have vocalized Arabic text only, without Turkish translation; 25×16.5 (21.5×13.5) cm; 18 lines (9 Arabic, 9 Turkish).

Paper: The original paper has chain lines and laid lines, but no watermark designs. The MS is undated but ca. 16th century, except for the supply leaves, which are ca. 17–18th century.

Decoration: No *ʿunwān*; red ink used for sura headings and marks for *ʿushr*, *ḥizb*, *sajda*, etc.; red ink dots between *āyāt*.

Ownership: In later hands than the MS: (1) f. 1[a], donated as *waqf* by al-ḥājj ʿUmar b. al-ḥājj Khalīl for the muftī ʿAlī Efendi; (2) in another hand, "1234" [1819]; (3) "Khānum Efendi ḥaḍratlari"; (4) Bought by E. Birnbaum, Istanbul, May 1994.

Binding: When this MS was rebound about the middle of the 20th century in maroon cloth covers over cardboard, it was so tightly sewn that the inner margins are very narrow, and the pages were trimmed too much, as is evident in the loss of part of many catchwords.

Other MSS and references: See **MS 28, T10**.

[30] **A14**

[*Qurʾān, juzʾ* 30]

[جزء ٣٠ من القران]

Begins (f. 1b, after *basmala*)

عمّ يتساءلون

Ends (f. 25b)

و لا الضالّين

Sūras 78–114 (i.e. last of the 30 *juzʾ* [sections] of the Qurʾān), followed by sura 1.

Colophon (f. 25b)

كتبه افقر الورئ على الوصفى

The copyist ʿAlī Waṣfī/Vaṣfī (d. 1255/1837) was a well-known calligrapher who also taught that subject at the Galatasaray Palace school in Istanbul. (See Şevket Rado, *Türk hattatları*. İstanbul [1985], p. 203. For another example of his calligraphy, see M. Uğur Derman, *Türk sanatında ebru*. Istanbul, 1977, p. 50).

Fully vocalized excellent *naskh*; f. 1–26 (f. 26 blank); 22.5 × 15 (17 × 9.5 cm); 9 lines.

Paper: Watermarked: Lion rampant.

Decoration: Good floral *ʿūnwān* (f. 1b) in gold, blue, pink, red and black; all pages multi-framed in gold, blue and red; gold roundels between *āyāt*.

Biding: Early 19th century; brown leather with *zanjīrak* around edges.

Ownership: Bought by E. Birnbaum, Istanbul, June 1981.

F. Tafsīr

[31] A18

al-Bayḍāwī, ʿAbdullāh b. ʿUmar, d. ca. 685/1286

البيضاوى ، عبد الله بن عمر

Anwār al-tanzīl wa asrār al-taʾwīl (f. 1b)

انوار التنزيل و اسرار التأويل

[*Tafsīr al-Bayḍāwī*]

[تفسير البيضاوى]

Begins (f. 1b)

الحمد لله الذى نزل الفرقان على عبده

End (f. 251b)

بما انعم عليه فى دار الدنيا و ان مات فى يوم تلاها او ليلة كان له من الاجر كالذى مات و احسن الوصيّه

The first part of one of the most famous standard medieval commentaries of the Qurʾān, comprising sūras 1–16. This basic work has been studied in *madrasa*s throughout the Muslim world since its composition, in the 7/13th century.

That this is an unusually early copy, probably 14th or perhaps early 15th century CE, is evident from the paleography and from the Egyptian/Syrian Mamlūk style of the binding's leather doublures, and the type of gilding of the headings in the first part of the manuscript.

The masses of interlinear and marginal notes in the first half of this large format book, written in many different but early hands, show that this manuscript

© KONINKLIJKE BRILL NV, LEIDEN, 2019 | DOI:10.1163/9789004389670_008

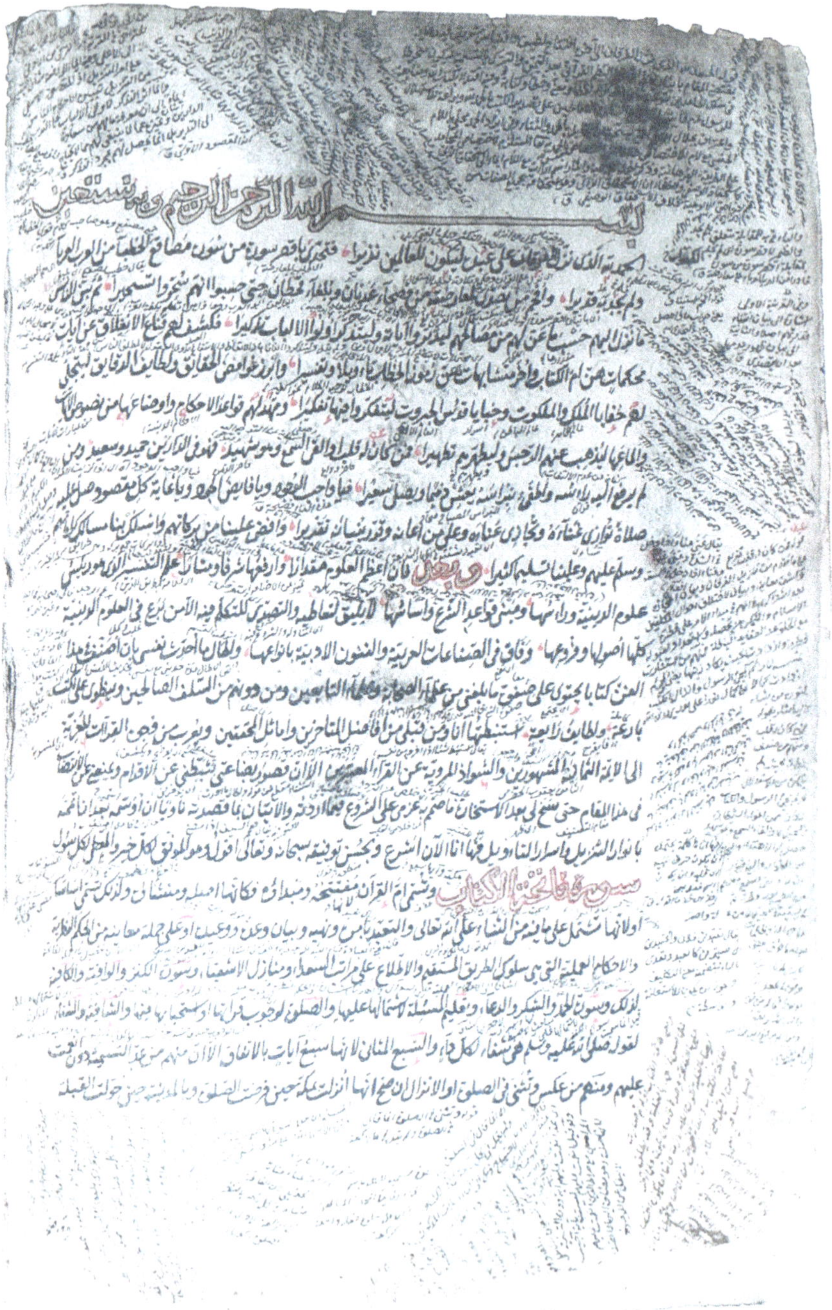

FIGURE 8 No. 31 (A18). al-Bayḍāwī, ʿAbdullāh b. ʿUmar, d. ca. 685/1286, *Anwār al-tanzīl*. [*Tafsīr*]; copied ca. 8/14th century; f. 1b

FIGURE 9 No. 31 (A18). al-Bayḍāwī, ʿAbdullāh b. ʿUmar, d. ca. 685/1286, *Anwār al-tanzīl. [Tafsīr]*; copied ca. 8/14th century; f. 1b. Part of Mamlūk binding doublure, inscribed *al-ʿizz al-dāʾim wa al-iqbāl*

was heavily used by scholars over several centuries. Due to intensive use a considerable number of pages fell out over the years and were replaced at various times later by supply leaves, most of them several centuries ago. However, a few folios at the beginning (f. 3–6) and the last 6 leaves (f. 246–251) were supplied much later, probably near the end of the 19th century.

Script is "proto-*nasta'līq*", partly vocalized; 27×18 (18×12.5) cm; 23 lines.

Paper: No watermarks, except on the later flyleaves, added at a mid-18th century rebinding (on p. 001 IASETMANDY; LANGVEDO; on p. 002, Crown above Grapes above VAMAN).

Binding: Original flap binding: pasteboard covered by dark brown leather, framed in blindstamped border; at centre is a quadruple-framed oval medallion; back cover in good condition, front cover stained and scraped; backstrip was partly replaced several centuries ago.

Doublure is typical Egyptian/Syrian Mamlūk style of the 14–15th century: block-pressed light brown leather, stamped with lozenges enclosing leaf patterns and frames, each repeating the blessing '*al-'izz al-dā'im wa al-iqbāl*';

This MS was rebound within its original covers, plus the addition of two new fly-leaves (f. 001 and 002), and an owner's note dated Muḥarram 1163 [December 1749], which corroborates the mid-18th century date of the watermarks on the additional fly-leaves which include the Christian date 1749 (see above).

Decoration: Some headings (*sūra* name, *basmala*, etc.) sometimes written in gold ink, outlined in red ink; Qur'anic citations usually overlined in red ink.

Ownership: (1) f. 001[a]: round seal (1.5 cm diameter) inscribed "Muḥammad ḥāfiẓ al-Qur'ān", and nearby the *shahāda* written in ink, with this owner's name and date, Muḥarram 1163; (2) Bought by E. Birnbaum, Istanbul, June 1981.

Other MSS: GAL I, 530; S I 738; Mach 748.

[32] A31

Ibn Kamāl Pāshā, Aḥmad b. Sulaymān, d. 940/1534

ابن كمال پاشا ، احمد بن سليمان

Tafsīr Kamāl Pāshāzāda (bottom edge and f. 1[a])

تفسير كمال پاشازاده

Sūras 7–31 only

[من سورة الاعراف الى سورة لقمان]

Begins (f. 1[b])

المص قد سبق الكلام فى مثله كتاب خبر مبتداء محذوف

Ends (sūra 31, middle of verse 33 [f. 328[b]])

فلا تغرنكم الحيوة الدنيا بزينتها فان نعمها داته (؟)// و لذاتها (catchword)

The original last folio of the MS is lost. It would have contained commentary on the end of verse 33 and all of 34, the end of *sūrat Luqmān.*

Ibn Kamāl Pāshā composed *tafsīr*s (commentaries) only on selected sūras of the Qur'ān. They mostly appear in the form of manuscripts of individual sūras: 1–38, 67, 78–79, 86. 89, 103. Only a minority of MSS contain many sūras copied together. The present manuscript contains the commentaries on the 24 sūras from sūra 7–31.

For a brief account of this polymath scholar's life and works see MS **67, M1/I.**

Professional *naskh,* a co-operative effort by several contemporary copyists; unvocalized; red ink for sūra names and for overlines on Qur'anic citations; f. 1–328; 30 × 18.5 (21.5 × 9.5) cm; 29 lines.

Paper: f. 1–89 buff colored thin "Oriental" paper without watermarks; on f. 90–328 there are at least three watermark designs in the following sequence: (1)

small Trelune; (2) small Crown, surmounted by a six-armed Star, surmounted by a recumbent Crescent; (3) from f. 303 on, several sheets have watermark of a small Cross enclosed in an oval with narrow lower part, and the letters I B below the oval; back doublure paper has a large Trelune. The MS is undated but similar watermarks are found in dated MSS of the late 17th century.

Binding: Spine and adjacent flap and edges of front and back covers are leather; the covers themselves are boards made up of pages recycled from an old Arabic MS in ugly naskh script. The exposed page used for the cover board describes denizens of heaven, the divine throne (*ʿarsh*), etc. The front and back covers and half of the flap are covered by soft-surfaced yellow paper, impressed with a scalloped long floral blind stamp and pendants (the flap has only one pendant); the yellow paper on the back cover is partly torn off. Bottom edge of the volume bears title: *Tafsīr Kamāl Pāshāzāda min sūrat al-Aʿrāf.*

Ownership: (1) On f. 1^{a}: Roundish seal-stamp (twice), inscribed "al-Sayyid Muḥammad ʿĀrif 1225" and two statements in ink signed by him, the first stating that he, Muḥammad ʿĀrif b. ʿAbdullāh al-Nūrī, known as ʿĀlimzāda acquired this MS on 1 Rajab 1234 [April 26, 1819] and the second his devoting it as waqf in 1237 [1821–1822]; (2) Bought by E. Birnbaum, Istanbul, July 1991.

References: İA vol. 6, pp. 561–565, art. Kemal Paşā-zade; DİA vol. 25, pp. 236–247; EI^{2} vol. 4, pp. 879–881.

G. Islām: Other (*Ḥadīth*, *ʿAqāʾid*, *Fiqh*, *Fatwā*, Eschatology, Prayer, etc.)

[33] T109/III

al-Ūshī, ʿAbdullāh b. ʿUthmān, Sirāj al-Dīn, fl. 569/1173

الاوشى ، عبد الله بن عثمان ، سراج الدين

Badʾ al-amālī (f. 18[a])

بدء الامالى

Alternative title:

al-Qaṣīdah al-lāmīya fī al-tawḥīd

القصيدة اللامية فى التوحيد

Begins (f. 18[a])

يقول العبد فى بدء الامالى * لتوحيد بنظم كاللآلى

Ends (f. 20[b])

جمعت جمعها سبعين بيتاً * بهذا البيت لم يجمع مثال

Copyist's colophon (f. 20[b]) 1112/1700.

This popular versified Islamic catechism in Arabic *mathnawī* has been widely used since the 6/12th century. This copy has 75 verses although its final couplet mentions only 70.

Naskh, fully vocalized; f. 18[a]–20[b]; 20.5 × 15 (16 × 10) cm. in two columns per page, framed in red rules; 15 lines. This copy is the last item in a 3 part MS by a single copyist (see E. Birnbaum, *Ottoman Turkish and Çağatay MSS in Canada*,

© KONINKLIJKE BRILL NV, LEIDEN, 2019 | DOI:10.1163/9789004389670_009

pp. 279–281): the first part is Turkish **MS 135, T109/I** *Münācāt-i Mūsā*, a dialogue between God and Mūsā, in Old Ottoman Turkish; the second is a book of prayers in Arabic with translation and interpretation in Old Ottoman Turkish, described below **MS 34, T109/II.**

Paper watermarked: Crown above Grapes.

Ownership: Seal stamp "al-Sayyid Ḥāfiẓ Ibrāhīm (or Ibrāhīm Ḥāfiẓ) 1252"/1836; round, diameter 1.5 cm (f. 18[a]). Other inscriptions in Turkish on f. 1[a] and inner cover, dated 1205/1790; Jumādā I 1210/1796; 1213/1799; 1218/1803.

Binding: Flap binding, front and back cardboard covers covered with faded marbled (*ebru*) paper (which remains bright on the flap): covers edged with brown leather, probably original; 18th century.

Ownership: Bought by E. Birnbaum in Istanbul, 1987.

Other MSS and references: Numerous copies in collections worldwide; many MSS listed in Brockelmann, GAL I 552 and S I 764; and Princeton-Mach, 2260 (13 MSS).

[34] T109/II

[*Kitab al-duʿāʾ*]

[كتاب الدعاء]

Begins (f. 15[a])

اعوذ بالله من الشيطان الرجيم بن الله تعالى يه استعانه ايده رم شيطاندن انجلين شيطانكى طاشلنمشدر

Ends (f. 15[a])

انك حميد مجيد تحقيقا سن اوكلمش سين و اولو پادشاهسين

Prayers in Arabic with phrase by phrase translation/interpretation in Old Ottoman Turkish; followed by heading (f. 16[a]) دعاء قنوت *Duʿā Qunūt* [a reverent prayer of trust in God, recited with the supererogatory prayers at night], beginning

انك نستعينك يعنى يا رب سندن طاعت و عبادت اوزرينه

and ending (f. 18[a])

الله تقبّل منى اى بنم اللهم بو قربانى قبول ايله ...

followed by instructions in Turkish to slaughter the sacrifice: *Bunı oḳıya, andan yatura, 'Bismillāh, Allāhü ekber diye boġazlaya.*

Naskh, fully vocalized: f. 15[a]–18[a] (in a MS of 20 f. [Turkish **MS 135, T109/I**]), dated 1112/1700–1701. Paper watermarked: Crown above a bunch of Grapes; (1) Seal-stamp "al-Sayyid Ḥāfiẓ Ibrāhīm, 1252"/1836; (2) -- Muṣṭafā; previous owner's family births noted 1205; 1210; 1213; 1218. Flap binding, ca. 18th century. Bought by E. Birnbaum, Istanbul, 1987.

[35] **A26**

[*Masāʾil wa ajwiba: ḥāshiya ʿalā kitāb majhūl fī uṣūl al-fiqh*]

[مسائل و اجوبه: حاشية على كتاب مجهول فى اصول الفقه]

Beginning missing; now begins (f. 1[a])

لكونه مسئلها (؟) لترك الواجب فلو لم قول من حيث هو فعل له اى للممنوع

First extant heading (f. 1[a])

قال مسئله الاتفاق الى اخره **اقول** يعنى ان العقلاء اتفقوا على ان الفعل الواحد باى معنى كان من معانى الوحده

Last heading (f. 209[b])

فان قلتَ المجاز واقع على قولهم ايضا لانه حينئذ [sic] اطلق المثل [--] **فقلْتُ** للطاهره [sic]

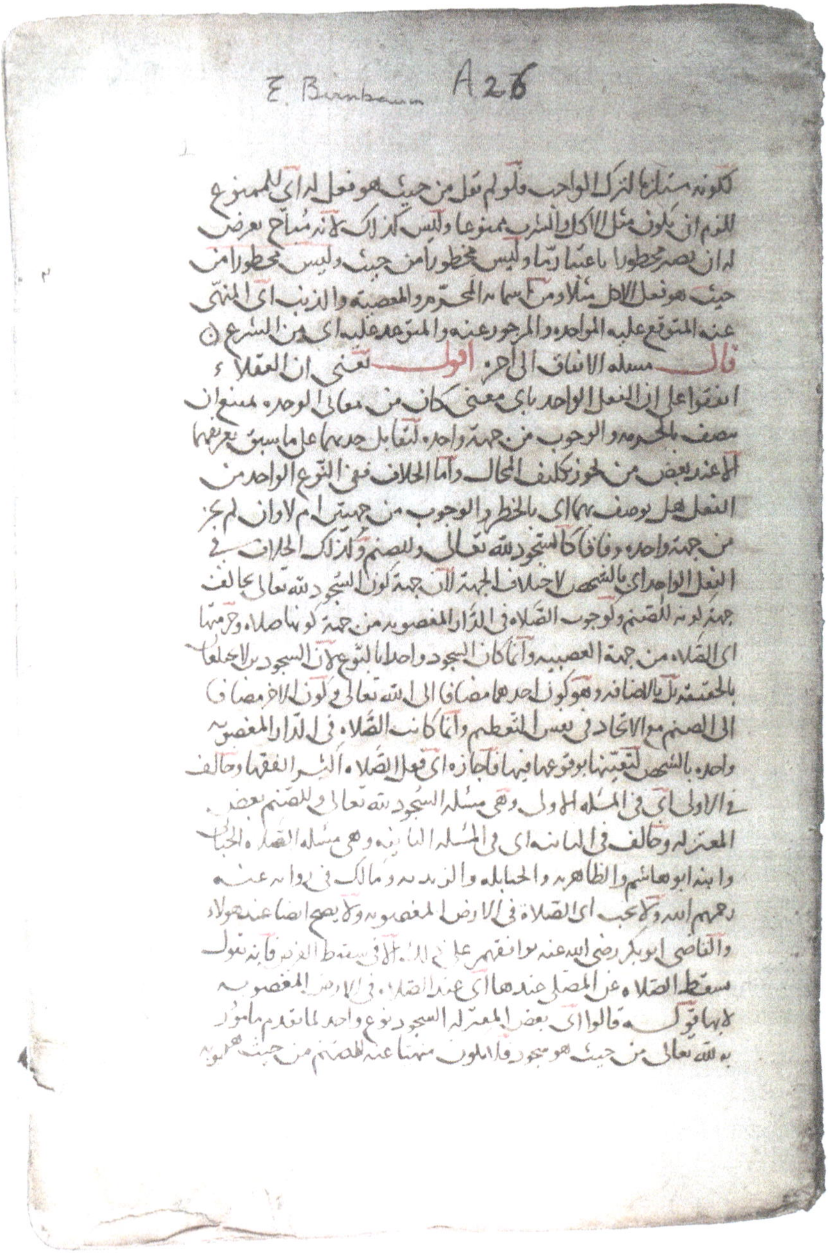

FIGURE 10 No. 35 (A26). [*Masāʾil wa ajwiba*: *ḥāshiya ʿalā kitāb fī uṣūl al-fiqh*]; copied ca. 7/13th century; f. 1a

A large fragment (210 folios) of an unidentified old commentary on an unidentified old Ḥanafī work on *uṣūl al-fiqh*. It is critical of the Muʿtazila, and sometimes cites al-Shāfiʿī. The general style is to cite two or three words of the targeted original work, followed by the words "*ilā ākhirihi*", and then explain or criticize the original citation. Much of the text is in the classic form of "Questions and Answers" (*masāʾil wa ajwiba*). The author frequently uses these formulas: ***fa-in qulta*** [citation] *ilā ākhirihi,* ***aqūl*** …; and ***qāl*** [citation] *ilā ākhirih* ***aqūl*** …; ***qāl*** *masʾala* [citation] *ilā ākhirih,* ***aqūl*** …

This work was probably composed in the 7/13th century. The latest authorities cited in it were by then already deceased, their names followed by the formula *raḍī Allāh ʿanh*. The most recent seems to be Fakhr al-Dīn al-Rāzī (d. 607/1210, f. 6[b]); there is a reference to his work *al-Maḥṣūl* [*fī uṣūl al-fiqh*], (f. 48[a]). Other authorities of the 5–7/11–13th centuries cited include al-Ghazālī (d. 505/1111, f. 78[b]); [Abū al-Yusr] al-Bazdawī (d. 482/1089, f. 184[b]; 186[a]); al-Bāqillānī (d. 404/1013) and al-Jawharī (d. 400/1009).

Paleographically this MS dates from about the 7/13th century.

Old *naskh*, not vocalized; diacritics omitted from common words; f. 1–210 (last folio extant f. 209; "f. 210" is a loose page detached from somewhere earlier in the MS); 26 × 17.5 (19.5 × 12) cm; 25 lines; headings in red ink. At least 2 contemporary copyists wrote this MS; both the original beginning and end of the MS are lost.

Paper: "Oriental", without watermarks; more than half the pages are discolored by the iron in the ink used by the copyist.

Binding: Front and back covers lost, but cloth backstrip and sewing of the quires are intact, holding the remaining leaves in place.

Ownership: (1) Old owner's oval seal (difficult to read), f. 107[a]; 152[a] (2) Bought by E. Birnbaum, Istanbul, July 1987.

[36] A27

[*Masāʾil wa ajwiba ʿalā kitāb fī uṣūl al-fiqh al-Ḥanafī*]

[مسائل و اجوبه على كتاب فى اصول الفقه الحنفى]

Beginning is lost; text at the *centre* of the page now begins (f. 1[a])

و سبب الطهارة الصلاة و هى شرطها فلم يجب قصدا بل عند ارادة الصلوة

First rubric (f. 4[b])

الاصل الرابع فى المحكوم عليه شرط التكليف العقل و الفهم

Marginal commentary: Beginning is lost: now begins (f. 1[a])

قوله و سبب الطهارة اى سبب وجود الطهارة الصلاه او ارادتها لان الطهارة مضاف اليها شرعا …

Center text: First heading (f. 4[b])

الاصل الرابع فى المحكوم عليه شرط التكليف العقل و الفهم

End: [f. 88[b]–137]. Most of these leaves are presently stuck together due to ancient water damage, and only small portions at the edges of the pages are legible. Museum conservation is required to separate the pages of this block of folios.

End of last legible page now (f. 88[a], centre)

الكلام موجبا الحكمه فى البعض كما منع الشرط العقاد العله لحكمها

A large part of an unidentified commentary (*sharḥ*) on an unidentified Ḥanafī work of jurisprudence (*uṣūl al-fiqh*), together with an equally unidentified marginal supercommentary (*hāmish*) on that commentary. The main commentary occupies the centre of the page. Much of it is in the form of the genre *Masāʾil wa ajwiba* ("Questions and Answers"). Until f. 20 the rubric *masʾala* heads each question; thereafter the copyist left a blank space for later insertion, merely marking the margin opposite with the word *masʾala* in tiny script.

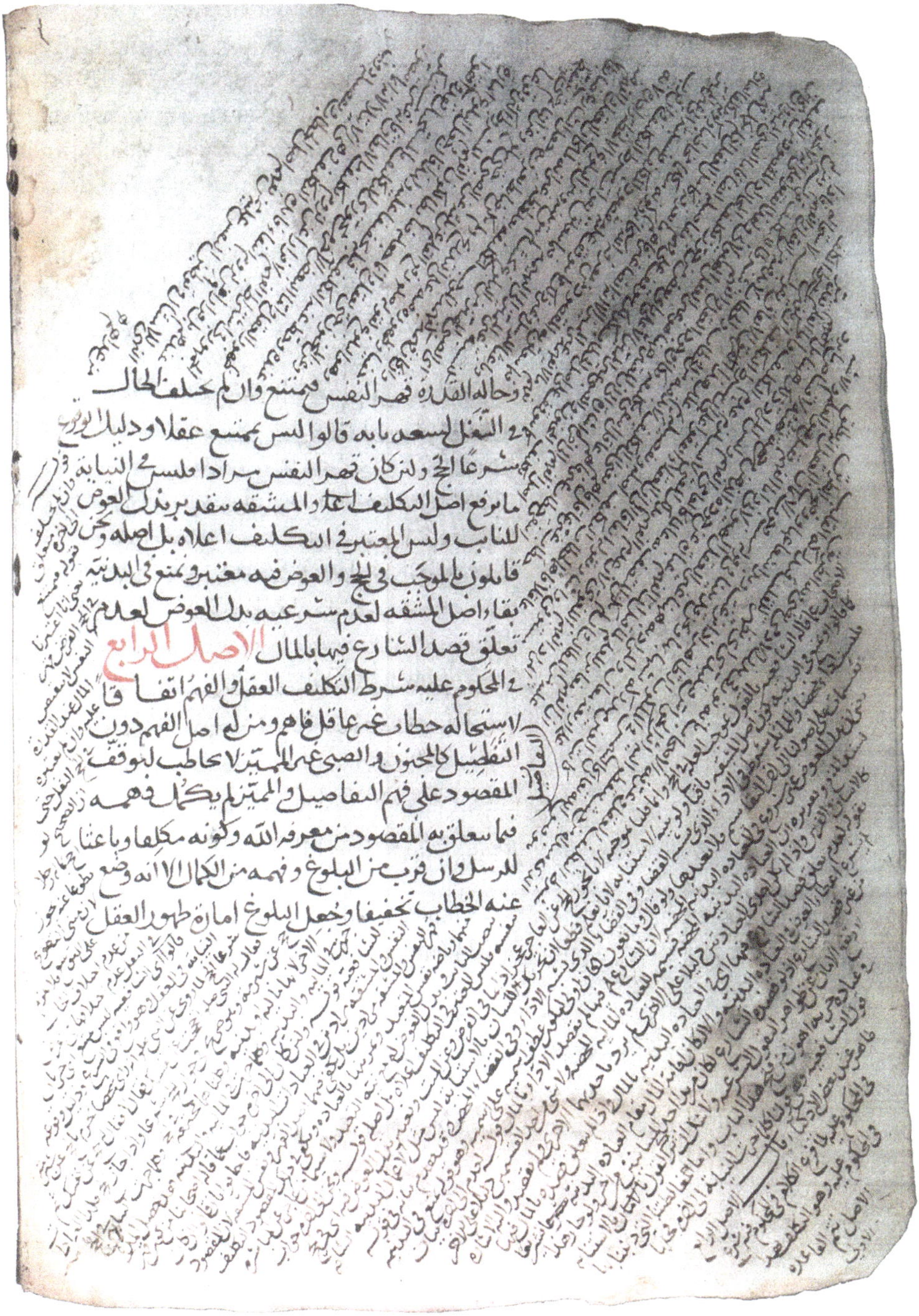

FIGURE 11 No. 36 (A27). [*Masāʾil wa ajwiba fī uṣūl al-fiqh al-Ḥanafī*]; copied ca. 7/13th century; f. 4[b]

The copyist also left blanks for the insertion of other headings such as *al-jawāb* and some section headings, noted in small script in the margins. The supercommentary in the margins discusses matters raised in the *sharḥ*, usually introduced by the word *qawluh*. Both the main text and the marginalia are in the hand of the same copyist, but the script of the marginalia is smaller, and sometimes the marginalia in the top half of the page are written upside down.

This MS includes several groups of folios in smaller format, which bear only the "central" text, without marginalia, but in script of about the same age as the main text. They are between: f. 1 and 2 (1 folio); f. 67 and 68 (1 fol.); f. 70 and 71 (7 fol.); f. 105 and 106 (1 fol.); f. 130 and 131 (5 fol.).

Age of works cited, and the age of this MS:

The main text cites many classical authorities. Among the *most recent* are:

al-Ghazālī (d. 505/1111, 69^{b}; 87^{a}; 105^{a}); al-Sakkākī (d. 626/1229, f. 105^{a}); al-Qāḍī [= al-Bayḍāwī] (d. 685/1286, f. 75^{b}; 105^{a}).

We may deduce that the work was composed no later than the first half of the 8th/14th century; paleographically the script is rather archaic, similar to dated MSS of the 13th century.

Good professional old *naskh*, unvocalized and *rather sparing of the diacritics which normally distinguish similar letters*. This MS is incomplete. Although foliated f. 1–137, the fol. 88^{b}–137 are now mostly stuck together, due to water damage many centuries ago, and so only the edges of these pages are legible. 26×17.5 (centre 11×9; margins 23×17) cm; 15 lines (centre); margin, 50 lines or less (varies).

Paper: "Oriental", buff color without watermarks.

Binding: Covers missing; but retains old brown leather backstrip; sewing loose and now partly detached.

Ownership: Bought by E. Birnbaum, Istanbul, July 1987.

[37] A16

[*Majmūʿa fī al-fiqh al-Ḥanafī*]

[مجموعه فى الفقه الحنفى]

Four works on Ḥanafī *fiqh*, all copied by the same copyist. The last three works are dated in different months of the year "93". This is probably 793/1391 because (1) the script is paleographically similar to that of MSS of the 7–8/13–14th centuries; and (2) the copyist refers to the author of the third work (*al-ʿUmda fī ʿaqīdat ahl al-Sunna*), Abū al-Barakāt ʿAbdullāh b. Aḥmad al-Nasafī who died in 710/1310, as being deceased (*raḥimahu Allāh*, f. 29[a]; *ghafar Allāh lahū*, f. 29[b]).

All four works in this *majmūʿa* are in good old-fashioned *naskh* and have occasional rubrications, including overlining, and section headings, and dots marking the ends of *miṣraʿ*s and *bayt*s in poetry; 17.5×14 (12×19) cm; 13 lines. For details of each work, see below **MS 38–41, A16, I–IV.**

Paper: Old "Oriental" beige paper without watermarks; worm holes mainly in inner margins; some pages roughly repaired with paper patches but rarely affecting legibility.

Binding: Leather spine and edges; front and back covers are now covered with old marbled (*ebru*) paper—a later rebinding, now loose, with later doublures. The one facing f. 1[a] mentions in Turkish:

> جاكر كوينلى حاجى داوده ينه قرية مزبور ... *Muḥarrem ġurresinde ʿAbd ül-Ḳādir māl* ...

On the originally blank f. 95[a], an old but later hand has written a 6-*bayt* Turkish hymn (*ilāhī*), beginning

كله هى جانمك جانى كل ذكر ايدلوم الله
وجودم اول دن فانى كل ذكر ايدلوم الله

Beneath it, in different ink, is an old poor imitation of an Ottoman *ṭughrā* including the name Süleymān. The back doublure is on later paper, and bears a note dated Jumādā II 1041/December 1631-January 1632.

Ownership: Bought E. Birnbaum, Istanbul, June 1981.

[38] **A16/I**

(Attributed to)

Abū Ḥanīfa, al-Nuʿmān b. Thābit, d. 150/767 (f. 1ᵃ; 1ᵇ)

ابو حنيفه ، النعمان بن ثابت

al-Fiqh al-akbar (f. 1ᵃ)

الفقه الاكبر

Begins (f. 1ᵃ)

قال حدثنا ابو الفضل محمد بن احمد بن الحسين قال حدثنا ابو بكر محمد بن عبد الله بن صالح قال حدثنا الفقيه ابو سعيد سعدان بن محمد بن بكر البستى ببلخ

Ends (f. 20ᵇ)

فاعطى بعضا و منع بعضا و هذا كمن له عبيد فاعطى واحداً و منع واحداً . و الله اعلم

A relatively old copy of a standard early Ḥanafī work on the Muslim creed. This MS is not dated but is in the same hand as the next MS in this volume, which is date 9 Rajab [7]93/June 1391. (See above **MS 37, A16**).

Other MSS: GAL (1st ed.), 170; S I, 285; Mach 2197.

[39] **A16/II**

al-Nasafī, Najm al-Dīn ʿUmar b. Muḥammad, d. 537/1142 (f. 21ᵇ)

النسفى ، نجم الدين عمر بن محمد

al-ʿAqīda al-Nasafīya (f. 27^b, 55^b)

العقيدة النسفية

Begins (f. 21^b after *basmala*)

قال الشيخ الامام الاجل العالم العابد المتقى استاذ الايمه و العلما امام الحرمين مفتى الخافقين ابو حفص عمر بن محمد ابن احمد النسفى تغمده الله بغفرانه ... قال اهل الحق حقايق الاشيا ثابته

Ends (F. 27^b)

المليكه [sic] افضل من عامة البشر و من المومنين افضل من عامة المليئكه [sic] و بالله التوفيق.
تمت العقيده النسفيه ... يوم الجمعه اليوم التاسع من شهر رجب الفرد احد شهور سنه ٩٣ هجريه

An early copy of a standard *fiqh* work on the Muslim creed; copy completed 9 Rajab "93", probably 793/June 1391. This work is more often titled *al-ʿAqāʾid al-Nasafīya*. (This author, Najm al-Dīn ʿUmar al-Nasafī should not be confused with Abū al-Barakāt ʿAbdullāh b. Aḥmad al-Nasafī who lived a century and a half later and is the author of *al-ʿUmda*, the next work in this *majmūʿa*. For calculation of this date, see **MS 37, A16**).

Other MSS: GAL I, 548; S I 758; Mach 2224.

[40] **A16/III**

al-Nasafī, Abū al-Barakāt ʿAbdullāh b. Aḥmad b. Maḥmūd, (d. 710/1310) (f. 29^a, 29^b)

النسفى ، ابو البركات عبد الله بن احمد بن محمود رحمه الله

al-ʿUmda fī ʿaqīdat ahl al-sunna wa al-jamāʿa (f. 29^b)

العمدة فى عقيدة اهل السنة و الجماعة

or

al-ʿAqīda al-Nasafīya (f. 55^b)

العقيدة النسفية

Begins (f. 29^b, after *basmala*)

الحمد لله ... قال العبد المفتقر الى الله الودود ابو البركات عبد الله بن احمد بن محمود النسفى غفر الله له ... جمعت فى هذا المختصر عمدة [sic] عقيدة اهل السنة و الجماعة

Ends (f. 55^b)

و قد قال عليه الصلوة و السلام الخلافة بعدي ثالثون سنه و قد تمت بعلى رضى الله عنهم و الله اعلم بالصواب

Colophon (f. 55^b)

تمت العقيدة النسفيه الحمد لله ... كان ذلك يوم الخميس يوم التاسع و العشرون من شهر رجب الفرد احد شهور سنه ٩٣ هجرية ...

A relatively old copy of this work of Ḥanafī *fiqh*, copied "29 Rajab 93", probably 793/July 1391. For calculation of this date, see **MS 37, A16**, above.

References: GAL II, 253 (X); S II 268 (XI); Mach 2286.

[41] **A16/IV**

"al-Imām Shaykh al-Islām" (f. 57^a)

"الامام شيخ الاسلام"

al-Jawāhir fī uṣūl al-dīn ʿalā madhhab al-Imām Abū Ḥanīfa (f. 57^a)

الجواهر فى اصول الدين على مذهب الامام ابو حنيفه نظم الامام شيخ الاسلام

FIGURE 12 No. 41 (A16). "al-Imām Shaykh al-Islām", *al-Jawāhir fī uṣūl al-dīn*, composed 570/1174/75; copied [7]93/[13]91; f. 57[b]–58[a]

Begins (after *basmala*) (f. 57[b]–58[a])

الحمد لله القديم الاحد * الدايم الفرد العظيم الصمد

مقدر الاقدار و الاقتسام * مدبّر الامور و الاحكام ...

علم اصول الدين بالتفصيل * فقيه منجات من التضليل

Ends (f. 95[a])

و قد مضت للامة المستحنه (المستحسنه ؟) خمسماءآتٍ ثم سبعون سنه

Colophon (f. 95[a])

تمت بحمد الله و منه و حسن توفيقه قُبَيل صلاه العصر يوم الاحد يوم التاسع من شهر شعبان

احد شهور سنه ٩٣ هجريه ...

A very rare treatise on Ḥanafī *uṣūl al-dīn*, entirely in verse, consisting of approximately 900 rhyming couplets by an author described on the "title page" (preceding the text) only a "al-imām shaykh al-Islām", an honorific title given to major scholars and mystics from the 4th/10th century onwards. The book is addressed to *ikhwatī fī al-dīn* (f. 57[b], line 13). The frequent subject headings are in red ink and are not verse. The author states in the last verse (f. 95[a], line 6) that the work was completed in 570 AH [= 1174–1175]. Beneath that, but in the same hand, is the copyist's date of completion: "9 Shaʿbān 93", presumably 793/July 1391. For calculation of this date, see **MS 37, A16** above.

This work in verse is not cited in GAL or Mach.

[42] **A24/I**

[*Risāla fī Yawm al-Qiyāma*]

[رسالة فى يوم القيامة]

Begins (first leaves lost; now begins f. 2[a])

يكون مايه و سبعه و ثمانين و هو عام زوال دولة البرامكه و انقراض ملكهم و انتها ايامهم المشهورة فى الدنيا

Ends (original end lost; now ends f. 77[b])

و كذلك اخذ ربك اذا اخذ القرا و هى ظالمه ان اخذه اليم شديد ق و القران المجيد //

An unidentified old eschatological and apocalyptic work in rhymed prose (*sajʿ*) with numerous sections in poetry, partly updated to the early 16th century. There are many diagrams. The text includes items typically found in books on *Yawm al-Qiyāma*. However, this work also refers to many historical events, including even some very recent and current ones: the collapse of the Umayyads; rise of the Saljuqs; collapse of the Fāṭimids; the expulsion of the Franks in 583 AH at the hands of Ṣalāḥ al-Dīn (Saladin); Jalāl al-Dīn Khwarazm Shāh; the invasion of the Tatars, etc. Dates are cited for many of the events. Among the many peoples named are the Egyptians, Iraqīs, Persians, Ottomans, Christians (*al-Naṣrānī*), "Bulghārī", "Iṣfahānī"; the appearance of the Banī al-Aṣfar and Yājūj, etc., etc.

FIGURE 13 No. 42 (A24/I). [*Risāla fī yawm al-Qiyāma*]: An eschatological and apocalyptic historical work in rhymed prose and poetry, about events ranging from antiquity to the early 10/16th century; f. 40[b]–41[a]

In its present form, this work probably dates from the period 1516–1520: it mentions "*Salīm Āl ʿUthmān yamluk jazīrat al-ʿArab fī ākhir zamān*" (f. 41[a]); i.e. the Ottoman sultan Salīm I ("the Grim") who reigned 1512–1520, and whose conquests in 1516 included Arabia.

The MS is divided into 12 sections (*juzʾ*), the first 6 untitled. However, *juzʾ* 7 is headed *fī khurūj al-Mahdī* (f. 23[a]). The year 922(/1516) is noted as the time when "the destruction" will occur (*yaẓhur al-kharāb*, f. 22[b]). In *juzʾ* 8, *fī ʿalāmāt al-sāʿa wa kharāb al-mudun*, there is a very long and detailed list of cities in the Middle East and Central Asia which will be destroyed (f. 27[b] ff). *Juzʾ* 9 is titled *fī taʾrīkh al-Qāhira* (f. 34[b]); *juzʾ* 11 … *fī dawlat al-Atrāk fī Miṣr* (f. 54[b]). The author had previously cited a *ḥadīth*: "I [God] have armies in the East which I have named al-Turk—horsemen by whom I take revenge on those who rebel against Me, … from the East, a people without religion, whose heads are big and their eyes small …, who will rule the lands of the Persians, and Khurasan, ʿIrāq, Ḥarrān, Rūm, Arzinjān and the Jazāʾir of the Firāh (Firāt) [Euphrates] and Shām … and those who know secrets and raise the Qurʾān … at the end of 903 years [1497–1498] which is 97 years before the millennium [i.e. 1000 AH/1591] …" (f. 44b–46a).

Naskh/taʿlīq mixture; f. 1–77 (in a volume of 86 folios; f. 78–86 are a different work: see **43**, **A24/II**); 20.5×15 (14×10) cm; 19 lines; headings, subheadings and division dots are usually in red ink; occasional words in gold ink. Selected words routinely written upside down. Copyist left f. 32a blank, noting that it marked a gap in his manuscript Vorlage.

Illustrations: Diagrams in red and black ink, on f. 1b, the Earth surrounded by 8 planets within a circle, marking the course of the Sun; other diagrams on f. 17b, 18a, 27a, 32a, 36a, 37a, 38a–b, 39a, 40a, 41a, [42a left blank for diagram], 43b, 44a–b, 45b, 46b, 56b, 57a, 58a–b, 59b, 61b, 74b–77b. Occasional marginal notes, largely translated into Turkish in 19–20th century hands; flyleaf f. 1a on later paper contains a note dated [1]211 = 1796–1797, and notes (of loans ?), naming Monla Ismāʿīl (8 *ghurūsh* 50 *pāra*) and "Imām" (3 *ghurūsh* 10 *pāra*).

Paper: Watermarked: (1) Anchor in Circle, topped by rounded Cloverleaf Trefoil (on 7 pages); (2) Anchor in Circle topped by *diamond-shaped* Trefoil (on 1 page). [Both watermarks are found in 16th century papers].

Binding: Rebound in 19th century.

Ownership: Bought by E. Birnbaum, Istanbul, July 1987.

[43] A24/II

al-Bisṭāmī, ʿAbd al-Raḥmān b. Muḥammad b. ʿAlī b. Aḥmad, d. 858/1454 (f. 85a)

البسطامى ، عبد الرحمان بن محمد بن على بن احمد

[*Risāla fī Yawm al-Qiyāma*]

[رسالة فى يوم القيامة]

Begins (f. 78ª; beginning missing)

قال عليه الصلاة و السلام انا و الساعه كفرس رهان قد سبقت اذ احدهما الاخرى
قال دانيال اذا مضى السابع ٩٦٤ سنة

Ends (f. 86ᵇ)

و من بعد ياتى على الناس ميمة يموت جميع الخلق فى قدر لمحة فتخلو الاراضى من جميع اناسها
و ذلك فعل الله رب البرية . و صلى الله على سيدنا محمد و اله و صحبه و سلم تسليما كثيرا

ʿAbd al-Raḥmān al-Bisṭāmī was a very prolific author on a wide range of subjects, including a major encyclopedic work and many treatises on Sufism, traditional Islamic sciences, eschatology, ḥurūfism, alchemy and magic arts, etc. After he settled in Bursa, which was then the capital city of the Ottoman Empire, he enjoyed the patronage of Sultan Murād II, to whom he dedicated several works.

This MS lacks at least the first folio, and its original title is unknown. The subject is *Yawm al-Qiyāma*, the Day of Resurrection—an eschatology largely in rhymed prose (*sajʿ*). It is now bound after a much longer eschatological work (**MS 43, A24/I**) written in a different old *naskh* hand, yet of similar scribal age. The author describes himself as *ʿAbd al-Raḥmān b. Muḥammad b. ʿAlī b. Aḥmad al-Bisṭāmī amātahu Allāh ʿalā al-Kitāb wa al-Sunna bilā miḥna*, and names his source as *Mafātiḥ al-faraj al-jāmiʿ wa miṣbāḥ al-nūr al-lāmiʿ*, stating that he transcribed it from the [unnamed] late author's own autograph. (f. 85ª).

Our writer goes on to describe how the Prophet appeared to him in a dream and told him a *ḥadīth*, which he cites (f. 85ᵇ–86ª). The work closes with a poetic prognostication in 15 verses, beginning (f. 85ᵇ)

فينزل عيسى جامع الشام جهرة * فتنظره جميع البلاد البعيده

It ends as noted above (f. 86ᵇ)

فتخلو الاراضي من جميع اناسها * و ذلك فعل الله رب البرية

Large old fashioned naskh; f. 78ª–86ᵇ; 20.5×15 (14.5×10) cm; 15 lines; headings and division dots in red ink; much later marginal notes in indelible purple pencil (ca. 19-early 20th century), mostly Turkish translations of uncommon Arabic words in this manuscript.

Paper: Watermarks, (probably 10–11/16–17th century): (1) small Trelune in descending sizes; (2) Unclear: possibly outline of letters C and B separated by a vertical line, topped by a Trefoil.

Binding: Mostly detached; this work follows **MS 43, A24/I**: see that entry.

Ownership: (1) Unknown owner who foliated it in "Oriental" Arabic numerals, perhaps in 18th century; (2) Bought by E. Birnbaum, Istanbul, July 1987.

Other MSS and references: No other MSS found; cf. GAL II, 232 (2nd ed., p. 300); S II 323–324; DİA, vol. 6, pp. 218–219; *Kashf al-ẓunūn*, (Istanbul, 1941), col. 1905, under *Mawḍūʿāt al-ʿulūm*.

[44] A37/I

Sharḥ al-Maṣābīḥ (f. 81ᵇ)

شرح المصابيح

Begins f. 7ᵃ [f. 1–6 missing]

الصحابى فى متن الكتاب و كتب بعضا من الرواة عن رسول الله ... فى الحواشى ... النسّاخون
فى المتن ما كتبه المصنّف فى الحواشى فصار الرواة المذكورون فى متن الكتاب كثيرا

Selected rubric headings:

f. 38a

باب الكبائر و علامات النفاق

f. 43a

فصل فى الوسوسه

f. 48b

باب الايمان بالقدر

f. 61b

باب اثبات عذاب القبر

f. 66b

باب الاعتصام بالكتاب و السنة

Ends (f. 81[b])

و كل امر مخاطب من وكل يكل كل [؟—] تكل و معنى وكل فوض اخره اى [؟—] و الله اعلم

This next paragraph [below] was crossed out until the word امين which just precedes the copyist's colophon:

هذه تمة نصف [sic] الاول من شرح الكتاب المصابيح لمولانا و سيدنا الامام و الجر اليهما و [؟—] مظهر الحق و المتوالدين قدس الله روحه و نوّر ضريحه و قد [و]قعت [sic] تحريره هذا الكتاب و تسطيره فى منتصف شهر المبارك ذى القعده سنه ثمان و ثمانمايه ...

مشقه العبد الواثق بالله فضل الله بن محمود بن فضل الله الشهير بكمال ...

The first half of a commentary (*sharḥ*) on the well-known work on *ḥadīth* titled *Maṣābīḥ al-sunna*, a classic *madrasa* textbook by al-Ḥusayn b. Masʿūd al-Baghawī (d. 516/1122).

The author of this commentary is not named. He cites the standard classic collections of the *sunna*: the *Ṣaḥīḥ* of both al-Bukhārī and Muslim.

On f. 82[a], the page after the end of this work, another work begins, headed *Bāb al-ʿilm min al-Ṣiḥāḥ* (see below **MS 46, A37/II**).

Fluent but untidy small old fashioned *naskh*; [f. 1–6 lost]; f. 7[a]–81[b]; 25 × 15 (14 × 11) cm; 25 lines; "Oriental" paper without watermark designs; there are a few large script headings in red ink; occasional old corrections in margins; copyist's colophon dated middle of Dhū al-Qaʿda 808/May 1406 (f. 81[b]).

Binding: Dark brown leather with medallion in center and edges framed in *zanjīrak*; covers originally stamped and painted in gold, but the gold has mostly disappeared. The present binding boards are about 1 to 2 cm too small for the text block; they have obviously been transfered from a smaller MS. The front and back cover boards are partly made of pages recycled many centuries ago from older manuscripts in Persian and Arabic.

Ownership: Bought by E. Birnbaum in Istanbul in July 1991.

Other MSS: Cf. Mach, 624 ff.

[45] A37/II

[***Sharḥ***] ***al-Ṣiḥāḥ*** (f. 82ª, 93ª and *passim*)

[شرح] الصحاح

Begins (f. 82ª, line 1)

[كتا]ب العلم من صحاح قوله بلغوا عنى و لو اية امر مخاطبين من التبليغ [—] ايصال الخير الى اصل الايه …

Ends (f. 326ᵇ, line 6)

كما فى عادة مصنّف المصابيح … احاديث المصابيح نحو حديث صلح الحديبيه فان ذلك حديث طويل اورد فى المصابيح

Last heading (f. 325ᵇ)

باب الوصايا من الصحاح

Last words (f. 326ᵇ)

قوله انّ الرجل ليعمل المراة بطاعة الله سنتين // سنه (catchword)

This MS is a commentary on the *Ṣiḥāḥ*, the six canonical collections of the *sunna* (by al-Bukhārī, Muslim, al-Tirmidhī, Abū Dāwūd, al-Nasāʾī, and Ibn

Māja). Many centuries ago this MS was bound, where it still remains, following a commentary on the *Maṣābīḥ al-sunna* of al-Baghāwī (d. 512/1122) and other works: **MS 45, A37/I**, f. 7ª–81ᵇ.

The MS contains main headings in red ink beginning with the word *kitāb*, most subdivided into many *bāb*s. Both of these headings are often followed by the words *min al-Ṣiḥāḥ*. Here is a selection of these headings and subheadings, which may help to identify the author of this work:

f. 82ª, *Bāb al-ʿilm min al-Ṣiḥāḥ*; f. 93ª, *Kitāb al-ṭahāra min al-Ṣiḥāḥ*; f. 96ᵇ, *Bāb mā yūjib al-wuḍūʾ min al-Ṣiḥāḥ*; f. 103ᵇ, *Kitāb al-ṣalāt* …; f. 104ª, *Bāb sunan al-wuḍūʾ*; f. 118ª, *Kitāb al-ṣalāt*; f. 120ᵇ, *Bāb taʿjīl al-ṣalāt*; f. 124ᵇ, *Bāb al-adhān*; f. 198ª, *Kitāb al-zakāt*; f. 205ª, *Bāb al-ṣadaqa*; f. 219ª, *Kitāb al-ṣawm*; f. 225ª, *Bāb laylat al-qadr*; f. 227ª, *Kitāb faḍāʾil al-Qurʾān*; f. 237, *Kitāb al-daʿwāt*; f. 261ª, *Kitāb al-nāsik*; f. 283ª, *Bāb ḥaram Makka min al-Ṣiḥāḥ*; f. 288ª, *Kitāb al-buyūʿ*; f. 306ª, *Kitāb al-salaf* …; f. 313ᵇ, *Bāb al-shifāʾ*; f. 315ᵇ, *Bāb al-ijāza*; f. 316ª, *Bāb iḥyā al-mawāt* …; f. 325ª, *Bāb al-waṣāya min al-Ṣiḥāḥ* [last heading in this MS].

f. 326ᵇ. The original end of this MS is lost; last folio ends

قوله انّ الرجل ليعمل و المواة بطاعة الله ستين // (catchword سنه)

Small naskh in several hands in cooperation; f. 82ª–326ᵇ [f. 320 lost]; 25×15 (19×11) cm; 25 lines; "Oriental" paper without watermark designs; headings in red ink; occasional corrections in margins; end of this work is missing, but the MS seems to be about the same age as the work **MS 45, A37/I** which precedes it in this bound volume: ca. 808/1406, although the work of different copyists.

Ownership: Bought by E. Birnbaum in Istanbul, July 1991.

[46] **A32**

[***Sharḥ ʿalā kitāb Maṣābīḥ al-sunna liʾl-Baghawī wa ghayrihi***]

[شرح على كتاب مصابيح السنه للبغوى و غيره]

Beginning and first 45 leaves lost, and the end is also missing; now begins at f. 46[a]

يعقل ان اجازه وَليُّه او كان آذن له يجوز و العبد كالضبي

First heading (f. 46[b])

كتاب ١٣ الماذون

Last heading (f. 134[a])

كتاب ٥٥ الوَصّيه

End lost; last words of the text (f. 136[b])

خاصة اوصى لورثة فلان فللذكر مثل حظ الانثيَيْن و ان قال لولد فلان فالذكرُ و الانْثى سواء //

A large fragment of an unidentified old manuscript (paleographically dated to approximately the 6th or 7th/12–13th century) of a work on *uṣūl al-fiqh*. The first part, f. 1–45, is lost.

This MS consists of numbered "books" (each headed *kitāb*), from the latter part of the 12th to a large part of the 55th "book". The first few extant are: 13, *al-ma'dhūn*; 14, *al-ikrāh*; 15, *al-daʿwā*; 16, *al-iqrār*; 17, *al-shahādāt*; 18, *al-wakāla*; 19, *al-kafāla*; 20, *al-ḥawāla*.

The last few extant are: 48, *al-jihād*; 49, *al-karāhīya*; 50, *al-ṣayd*; 51, *al-dhibāḥ*; 52, *al-uḍḥīya*; 53, *al-khanāyat*; 54, *al-diyyāt*; 55, *al-waṣīya*.

The *margins* bear notes in many different hands added later at various periods from about the 13th to the 17th centuries. Many are references to standard early Islamic commentaries on *fiqh* works of various periods, cited mostly by title only: *Dhakhīra*; *Kifāya*; *Sharḥ al-Hidāya*; *Wiqāya*; *Kāfī*; *Sharḥ al-Mukhtār*; Qāḍī Khān [d. 592/1196]; Ḥusāmzāda [d. 893/1438]; *Nāfiʿ*; *Ikhtiyār*; *Mushkilāt al-Qudūrī* [d. 428/1037]; *Nihāya*; *Khizānat al-Fatwā* [completed before 522/1128]; *Bazzāzīyīn*; *Nawādir*; *Hidāya*; Ibn Mālik, etc.

This MS was owned for the past few centuries by Turkish speakers, who inserted or added a few items some four centuries after the Arabic text was copied. These included some Turkish translations of uncommon Arabic words e.g. / انت طالق سن بوشنمق لق سن [f. 83ª].

The originally blank f. 137ª–138ª are entirely in Ottoman Turkish, perhaps written at various times in the 16th and 17th centuries. On f. 137ª, 2 *fatwā*s sourced to *Fatāwā-yi ʿAlī Efendi Shaykh al-Islām* [i.e. Zenbilli Ali Efendi (also known as ʿAlī al-Jamālī, who served 908–932/1503–1526)]; on f. 137ª⁻ᵇ, Arabic citations from *Sharḥ al-Ashbāh* by "Muḥammad al-Shahrī"; and a *fatwā* in Arabic by Abū al-Suʿūd (who served as Shaykh al-Islām of the Ottoman Empire, 952–982/1545–1574), and another by him in Turkish on f. 138ª, followed by a long explanatory commentary on it in Turkish, beginning *yaʿnī*, sourced to "*al-faqīr mawlā al-marḥūm Shaykh al-Islām Muḥammad Efendi Anqaravī*", who may be Abū al-Suʿūd's former student Maʿlūlzāda Muḥammad (d. 992/1584).

Old *naskh*; f. 46ª–137ª; 18 × 12.5 (10 × 7.5) cm; partly vocalized; 13 lines.

Paper: "Oriental"; not watermarked.

Binding: Brown leather with oval floral medallion on front and back covers, both enclosed in originally gold *jadwal* frames; leather backstrip is a replacement made centuries ago; binding block still sewn, but its leather cover boards have long been detached from it.

Ownership: Bought by E. Birnbaum, Istanbul, July 1991.

[47] **A15**

al-Kisāʾī, Muḥammad b. ʿAbdullāh, Abū Jaʿfar, 5/11th century (f. 1ᵇ)

الكسائى ، محمد بن عبد الله

Kitāb al-malakūt (f. 1ᵇ)

كتاب الملكوت

FIGURE 14 No. 47 (A15). al-Kisāʾī, Muḥammad b. ʿAbdullāh, 5/11th century. *Kitāb al-malakūt*; copied apparently in the author's lifetime; f. 1b–2a

Begins (f. 1b, after *basmala*)

قال الشيخ الجليل ابو جعفر محمد بن عبد الله الكسائى ابقاه الله الحمد لله الذى كان قبل تكوين الاكوان ... هذا كتاب المَلَكُوت جمعت فيه عجايب صنع ربنا

Ends [*in a later hand and on a different paper*] (f. 101a)

و اذا دَخَلْتَ عليها لَهَزَتَك يا ناظراً فيه اسئل الله مرحمةً على المصنّف استَغْفِرْ و اطلب لنفسك من خير تُريد بها من بعد ذٰلك غفراناً بكتابته

تمت بعون الله تعالى و حسن توفيقه على اضعف عباد الله و احوجهم الى رحمة ربّه الكريم سنه تسع و سبعين [و] ثمانمانه الهجريه ...

A rather rare work, mostly on Muslim doctrines about the Creation of the Universe. This is a work of many unnumbered chapters. It was categorized by Rudolf Mach as "sermon" (*Catalogue of Arabic Manuscripts* [*Yahuda section*] *in the Garrett Collection, Princeton University Library*, no. 4393). It was composed early in the 5/11th century (Brockelmann). **Our manuscript was apparently copied in the author's lifetime**, judging from the copyist's blessings on the author: "*abqāhu Allāh*" ("may God grant him a long life", f. 1[b]) and the calligraphy is consistent with this period. Some MSS of this work bear the variant title *ʿAjāʾib al-malakūt*.

The last 6 folios (96–101) are supply leaves (replacing lost originals), and are dated 879 /1474–1475 in the colophon (f. 101[a]) by an anonymous copyist.

The margins throughout the MS are heavily annotated with later Ottoman Turkish explanations of difficult Arabic words, most often citing one of several dictionaries, such as *Akhtarī* (Aḫterī, d. 968/1560, an Arabic-Turkish dictionary completed in 952/1545), *Anwar* (*Enver*), *Ṣiḥāḥ* or simply *Lugha*.

Old fully vocalized *naskh*; f. 01–02; 1–101 (of which f. 14 and 96–101 are 15th century supply leaves); 17.5×13 (12.5×9) cm; 15 lines; partial table of contents on 17–18th century paper (f. 01).

Paper: Old oriental, without watermarks (except for 2 leaves [01 and 02], which were added later before the main text; these two have a Shield watermark). Many wormholes especially on inner margins and the lower edge of pages, but legibility is not affected.

Binding: in bad condtion; the leather backstrip and leather edges of the cover boards are evidence of an old rebinding; paper now mostly covers the older boards.

Ownership: Bought by E. Birnbaum in Istanbul in June 1981.

Other MSS: Mach 4393.

[48] A23

al-Ṣaghānī, al-Ḥasan b. Muḥammad b. al-Ḥasan, d. 650/1252 (f. 1[b])

الصغانى ، الحسن بن محمد بن الحسن

FIGURE 15 No. 48 (A23). al-Ṣaghānī, d. 650/1252. *Mashāriq al-anwār*; copied 756/1355; f. 120[b]–121[a]

Mashāriq al-anwār al-nabawīyah min ṣiḥāḥ al-akhbār al-Muṣṭafawīya (f. 2[b]; 121[a])

مشارق الانوار النبوية من صحاح الاخبار المصطفوية

Begins (f. 1[b])

الحمد لله مُحْيي الرمم و مُجْرى القلم ... قال الملتجى الى حرم الله تعالى الحسن بن محمد ... الصِغانى

Ends (f. 121[a])

كان يلي بهذه التلبية و عمرته م انس لبيك عُمرةً و حَجّاً انس لبيك عمرةً و حجاً

FIGURE 16 No. 48 (A23). al-Ṣaghānī, d. 650/1252. *Mashāriq al-anwār*, copied 756/1355. Fine Mamlūk flap binding, with repeat pattern of 6-pointed star within a hexagram

End and colophon (f. 121[a])\

تم كتاب مشارق الانوار النبوية ... فرغ من تحريره فى اواخر جماذى الاولى سنه ست و خمسين و سبع مايه ...

This author (here vocalized al-Ṣighānī, f. 1[b]) gained fame for his contributions to two major fields of traditional Islamic scholarship: Arabic lexicography and *ḥadīth*. In the present work he brings together the traditions recorded in two basic works of classical *ḥadīth*, the *Ṣaḥīḥ* of al-Bukhārī (d. 256/870) and the *Ṣaḥīḥ* of Muslim (d. 261/875), reorganized according to an unusual linguistic classification. This manuscript is *a fine early copy*, made about a century after the author's death. Many marginal notes were added over the centuries by generations of scholars.

Fine calligraphic *naskh*, often vocalized; f. 1–122; 21.5×14.5 (15×10) cm; 17 lines;

Paper: Thick burnished "oriental" paper; colophon (121[a]) "*awākhir Jumādhā I, 756*"/June 1355; first of each 8-leaf quire is usually numbered *in words* in the upper left corner of the outer margin.

Decoration: Red ink for headings and for 3 frequent abbreviations: خ for *akhbaranā*, ق for *qāla*, and م for ?. Occasional old interlinear and marginal notes added.

Binding: *Finely restored Mamlūk flap* binding decorated with repeat pattern of a six-pointed star ("Star of David"), each within a hexagon on both front and back covers and on the outside of the flap. The binding was evidently restored by the addition of a new backstrip in the 20th century.

Notes later added to the originally blank f. 121[b] (in later hands, ca. 17–18th century):

(1) From *Iḥyā ʿulūm al-dīn* [of al-Ghazālī, d. 505/1111]: a passage on the names of *aṣḥāb al-kahf*;
(2) From *al-Shaqāʾiq al-nuʿmānīya* of Ṭāshkūprīzāda (d. 968/1560): biography of Ibn Farishta ʿAbd al-Laṭīf (Ibn Malak), the author of a standard Arabic-Turkish vocabulary (*Luġat-i Ferişteoğlu-i ʿAbdüllaṭīf Ibn Melek*) who died some time after 821/1418.

Ownership: Bought by E. Birnbaum, Istanbul, July 1981.

Other MSS: GAL I, 443, S I, 613; Sezgin VIII 327; Mach 643.

[49] **A29**

ʿIyāḍ b. Mūsā al-Yaḥṣubī, d. 544/1149 (f. 1[a]; 1[b])

عياض بن موسى اليحصبي

al-Shifā bi-taʿrīf ḥuqūq al-Muṣṭafā (f. 1[a])

الشفا بتعريف حقوق المصطفى

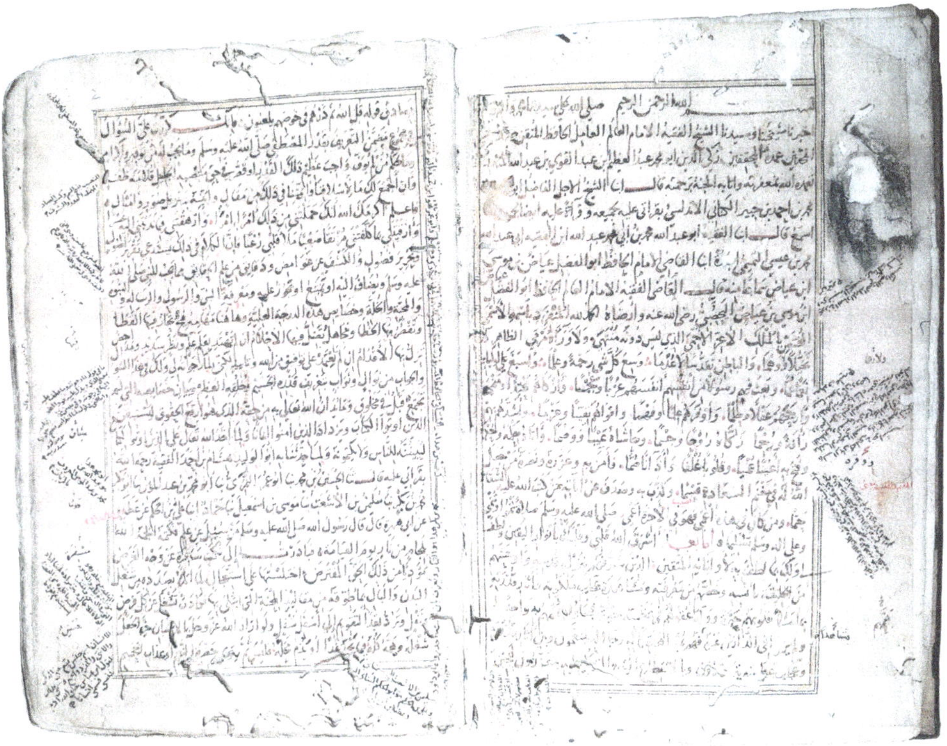

FIGURE 17 No. 49 (A29). ʿIyāḍ al-Yaḥṣubī, d. 544/1149. *al-Shifā' bi taʿrīf ḥuqūq al-Muṣṭafā*; copied 757/1356; f. 1b–2a

Begins (f. 1b, after *basmala*)

اخبرنا شيخي و سيدنا الشيخ الفقيه الامام العالم العامل الحافظ ... ابو محمد عبد العظيم ابن عبد القوى بن عبد الله المنذرى ... ابو الفضل عياض ابن موسى ابن عياض اليَحْصُبِي رضى الله عنه ... اما بعد اشرق الله قلبي و قلبك بانوار اليقين

Ends (f. 165a)

و لا ينتصر مَنْ خَذَلَهُ و لا يرد دعوه القاصدين و لا يُصلح عمل المفسدين و هو حسبنا و نعم الوكيل

Colophon (f. 165[a])

وافق الفراغ من تعليقه فى الخامس عشر من المحرم افتتاح شهور سنه سبع و خمسون و سبع مایة ... على يد ... محمد بن على النشاى ...

This classic of popular piety, extolling reverence for God, and especially for the Prophet Muḥammad, retained its popularity for many centuries. Its author was a Mālikī *qāḍī*, a prolific North African scholar, who lived and held office mainly in Sabta/Ceuta, but also in Granada in Islamic Spain. This work consists of an introduction and 4 parts (*qism*), each subdivided into chapters (*bāb*), themselves made up of sections (*faṣl*). This copy is dated "15 Muḥarram 756"/January 1356. The margins contain many added brief marginal notes of considerable age.

Old *naskh* (not Maghribī), fully vocalized; f. 1–165; 25.5×17.5 (21×12.5) cm; 23 lines; wormholes in upper margins, but not affecting legibility.

Paper: "Oriental", buff colored, without watermarks.

Decoration: (f. 1[a]) Ornamental gold and black frame around the "title page" includes a citation, in the same copyist's hand, of the author's biography, sourced to Muḥyī al-Dīn al-Nawawī (d. 676/1277), *Tahdhīb al-ʿasmā wa al-lughāt*. The two pages comprising the first opening (f. 1[b]–2[a]) are framed in gold; all other pages are double-framed in red ink; headings in red throughout.

Binding: Good brown leather Ottoman flap binding, decorated with good medallion with a floral motif and pendants; probably an 18th century rebinding. The present doublures at front and back, watermarked with Trelune Crescents in descending size, were added when the manuscript was rebound.

Ownership: (1) A hole and a smudge in the outer margin of f. 1 indicates that a stamp or inscription of previous ownership has been deliberately removed by a later owner; (2) bought by E. Birnbaum, Istanbul, 1991.

Other MSS: GAL I 455 (no. 1); S I 630; Mach 4501.

[50] A25/I

al-Bābilī, Aḥmad b. Muḥammad b. Aḥmad, fl. 964/1557 (f. 32b)

البابلي ، احمد بن محمد بن احمد بن عمران ، البابلي بلداً و الشافعي مذهباً (f. 32b)

Muqaddima fī al-basmala wa al-ḥamdala

مقدمة فى البسمله و الحمدله

Begins (after *basmala*, f. 1b)

و به نستعين على كل صعب شديد و بعد فلما ان عزمت و انا الفقير احمد بن محمد البابلى

Heading (f. 21b)

المبحث الثانى فى الحمد

Ends (f. 32b–33a)

و الله ... اعلم و قد اذنت لمن اشتهر فضله و على قدره انه اذا راي فى تاليفى هذا خطا فاليصلحه
بعد مراجعته الفضلا الاماثل فانى ما وضعت فيه تركيبا الا بعد تامل كثير و كان الفراغ على
يد مولفه احمد بن محمد بن احمد بن عمران البابلى بلداً و الشافعى مذهباً فى سابع عشري شعبان
المعظم قدره سنة اربع و ستين و تسعمايه ...

Colophon (f. 33a)

... هذا اخر لفظ مولفه و كان الفراغ من كتابتها تاسع عشرين شهر رمضان المعظم قدره سنه
اربع و ستين و تسعمايه ختمتها ... بخير و كتبتها حسن بن حسين البرديني الشافعى

Colophon of author, dated 17 Shaʿbān 964/June 1557 (f. 32b),

Colophon of copyist: Ḥasan b. Ḥusayn al-Bardīnī [probably from Bardonya (Marathonisi in southern Greece)], dated 19 Ramaḍān 964/July 1557 (f. 33a), about one month after the author completed composing it.

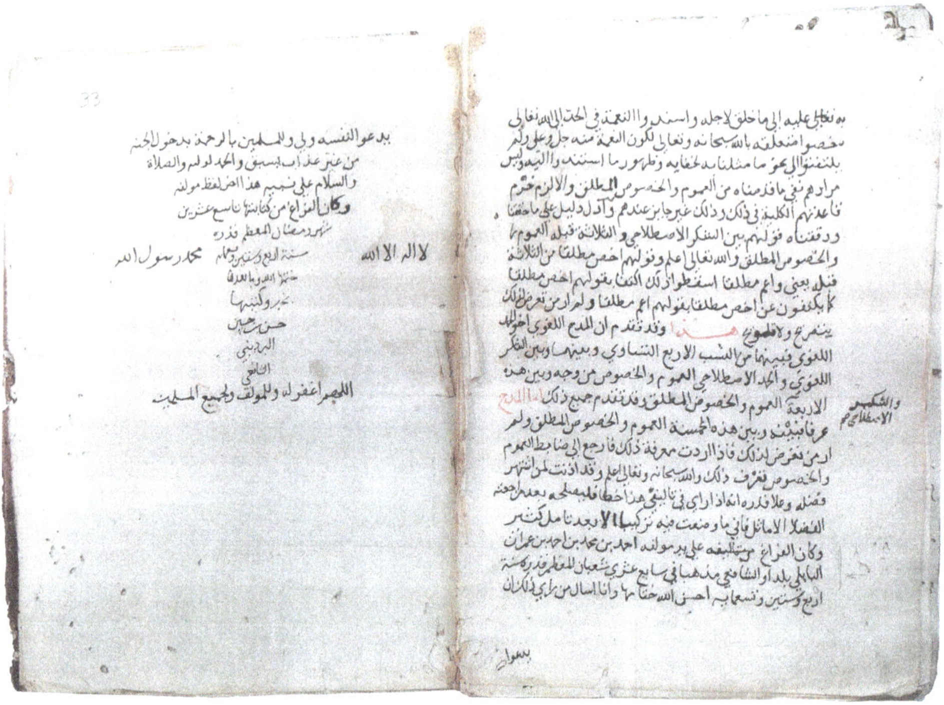

FIGURE 18 No. 50 (A25/I). al-Bābilī, Aḥmad, fl. 964/1557. *Muqaddima fī al-basmala wa al-ḥamdala*; composed and copied 964/1557; f. 32[b]–33[a]

A rare treatise on the use of the expressions *Bism Allāh al-Raḥmān al-Raḥīm* and *al-Ḥamd li'llāh*. **No other copies found.**

Naskh; f. 1–33 (in a volume of 35 fol., preceded by a later flyleaf, with a Turkish note dated 1155/1761–1762); 21 × 15.5 (15.5 × 11.5) cm; 21 lines.

Paper: Watermarked: (1) Crown (?); (2) Six-pointed Star; mid-10th/16th century.

Binding: Flap binding very loose; paperboards covered with Turkish marbled (*ebru*) paper; probably 18th century.

Ownership: (1) Muḥammad al-Ṭūsyawī [from Tosya, near Kastamonu in Anatolia], f. 1[a]; (2) Muṣṭafā b. ʿAlī al-Istānbūlī al-Miṣrī, 1188[/1744], f. 1[a]; [(3) Bibliophile bookseller Raif Yelkenci, Istanbul, 20th century]; (4) another Istanbul bookseller; (5) E. Birnbaum, July 1987.

Other MSS: GAL, SN II 186 (?)

Note: On f. 0[a] (the flyleaf) a note of the contents in a different hand:

Fī hādhā al-mujallad fawāʾid mutafarriqa:1. Muqaddima fī mabḥath al-basmala wa al-ḥamdala; 2. Ḥāshiya ʿala[—]Abī Fatḥ fī ādāb liʾl-muftī al-sābiq Yaḥyā Efendi; 3. Ḥāshiya Mīr Ṣadr al-Dīn; 4. Bir risāla Ḥanafīya fī al-adab; 5. Unmūdhaj al-[?] maʿ ajwibatih fī hāmish li-wāḥid min al-ʿulamāʾ.

[51] M4/II

Asrār al-ṭahāra

اسرار الطهارة

Begins (f. 52[b])

الحمد لله الذى تلطّف بعباده فتعبدهم بنظافة

Ends (f. 55[b])

و ما ياكُل لحمه و جزء طير لا ياكل عوف

An anonymous brief tract on physical and spiritual purity, in naskh script, added on the blank pages of a Turkish MS copied in Jumādā I 966/March 1559. (See E. Birnbaum, *Ottoman Turkish and Çağatay MSS in Canada*, pp. 96–97).

Ownership: Bought by E. Birnbaum in Istanbul in 1987.

[52] A17

al-Futūḥī, ʿUthmān, before mid-17th century (f. 1[a])

الفتوحى ، عثمان

Bushrā al-karīm al-amjad bi-ʿadm taʿdhīb man tusammā biʾsm nabīhi Aḥmad aw Muḥammad, (f. 1a, 2b)

بشري الكريم الامجد بعدم تعذيب من تسمّى باسم نبيه احمد او محمد

Begins (f. 1b, after *basmala*)

الحمد لله الذى اطلع فى سَماء الازل شمس انوار نبوة نبيه احمد ... و بعد فلا يخفى على اولى العرفان

Ends (f. 23a)

فنسال الله سبحانه و تعالى ان يَمّن علينا بالموت على الاسلام و ان تجعلنا من امة محمد عليه افضل الصلوة و السلام و الحمد لله وحده و هو حسبنا و نعم الوكيل

A treatise on the benefits accruing to those who bear the same names as the prophet: Aḥmad or Muḥammad. It is based on the interpretation of sura 61:6. The work concludes with a *khātima* (f. 19b–23a) emphasizing the good news ("*bushrā*") for those bearing such names.

This work is ***rare***: it is not recorded in GAL and Mach, but Ḥājjī Khalīfa [Kātib Chelebi] (d. 1067/1657) included it in his *Kashf al-Ẓunūn* (I, col. 245) and therefore it must have been composed before the middle of the 17th century.

Naskh, occasionally vocalized; f. 1–23 (previously numbered 54–76, and so clearly extracted from a larger bound volume); 19.5×12 (15×6.5) cm; 17 lines.

Paper: Watermarked with Trelune in decreasing size; ca. 17–18th century.

Binding: Disbound when it was removed from its previous binding.

Decoration: "Title page" (f. 1) in alternating lines of red and black ink. First opening framed in gold rules, subsequent pages double-framed in red ink; headings throughout in red ink.

Ownership: Bought by E. Birnbaum, Istanbul, June 1981.

[53] **A13**

[*Kitāb al-duʿāʾ*]

[كتاب الدعاء]

Begins (f. 1b, after *basmala*, sūra Yāsīn)

يٓس و القران الحكيم

Ends (f. 18b)

اللهمّ صل على سيدنا محمدُ آدم ... صلوات الله على نبينا و عليهم اجمعين

A prayer book consisting of 5 suras of the Qurʾān nos. 36, 67, 78, 113, and 1, (f. 1–13) followed by prayers (f. 14a–18b). This small volume was beautifully copied in 1293/1876 by Sayyid ʿUthmān, librarian of the Wālida Sulṭān/Sulṭān Vālide Mosque [at the southern end of the Galata Bridge] in Istanbul (colophon 18b).

Turkish style *naskh*; fully vocalized; each page multiframed in blue and red; the end of each *āya* is marked by a gold ball; 19.5 × 13 (13 × 8) cm; 9 lines; gold *ʿunwān* (f. 1b).

Paper: Buff colored, without watermarks.

Binding: Originally edged in decorated brown leather; rebound in the second half of the 20th century, when the leather was covered by green marbled (*ebru*) paper.

Ownership: 3 seals: (1) Ḥasan Ḥusayn b. ʿUthmān (f. 1a); (2, 3) Ḥasan Taḥsīn [Jaʿfar?] (f. 1a; 25b); bought by E. Birnbaum, Istanbul, August 1980.

H. Sufism

[54] **A1**

al-Jazūlī, Muḥammad b. Sulaymān, d. ca. 877/1472

الجزولى ، محمد بن سليمان

Dalāʾil al-khayrāt

دلائل الخيرات

Begins (f. 1ª)

محمد احمد حامد محمد احيد وحيد

(f. 5ᵇ heading)

هذه صبه الروضه المبركه [sic]

Ends (f. 140ª)

محمد خاتم النبيين امام المرسلين على اله و صحبه و سلم تسليماً

Al-Jazūlī was a major Moroccan mystic who established the Jazūlī branch of the Shādhilī sufi order. His *Dalāʾil al-khayrāt*, consisting largely of prayers for the Prophet, became extremely popular, not only in the Maghrib, but also throughout the Sunnī Middle East. This MS, which begins with several pages listing the many names of the Prophet, consists of small single unbound leaves of thick paper. It lacks the author's introduction.

West African Maghribi script, fully vocalized; 140 unbound leaves; 16×10.5 (12×7) cm; 9 lines; each leaf ends with catchword, which is repeated as first word of the next leaf; f. 1–13 have watermark laid and chain lines, but no designs; f. 14–140 lack laid and chain lines.

Date: Probably 19th century.

© KONINKLIJKE BRILL NV, LEIDEN, 2019 | DOI:10.1163/9789004389670_010

Binding; Unbound single leaves, in style typical of MSS from the region of Nigeria, placed between two pieces of cardboard, the lower one pierced by a hole, into which a thin strip of leather (77 × 0.6 cm) has been inserted and is wrapped around the cardboards.

Decoration: Red ink used for divine names, for Muḥammad, the Companions, and the Qur'anic citations. On f. 6[a] a half page geometric design within a square in brown, yellow, and black ink.

Ownership: (1) a pencil note on f. 1[a]: "Stev 35, 24/9/08"; (2) bought from a second hand bookstore in southern England by (3) Joseph Goodman of London, who presented it to (4) E. Birnbaum, in May 1959.

Other MSS and references: Birnbaum collection **MS 56, A12** (18th century); many other MSS in major libraries; GAL II, 327(4); Mach 1938.

[55] **A12**

al-Jazūlī, Muḥammad b. Sulaymān, d. ca. 877/1472

الجزولى ، محمد بن سليمان

Dalā'il al-khayrāt

دلائل الخيرات

Begins (after *basmala*, f. 1[b]–2[a])

الحمد لله الذى هدانا للايمان و الاسلام ... و بعد هذا فالغرض فى هذا الكتاب ذكر الصلواة على النبي ... و فضائلها اذكرها ... و سميته **دلائل الخيرات**

Ends (f. 98[a])

فى قلبي معرفتك حتى اعرفك حق معرفتك كما ينبغى ان نعرف به و صلى على سيدنا و نبينا و مولانا محمد خاتم النبيين ... و نعم الوكيل

Colophon (f. 98[a])

حرره الفقير المذنب السيد حافظ عبد الله النورى بن الحاجى احمد الجزرى من تلاميذ محمد صالح الفيضى الآمدي

(The words *ʿAbdullāh al-Nūrī* and *Muḥammad Ṣāliḥ al-Fayżī al-Āmidī* seem to have written over a smudge which may have contained other names too.)

Seal stamp (f. 98[a])

حافظ

السيد

عبد الله

A well calligraphed pocket sized copy of al-Jazūlī's sufi mystical prayer book. This MS was probably made in Turkey; the copyist's teacher is described as al-Āmidī (f. 98[a]), i.e. from Diyār Bakr in Anatolia.

Our other MS of this work, **MS 54, A1**, is in a West African Maghribī hand.

Very nicely calligraphed Turkish style *naskh*, fully vocalized; f. 1–100 (last two folios blank); 16×10.5 (10×5) cm; 11 lines; rubrics in green ink; a few notes added in Turkish.

Paper: Watermarked: Crown and letters GA and F; probably late 18th century.

Binding: Flap binding, cardboard, covered by faded red marbled (*ebru*) paper, now detached; leather backstrip.

Ownership: Bought by E. Birnbaum, Istanbul, August 1980.

References: GAL II, 327 (4); Mach 1938.

I. Druze

[56] **A4**

[*Rasāʾil al-ḥikma*]

[رسائل الحكمة]

Begins (f. 1^{b}, heading)

الرسالة الدامغة للفاسق الرد على النصيرى لعنه المولى

Last *risāla* (begins f. 145^{b})

شعر النفس و ما توفيقى الاّ بالله . قال الشيخ ابو ابراهيم اسمعيل ابن محمد التميمى الداعى

Ends (f. 146^{b})

فى كل يوم جديد بخز و السلام و السلام بحمد مولانا و منّه

The canon of Druze scripture consists of 111 tracts (*rasāʾil*). The authorship of most them is ascribed to Ḥamza b. ʿAlī and to Ismāʿīl b. Muḥammd al-Tamīmī "al-Dāʿī". Their composition goes back to the rise of the Druze religion in the 5/11th century. Silverstre de Sacy was the first to print a complete edition, accompanied by a detailed study (Paris, 1838, based on the Bibliotheque National, Paris MS 1581).

The present MS contains the text of the 25 *rasāʾil* numbered 15–40 in Silvestre de Sacy's edition, a grouping found in a number of other independent manuscripts in various libraries.

Script: Bold *naskh*, fully vocalized; f. 1^{b}–146^{a} in black ink, with headings and citations in red ink. The originally blank folios 146–148 are now filled with fully vocalized non-calligraphic prayers. (Begins: *Mīthāq walī al-zamān. Tawakkaltu ʿalā mawlānā al-Ḥākim al-aḥad*, and followed by *mīthāq al-nisāʾ*); 20.5×14.5 (15.5×10.5) cm; 13 lines.

© KONINKLIJKE BRILL NV, LEIDEN, 2019 | DOI:10.1163/9789004389670_011

Paper: Beige, with several watermark designs, probably 11/17th century: (1) Tre-lune (most frequent); (2) 3 Mountains; (3) Heart with letters PS in middle; (4) letter X with serifs.

Decoration: First opening is highly decorated, including a gold, red and green *ʿunwān*, framed in red and green; at head of each *risāla*, a title decorated in gold, often on a red and green background; all pages from 2^b to end framed in red ink.

Binding: Dark brown leather flap binding with floral central medallion and ornamented panels above and below, and corner pieces, all similarly decorated; on the leather flap a stamped lozenge bearing the formula لا يمسها الا المطهرين; doublures are Ottoman style gilded flowers and leaves on a pink background.

Ownership: Bought by E. Birnbaum in Istanbul, June 1973.

Other MSS and references: See *EI*² art. Durūz; N.M. Abu-Izzeddin, *The Druzes*. Leiden, 1984; DİA art. Dürzilik, vol. 10, pp. 39–48.

J. Ethics

[57] **A19**

al-ʿĪshī, Muḥammad al-Tīrawī, d. 1016/1607 [?]

العيشى ، محمد التيروى

Rawḍat al-ʿulamāʾ (f. 67ᵃ)

روضة العلماء

Begins (f. 2ᵇ–3ᵃ)

الباب الاول فى فضل قول لا اله الاّ الله **الباب الثانى** فى فضل طلب العلم ...
الباب الاول ... روى عن انس بن مالك ... عن رسول الله ... انه قال لا اله الا الله

Ends (main text, f. 67ᵃ)

قال رجل لرجل اموال اهل الذمّة و دماءهم حلال علينا كفر و كذلك لو قال شُرب الخمر حلال و دع قول من يقول انّها حرامٌ كفر تمت [sic] كتاب **روضة العلماء** بعون الله الملك الوهاب ... كتبه عبد الضعيف [sic] ... محمد بن يوسف المولوى عن قصبةِ يكُيجة واردار ... تم روز پنجشنبه فى وقت عصر من اوآخر شهر صفر المظفر سنه ١٠٣١ تم

This work on Islamic ethics (*akhlāq*) is rare. It consists of 40 numbered chapters, followed by one unnumbered final chapter, each citing the words of classical Arabic sources on the topic of that chapter. The opening page (f. 1ᵇ) consists entirely of a listing of the subject of each chapter, immediately followed by the beginning of *bāb 1*, on the virtues of learning (*faḍāʾil al-ʿilm*), citing Mālik b. Anas, Abū Zar al-Ghaffārī, Saʿīd b. Jubayr and others; *bāb 2* (f. 5ᵃ) on seeking *ʿilm*, cites Abū Mūsā al-Ashʿarī, Ḥasan al-Baṣrī and others. *Bāb 40* (f. 64ᵃ) discusses giving a drink of water to a Muslim, citing various authorities including Muḥammad b. Isḥāq and "Asad b. Khalīl al-muʾallif". In our MS an unnumbered final chapter titled *Bāb al-kalām alladhī yakūn al-rajul bihi kāfirān* (f. 66ᵃ–67ᵇ) completes the work. Old occasional notes in Arabic, Persian and Turkish are found in margins.

© KONINKLIJKE BRILL NV, LEIDEN, 2019 | DOI:10.1163/9789004389670_012

FIGURE 19 No. 57 (A19). al-ʿĪshī, Muḥammad, d. 1016/1607. *Rawḍat al-ʿulamāʾ*; copied 1031/1622; f. 1b

The great bibliographer Ḥajjī Khalīfa (Kātib Çelebi, d. 1657) describes in his *Kashf al-ẓunūn* (Istanbul, 1940–1941, col. 922) a work titled *Rawḍat al-ʿulamāʾ wa jannāt al-khulafāʾ* by ʿAlī b. Yaḥyā al-Zandawaysitī (d. 382/922), and records also an abridgement of this title by Muḥammad al-ʿĪshī al-Tīrawī (d. 1016/1607). Our manuscript is probably a copy of al-ʿĪshī's abridgement. *İzmir Millî Kütüphanesi Yazma Eserler Katalağu*, haz. Ali Yardım (cild I, no. 1521) records a copy of *Rawḍāt al-ʿulamāʾ wa jannāt al-ʿūrafāʾ*, probably of Zandawaysitī's text.

In his colophon (f. 67[a]) the copyist Muḥammad b. Yūsuf of the Mawlawī sufi order states that he completed this copy in the last decade of Ṣafar 1031/1622 at Yeñije-i Vārdār (Giannista, east of Salonica).

At the end of the MS, this copyist added versified formulas, one in Turkish and the other in Persian, requesting readers to recite the *Fātiḥa* for him:

*Her ki diler raḥmet çok kazana * Fātiḥa oḳıya bunı yazana*
*Navīsandarā har ki gūyad duʿā * Khudāya ba-kun ḥājatashrā ravā*

Turkish *taʿlīq*, partly vocalized; f. 2–69; 20×14 (16×9) cm; 23 lines; headings and overlining in red ink; inner margins heavily wormholed; illegible stamp-seals.

Paper: watermarked: (1) Crossbow within small Circle surmounted by a small Clover; (2) Small Anchor in small Circle, surmounted by a six-armed Star.

Binding: Old brown leather, with central medallion with floral motif; leather covers framed in double rules. Beneath the torn leather of the front cover, part of the paper board beneath has been recycled from an old Persian MS (ca. 7/13th century) in old style calligraphy and orthography (e.g. use of *dhāl* where later Persian uses *dāl*). "*Khwāja Mufaḍḍal*" is mentioned. Old Turkish marbled (*ebru*) papers are used for doublures. The binding twine is mostly disintegrated. Notes, most in Arabic but some in Turkish, have been written on the originally blank pages, f. 1[a], and f. 67[b]–68[a], and in some margins.

Ownership: Bought by E. Birnbaum in Istanbul in June 1981.

K. Encyclopedic; Sciences and Pseudosciences; Medicine; Mixed

[58] A2

Rasāʾil Ikhwān al-ṣafāʾ (f. 1b)

[رسائل إخوان الصفاء]

Begins (after *basmala*; f. 1b)

ثبت رسايل اخوان الصفا و الاصدقاء الكرام و ما هيئه اغراضهم فيها و هى احدى و خمسون رسالة فى فنون العلم و غريب الحكم و ظرايف الاداب من كلام الصوفيه

Ends (f. 282b)

و تعلم العلم اى علم كان فلسفيا او شرعيا او رياضاً او طبعاً او الهياً فانها كلها غذاء للنفس و حيوٰة لها فى الدنيا و الاخرة جمعاً و لا تتبع سبيل الذين لا يعلمون و هم الذين وصفهم الله تعالى في كتابه و من الناس//

Our MS is the first quarter of a remarkable encyclopedia, originally containing 51 treatises of philosophy, theology, and other sciences, composed in the 4/10th century by the group collectively known as the *Ikhwān al-ṣafāʾ* ("Brethren of Purity"). The copyist of this MS did not complete his task: this MS contains about of quarter of the complete work. The remainder of the last quire remains blank. A.G. Ellis, who was a cataloguer at the British Museum and later at the India Office, had previously owned this manuscript. He described its contents thus (on an open envelope postmarked "21 Feb. 1939," found in the volume): "*MS, ca. A.H. 1000*[1] (*unfinished*). *Parts 1–3 and the beginning of part 4* (*nearly to the end of Risālah 1, i.e.* [corresponding to] *96 pages out the 407 pages of the Bombay edition* [of 1888]) ... *Compare British Museum, Arab. Suppl. Pp. 480–483 for contents.*"

1 An error; rather "ca. early 18th century", as shown by the watermark described below.

© KONINKLIJKE BRILL NV, LEIDEN, 2019 | DOI:10.1163/9789004389670_013

In our MS: *qism* 1, f. 1–88ª; *qism* 2, f. 89ᵇ–216ᵇ; *qism* 3, f. 217ᵇ–254ª; *qism* 4, f. 254ᵇ–282ᵇ only.

This manuscript is a fine example of the traditional physical procedures and stages of Ottoman bookmaking at the time of this copy, shown by the watermarked paper to have been about the 18th century. Each quire consists of 4 large unbound sheets (45 × 31 cm), dyed buff, burnished and folded to provide 4 pages, in a total of 8 folios comprising gatherings of 16 pages per quire (except the last quire, which consists of only two folded sheets, f. 281ª–282ᵇ), each ending with a catchword; (folios [283ª–284ᵇ] have been left blank). Each page has been rubbed on a *misṭar*, providing guideline indentations on the paper to ensure that the copyist keep his lines straight. Within the text the copyist left spaces for the later inclusion (probably in red ink) of headings, rubrics, and sometimes diagrams, and—in the geographical sections—spaces for maps of the Seven Climes, major rivers, etc., on the relevant pages (p. 32a–45b). Occasionally the copyist added marginal notes in tiny script, indicating where headings/rubrics should be later inserted in the blanks of the body of the text.

f. 1ᵇ–282ᵇ; 31 × 22.5 (20 × 11) cm; 29 lines; watermarked throughout with a large Cross within a large fancy Shield, and—elsewhere on the folio—the serifed letters GC, or GPP, or GQ. The MS is not dated, but is approximately early 18th century (rather than "ca. 1000" AH/ ca. 1592 suggested in a note by Ellis, the previous owner).

Ownership: (1) A.G. Ellis (d. March 17, 1942, see above); (2) Luzac, London bookseller; (3) E. Birnbaum, London, August 1966.

Other MSS and references: GAL I, 214; S I, 380; Mach 23; printed edd. Bombay 1888; Cairo 1928; Beirut 1957.

[59] T77/V

al-Barmakī, Yaḥyā b. Abī Bakr b. Muḥammad, d. 3rd/9th century (f. 56ᵇ)

البرمكى ، يحيى بن ابى بكر بن محمد

Sirāj al-ẓulma wa al-raḥma (f. 56b–57a)

سراج الظلمة و الرحمة

Begins (f. 56b)

الحمد لله الذى خلق الاشيا على مايشاء الحكيم المخترع من مكنون سره ... فيقول الحكيم الفاضل يحيى ابن ابى بكر ابن محمد البرمكى انى كنت برهمة من الزمان صحبة الحكيم جابر ابن حيّان و كنّا نضّف كتب للعامه

Ends (f. 61a)

مخلصت من النوايب ومن عسل مصنّفى بسايغ يا شارب . تمت هذه الرسالة

A very rare treatise on alchemy claimed to be by Yaḥyā al-Barmakī, a scion of the famous Barmakī family, in which he is described (f. 56b) as a student and collaborator of Jābir b. Ḥayyān (d. 200/815), famous as both a dream interpreter and an alchemist. It is preceded in this physical volume by 4 other works on alchemy, all in Turkish (f. 1b–56a), all written by a different copyist than *Sirāj al-ẓulma*. (For details, see E. Birnbaum, *Ottoman Turkish and Çağatay MSS in Canada*, pp. 391–396).

Good professional naskh; f. 56a–61a; 19 × 11.5 (12.5 × 7) cm; 17 lines; headings overlined in red ink. This MS is not dated but other papers in this *majmūʿa* have watermarks used in the 18th century.

Binding: Rebound in mid-20th century in embossed red cloth.

Other MSS: Majlis Library, Teheran. (See GAL SI, 429; this Tehrān MS was the only one known to Brockelman); F. Sezgin, GAS, Bd. 4, p. 271, no. 117.

[60] A30

Ibn Kamāl Pāshā, Aḥmad b. Sulaymān, d. 940/1534

ابن كمال پاشا ، احمد بن سليمان

[Kemālpaşazāde, Aḥmed b. Süleymān]

[كمال پاشازاده]

[*Rasāʾil Ibn Kamāl Pāshā*]

[رسائل ابن كمال پاشا]

Ibn Kamāl Pāshā was a talented and very productive scholar who authored more than 200 works of varying length in many different fields of knowledge. Most of them are in Arabic, but others are in Turkish and Persian. Trained in prestigious *madrasas*, he rose from being a *mudarris* to become a *qāḍī*, and later *Qāḍī al-ʿAskar* of Rūmili. In the last eight years of his life he was *Shaykh al-Islām*, the supreme religious authority of the Ottoman Empire.

The original first half of this MS, f. 1–108, has been lost, and only f. 109–209 remain. For convenience, in the description below, each tract or treatise in this MS has been assigned a consecutive *risāla* number, and at the end of each description references have been given to other MSS of the same *risāla* which are described in the *Catalogue of Arabic Manuscripts* (*Yahuda section*) *in the Garrett Collection, Princeton University Library*, by Rudolf Mach; and/or in Atsız, 'Kemalpaşaoğlu'nun eserleri' *Şarkiyât Mecmûası*, cilt 6 (1966), s. 71–112; cilt 7 (1972), s. 83–135.

The present MS includes 25 of Ibn Kemāl Pāshā's tracts (*rasāʾil*), plus his *tafsīr* on sūra 1 of the Qurʾān. These are followed by the *tafsīr* on the same sūra by (1) Jalāl al-Dīn al-Dawwānī (d. 907/1501); (2) a treatise on the *kalimat al-tawḥīd*, by the major Persian mystic and poet Jāmī (d. 898/1492); and finally an anonymous short tract.

The MS now begins in the middle of [*Risāla* 1] f. 109[a].

لان ولد ولد اسم لمن ولد ولده و ابنته ولده و من ولدته و ابنته يكون ولد ولده حقيقه

The main text of this MS volume ends on f. 209[b], at the conclusion of *Risāla* [28] *fī iṣṭilāḥāt al-muḥaddithīn*:

و لم يسند الى النبي ع م و المرفوع هو الذى رواه الصحابى اسند الى النبي ع م تمت

f. 109^{b} [*Risāla* 2. Marginal heading added in a later old hand:] *Risāla fī bayān ṭabaqāt al-mujtahidīn*. (Mach—).

f. 110^{b} *Risāla* [3] *fī bayān taḥqīq al-khawāṣṣ wa al-mazāyā*. (Mach 3958; Atsız 145).

f. 113^{b} [*Risāla* 4] *Majʿūla*. (Mach—).

f. 113^{b} [*Risāla* 5: *al-Faqr*] (Mach 1136; Atsız 46).

f. 114^{a} *Risāla* [6] *murattaba fī taḥqīq taʿrīb al-kalima al-Aʿjamīya* (Mach 3793; Atsız 182).

f. 123^{a} *Risāla* [7] *fī bayān al-qaḍāʾ wa al-qadr* (Mach 2513; Atsız 56).

f. 136^{a} *Risāla* [8] *fī bayān masʾalat khalq al-Qurʾān* (Mach 125; Atsız 114).

f. 139^{a} *Risāla* [9] *fī bayān iʿjāz al-Qurʾān* (Mach 127; Atsız 37).

f. 144^{b} *Risāla* [10] *fī bayān al-jawāz liʾl-qāḍī iqāmat al-ghayr maqāmihi bi-lā tafwīḍ min al-sulṭān* (Mach—).

f. 146^{a} *Risāla* [11] *Rāḥat al-arwāḥ fī dafʿ al-ʿāmmat al-ashbāh* (Mach 5214; Atsız 205).

f. 149^{a} *Risāla* [12] *fī bayān ḥashr al-ajsād* [heading]. (In the body of text:) *Risāla murattaba fī bayān al-maʿād al-tafṣīl al-jismānī* (Mach 2557).

f. 155^{a}–165^{b} [*Risāla* 13]. Title at end, (f. 165^{b}): *al-Qaṣīda al-khamrīya lʾ-Ibn al-Fāriḍ maʿ sharḥihi lʾ-Ibn Kamāl Pāshā* (Mach 4110; Atsız 160).

f. 165^{b} *Risāla* [14] *fī bayān uslūb al-ḥakīm* (Mach 3959; Atsız 143).

f. 168^{b} *Risālat* [15] *haykal* (Title at end, f. 170^{b}: *Risālat taʿrīf al-insān al-musammā bi-Risālat haykal*) [Neither title in Mach].

f. 170^{b} *Mabḥath fī al-īmān al-sharʿī* [This *risāla* is **not** by Ibn Kamāl Pāshā: at its end [f. 175^{b}] its authorship is stated: "*Nuqila min Shaykhzāda ʿalā al-Qāḍī al-Bayḍāwī*". [Shaykhzāda, a contemporary of Ibn Kamāl Pāshā, died in 950/1543].

f. 175[b] [*Risāla* 16]. *Ḥāshiya liʾl-Mawāqif* [*fī ʿilm al-kalām liʾl-Ījī*] (Mach—).

f. 178[a] *Risāla* [17] *fī ʿulūm al-ḥaqāʾiq wa ḥikmat al-daqāʾiq* (Mach 2409; Atsız 106).

f. 180 *Risāla* [18] *murattaba fī waḥdat al-wujūd ʿalā aṣl al-taṣawwuf* (Mach—).

f. 184[a] *Risāla* [19] *fī tafṣīl mā qīla fī abaway al-Rasūl* (Mach 4579; Atsız 111).

f. 186[a] *Risāla* [20] *fī ādāb al-baḥth* (Mach 3371; Atsız 164).

f. 187[b] *Risāla* [21] *fī anna al-aʿmāl hal tūzanu am lā* (Mach—).

f. 188[b] *Risāla* [22] *fī madḥ al-saʿy wa dhamm al-baṭāla* (Mach 2007; Atsız 172).

f. 191[a] *Risāla* [23] *fī taḥqīq ʿan mā yaṣdur biʾl-qudra wa al-ikhtiyār* (Mach 2411; Atsız 105).

f. 192[b] *Risāla* [24] *fī bayān sirr ʿadam nisbat al-sharr ilā Allāh* (Mach 2410; Atsız 104).

f. 195[a] *Risāla* [25] *fī kitāb al-riḍāʿ* (Mach 1141; Atsız 50).

f. 196[b] [26] *Tafsīr sūrat al-Fātiḥa* (Mach 413; Atsız 27).

f. 204[b] [27] *Tafsīr sūrat al-Fātiḥa li-mawlānā Jalāl al-Dawwānī raḥmat Allāh ʿalayhi.*

f. 206[b] *Risāla* [28] *fī bayān Kalimat al-tawḥīd li-mawlānā ʿAbd al-Raḥmān al-Jāmī.*

f. 209[b] *Risāla* [29] *fī bayān iṣṭilāḥāt al-muḥaddithīn.* [last page] [short anonymous tract].

Scholars' small *naskh*, not vocalized; f. 109–210; 20×14 (15×7.5) cm; 21 lines; headings, overlinings and some poetic citations in red ink; occasional marginal notes by readers of various periods.

Paper: Watermarked: Anchor suspended from Ring within a Circle, surmounted by 6-armed Star. This watermark appears in many dated MSS of the 10/16th century.

Date: The copyist ends *Risāla* [7] with the note *Tamm tanmīq al-risāla ... li'l-'ālim ... Aḥmad b. Sulaymān Ibn Kamāl, 'ufiya 'anhumā* ... (f. 136ª), so this MS must have been copied after Ibn Kemāl Pasha's death in 940/1534.

Binding: Worn paperboards edged with leather; replacement cloth spine; in bad condition; sewing loose.

Ownership: (1) An anonymous owner (ca. 18th century?) cited two verses in *Turkish* on previously blank f. 110ª attributed respectively to "Shaykh Bāyazīd", and "Dede Rūshānī" (d. 892/1487); (2) f. 110ª: A late 19th century owner wrote a pencil note, referring to military mail (*'askarī posta*), accompanied by a red postage stamp bearing the contemporary sulṭān's *tughrā* and the words "20 *para*" in both Ottoman and Latin alphabets, and various calculations; (3) On f. 110ᵇ: Notes of calculations and prices in Turkish, ca. 18th and 19th centuries; (4) Bought by E. Birnbaum, Istanbul, July 1991.

[60a] **A11**

[***Risāla fī al-qiyās***]

[رسالة فى القياس]

Begins (f. 1ª)

اعلم خطاب عام شامل لكل واحد ممن يصلح لان يخاطب في هذا المقام ... سبب تاليف هذه الرسالة طلب ببعض تلامذه بيان طريق استخراج القياس من العبارة ...

Ends (f. 10ᵇ)

تعمل في هذا المقام فانّه طريق الاقدام والحمد لله ... و اصحابه الراشدين الكرام . تم الرسالة بعون الله ...

A short, anonymous treatise on *qiyās* (logic) and analogy, composed in traditional scholarly Arabic.

Rather untidy Ottoman style *ta'līq* script; f. 1–10; 20 × 14.5 (17 × 12.5) cm; 16 lines; cheap 19th century paper without watermarks; sewn but not bound. This MS was found inserted in an Old Ottoman Turkish manuscript dated Rabīʿ II, 836/1432 of the *Muḳaddime* of Ḳuṭbeddīn İznīḳī [d. 821/1418] (See E. Birnbaum, *Ottoman Turkish and Çağatay MSS in Canada*, p. 214).

Ownership: Bought by E. Birnbaum in Istanbul, August 1980.

L. Ijāza

[61] A7

Khaṭībzāda, ʿUthmān al-Chūnkushī, fl. 1261/1845

خطيب زاده، عثمان الجونكشي

[*Ijāza*]

[إجازة]

Begins (f. 1ᵇ–2ᵃ)

الحمد لله الذى انزل على سبعة الحرف تيسيراً ... **امّا بعد** فقد قرأ القران العظيم علىّ من اوّله الى آخره ... السيد شيخ محمد الآمدى ... التمس منى ان اَذَن له بالإقرا كما اخذ منى فاذنت له و اجزت بذلك ...

Ends (f. 5ᵃ)

و انا الفقير الى عناية ربه القدير السيد عثمان الجونكشى الشهير بخطيب زاده ... فى سنة احدى و ستين و ماتين و الف ...

Ijāza, a license to teach the *tajwīd* of the Qurʾān, issued to his student al-Sayyid Muḥammad al-Āmidī [Meḥmed el-Āmidī] by ʿUthmān al-Chūnkushī, known as Khaṭībzāda [Ḫaṭībzāda ʿOs̱mān Çüngüşī]. Most of the text consists of a chain of teachers going back to the Prophet, and from him to the archangel Jabrāʾīl, and the *lawḥ al-maḥfūẓ*. Dated 1261/1845 (f. 5ᵃ). Çüngüş is in the region of Diyārbakr.

Excellent professional scribe's fully vocalized *naskh*; f. 1–6 (f. 5ᵇ–6ᵇ blank); 20.5 × 12.5 (13 × 8.5); 9 lines.

Paper: Watermarked: (1) Lion rampant in a Shield, surmounted by a Crown; (2) Eagle.

© KONINKLIJKE BRILL NV, LEIDEN, 2019 | DOI:10.1163/9789004389670_014

Decoration: Each page framed in gold, as is the colophon statement of the issuer (f. 5[a]).

Never bound or sewn.

Ownership: Bought by E. Birnbaum, Istanbul, August 1980.

[62] A5

Ḥasan Efendizāda, Yaḥyā b. Aḥmad al-Deñizlī, fl. 1268/1852 (f. 1[b]; 9[a])

حسن افندى زاده ، يحيى بن احمد الدڭزلى

Ijāza (f. 9[a])

[اجازة]

Begins (f. 1[b], after *basmala*)

الحمد لله الذى انبت دوحة العلم فى صدور العلماء و جعل ثمارها احكام الشريعة الغراء ... و بعد
فيقول الفقير ... يحيى بن احمد العريف بحسن افندى زاده ... ان العلم انفس ما صرفت فيه

Ends (f. 8[b])

الى لقا الله عزّ و علا و هو اعلى المقاصد و اسنى المأرب و وقنا كون اخر كلامنا لا اله الّا الله
محمد رسول الله ...

Colophon (f. 9[a])

هذه صورة اجازتى و سندى فى الكتاب و السنة و فى شرعيّات العلوم و عقلياتها و ادبياتها على
ما اجازنى الاستاذ المذكور فاجازت حافظ القران محمد الحلمى بن ابراهيم المرزيفونى العريف
باويس خواجه زاده المزبور و انا افقر الورى ... يحيى بن احمد الدڭزلى المدرس بجامع السليمانية
و المقرب بحضور مجلس السلطانية و ذلك فى يوم الخميس من شهور ربيع الاخر لسنه ثمانية و
ستين و ماتين [sic] و الف

[Seal: يحيى توفق]

Ijāza, a certificate license to teach, granted by Yaḥyā b. Aḥmad al-Deñizlī, a teacher (*mudarris*) at the Sulaymāniya/Süleymāniye *madrasa* in Istanbul to this student, a *ḥāfiẓ* of the Qur'ān, Muḥammad al-Ḥilmī b. Ibrāhīm al-Marzīfūnī, commonly known Uways Khwājazāda (Meḥmed Ḥilmī b. Ibrāhīm el-Merzīfūnī, Üveys Ḫōcazāde) for all sciences: *naẓarīya, ʿamalīya, ʿaqlīya, naqlīya* for *ḥadīth* and *tafsīr, uṣūl* and *furūʿ*. The *mudarris* lists the sequence of teachers, starting with his father Aḥmad b. Ḥasan of "*Qaryat qāḍī*" (i.e. Ḳaḍıköy, on the Anatolian shore opposite Istanbul) going back several generations [to f. 6ᵃ, line 10]. Date of issue/colophon 5 Rabīʿ II 1268 [= January 29, 1852].

Excellent professional small *naskh*; f. 1–10 (f. 9ᵇ–10ᵇ blank); 18.5 × 12.5 (12 × 6) cm; 15 lines.

Paper: Watermarked (1) Eagle, looking right, above serifed letters TS (fol. 4/7), (2) Shield (containing a Lion (?) rampant), surmounted by a Crown. Last page bears the seal of the *mudarris* "Yaḥyā Tawfīq" (f. 9ᵃ).

Never bound or sewn.

Ownership: Bought by E. Birnbaum, Istanbul, June 1974.

References: Hüseyin Atay, 'Fatih Süleymaniye medreseleri ders programları ve icazet-nameler.' *Vakıflar Dergisi*, cilt 13, 1981; *EI*² art. Idjāza.

[63] A35

al-Qoyulḥiṣārī/Ḳoyulḥiṣārī, Ṭāhir Ḥilmī b. Aḥmad, fl. 1317/1899 (f. 2ᵇ)

القويلحصارى ، طاهر حلمى بن احمد

Ijāza (f. 2ᵇ; 10ᵇ)

إجازة

Begins (f. 1ᵇ)

الحمد لله الذى علمنا ما لم نعلم و اسعدنا بتعليم العلوم

Ends (f. 9^b^–10^a^)

رواه البيهقى رحمه الله ... ربنا اغفر لنا و لولدينا و المؤمنين و المؤمنات الاحياء منهم و الاموات برحمتك يا ارحم الراحمين ...

On f. 10[b] (in a different hand): A statement by "al-Sayyid ʿAbd al-Qādir Rāshid al-Islāmbūlī b. al-Sayyid al-shaykh Muṣṭafā Khulūṣī al-Barghamawī b. al-Sayyid al-shaykh ʿAlī al-Ṭantāwī," that this is a "second copy of my *ijāza*, [dated] in the second decade of Jumādā II 1317" [= mid-October 1899]. Beneath it is a seal-stamp with date engraved [1]279/[1862–1863].

This is an *ijāza* (license or permit) issued by a *madrasa* teacher, Ṭāhir Qoyulḥiṣārī, permitting his student ʿAbd al-Qādir Rāshid al-Islāmbūlī to teach *al-funūn al-ʿaqlīya wa al-naqlīya* ("rational and traditional sciences"). It includes a chain of teachers going back many generations. Qoyulḥiṣār is a town near Sivas.

Professional scribal *naskh*; 22.5×13.5 (14×7.5) cm; 13 lines; on paper without watermarks.

First opening (f. 1[b]–2[a]) decorated with colored *ʿunwān* (headpiece) in gold, crimson and blue, and gold painted marginal decoration; all pages framed in gold, blue and red ink; gold circles at phrase ends. The final page (f. 10[a]) decorated with a laurel wreath and a leaf pattern in gold ink.

Binding: Green cloth-covered paperboards, apparently recycled from a late 19th century book. Contemporary label on front cover: "Ṭāhir Ḥilmī al-Qoyulḥiṣārī, sana 1317."

Ownership: Bought by E. Birnbaum, Istanbul, July 1991.

[64] A8

al-Maʿlqarawī, Muḥammad Amīn b. Muḥammad, fl. 1332/1913 (f. 6[b])

المعلقروى ، محمد امين بن محمد بن عثمان بن مصطفى

Ijāza (f. 2b)

إجازة

Begins (f. 1b, after *basmala*)

الحمد لله الذى علمنا ما لم نعلم و اسعدنا بتعليم العلوم ... اعلم وفقك الله ... ان السبب لنيل الكرامات العلية

Ends (f. 6b)

و الحمد لله بعزته سبحان ربك رب العزة عما يصفون و سلام على المرسلين و الحمد لله رب العالمين

This MS is a *madrasa* teacher's license to his student ʿUmar [ʿÖmer] Luṭfī b. Ibrāhīm al-Sīwāsī to teach the "rational and traditional" (*maʿqūl wa manqūl*) sciences, listing a chain of teachers going back to the Prophet and the angel Jabrāʾīl. While the body of the text seems to be written by a professional calligrapher, the colophon dated 4 Jumādā I 1332/1 April 1913 is in the hand of the teacher, "al-ʿabd al-faqīr Muḥammad Amīn b. Muḥammad b. ʿUthmān al-Maʿlqarawī", followed by his stamp-seal (*muhr*) inscribed "Muḥammad Amīn, 1321". (Maʿlqara/Malḳara is a town near Gallipoli/Gelibolu in Anatolia).

Naskh; f. 1–6; 20.5×12.5 (14×7) cm; 15 lines; unwatermarked green paper; sewn but not bound.

Ownership: Bought by E. Birnbaum, Istanbul, August 1980.

M. Calligraphy

[66] A38

Calligraphy model (*mashq*) for writing in *thulth* script the letter ط *ṭāʾ* followed by every letter from *ṣād* to *yāʾ*. Text framed in two lines, the first from *ṭāʾ ṣād* to *ṭāʾ mīm*, the second from an alternative form of *ṭāʾ mīm* to *ṭāʾ yāʾ*. Between these frames another smaller frame encloses the text of a riddle in smaller letters:

تجدنى واسعاً بالخلق عبدي انا المذكور فاطلبنى

The whole composition is within multiple ink frames, surrounded by an outer gold frame.

Calligraphed on thin cardboard.

Not dated, but probably produced in the Ottoman Empire in the 13/19th century; 25.5 × 37.5 cm; innermost frame 9.5 × 17.5 cm.

Ownership: Gift of Mr. Altman of the bookseller H.P. Kraus, New York, to E. Birnbaum, November 1969.

© KONINKLIJKE BRILL NV, LEIDEN, 2019 | DOI:10.1163/9789004389670_015

N. Persian Philology

[Numbers 67–69 are in Arabic, but included in a *majmūʿa*, which also contains 2 *rasāʾil* in Persian by Jāmī. For a general description of the *majmūʿa*, see the catalogue of our Persian MSS, nos. 33–34]

[67] **M1/I**

[**Ibn Kamāl Pasha, Aḥmad b. Sulaymān**, d. 940/1534]

[ابن كمال پاشا، احمد بن سليمان]

Risāla ʿalā al-qawāʿid al-Fārisīya (f. 1b)

رسالة مشتمله ... على القواعد الفرسية [sic]

Tadwīn qawāʿid al-Furs (f. 1b)

تدوين قواعد الفرس

Begins (f. 1b)

الحمد لله الذى منحنى من تواتر نعمائية تدوين قواعد الفرس ... و بعد فهذه رسالة مشتملة على قواعد الفرسية [sic]

Ends (f. 19b)

براى تعليل ايچوندر مثلا براى خداى . بغير تكرى ايچندكلدر . سنه ١١ را سنه ١٠٨

(f. 20a): [In a different and later hand, the text of 3 *murabbaʿāt* in Turkish]

A philological treatise on the Persian language, in four chapters. The first three are written in Arabic; the last one is in Turkish (f. 17b–19b). The copyist did not include the name of its author, Ibn Kamāl Pasha, who was the Ottoman *Shaykh al-Islām* and a famously productive scholar. He composed several major works

© KONINKLIJKE BRILL NV, LEIDEN, 2019 | DOI:10.1163/9789004389670_016

and more than 180 short tracts (*rasāʾil*) on many subjects, mostly in Arabic,[1] even when the subject was Persian or Turkish. The present *risāla* contains four chapters (*bāb*): 1. (f. 20[a]): *al-ism*; 2. (f. 9[a]): *fī aḥvāl al-fiʿl*; 3. (f. 14[a]): *fī aḥvāl al-ḥarf*; 4. (f. 17[b]–19[b]): *fī tiʿdād al-ism.*

Turkish *taʿlīq*; 20.5×12.5 (14×17) cm; 17 lines; headings in red ink; colophon (f. 19[b]): ١١

Date (f. 19[b]): *Rabīʿ I,* $^{1}{}_{8}{}^{0}$ (= either [1]108 = 8 October 1696, or [1]008 = 2 October 1599).

Watermarks: (1) Horn; (2) Crown and Grapes; (3) Other faint designs.

Decoration: Headings in red ink.

Ownership: Bought by E. Birnbaum in Istanbul, August 1980.

Other MSS: See Rudolf Mach, *Catalogue of Arabic Manuscripts (Yahuda section) in the Garrett Collection, Princeton University Library*. Princeton, 1977, no. 3822; Atsız, *Kemalpaşaoğlu'nun eserleri*, no. 202 (in *Şarkiyat Mecmuası*, 6 [1966–1972]); Hivzija Hasandedić, *Katalog arabskih, turskih i persijskih rukopisa ... Mostar*, no. 634/26, p. 243.

[68] M1/IV

[Ibn Kemāl Pasha, Aḥmad b. Sulaymān, d. 940/1534]

[ابن كمال پاشا ، احمد بن سليمان]

[*Risāla fī ḍabṭ al-muḍāriʿ*]

[رسالة في ضبط المضارع]

1 See above, MS 60, A30 for 26 *rasāʾil*.

Begins (f. 40b)

الحمد لله الذى زيّن بنى آدم بالنطق و الكلام و الصلاة و السلام على سيد الانام ... و بعد فقد سألنى من خلايق المكرم لضبط المضارع من لسان العجم ... اعلم ان المصادر باعتبار

An Arabic tract on Persian infinitives (*muḍāriʿ*). After an introduction in Arabic, each Persian infinitive is written (in red ink), accompanied by its translation into Turkish (in black ink), often with an extended comment, also in Turkish, explaning the meaning and usage; e.g., (f. 40b) بشمك ، بشورمك, followed by a note in Turkish:

لازم و متعدى استعمال اولنور بالباء الفارسيه والرّاء العربيه بمعنى پختن

Ends (f. 46b: End of section on infinitives. The last one is:

برفتن

قبول ايلمك

(Another MS: see H. Hasandedić, *Katalog arabskih, turskih, persidskih rukopisa. Mostar*, 1977.)

[69] M1/V

[Ibn Kamāl Pasha, Aḥmad b. Sulaymān, d. 940/1534]

[ابن كمال پاشا ، احمد بن سليمان]

[*Risāla fī*] *al-maṣdar fī al-Fārisīya* (f. 46b)

[رسالة في] المصدر في الفارسية

Begins (f. 46b)

اعلم ان علامة المصدر في الفارسية كون اخرها نونا ساكنة

Ends (f. 55b)

و الجمع مطلقا معناسی ایلمك . م [= تم]

A treatise in Arabic on the *maṣdar* (infinitive verbal form) in Persian. Many examples are accompanied by interlinear or marginal translations or interpretations in Turkish.

∴

Indexes and concordance to the Arabic manuscripts: see pages 220–224.

Persian Manuscripts

Introduction to the Persian Manuscripts

It was as a student at the University of London's School of Oriental and African Studies, "SOAS" (1947–1953) that I first encountered Middle Eastern manuscripts.* There I studied the Arabic, Turkish, and Persian languages and literatures, Middle Eastern history and civilizations, and Hebrew palaeography. In those years, I was increasingly exposed to original manuscripts and facsimiles. Though I did most of my reading from printed texts, I found the manuscripts much more fascinating. At that time photocopying was expensive and not readily available. Cyril Mundy, one of my teachers of Turkish, who had assembled a collection of Ottoman Turkish manuscripts, would cheerfully lend me and my classmates 16th or 17th-century originals to take home in order to prepare sections for discussion in class. Another teacher, Professor Fahir İz, had us study the original Çaġatay Turkish text of the *Bāburnāma* using the Gibb series facsimile edition. The Hebrew palaeography course at SOAS involved the study of photographs from the huge collection of photocopies of dated items assembled by my father Dr. Solomon Birnbaum. This early exposure to Middle Eastern manuscripts developed my life-long passion for them.

As a student I frequented the "oriental" bookshops on Great Russell Street near the British Museum in London, but it was not until I began to earn a very modest living as Assistant Librarian for Middle Eastern Studies at Durham University Library in England (1953–1960) that I had enough money to buy my first manuscripts. Rummaging through the stocks of the bookstores in London became a favorite vacation activity. After becoming Near Eastern Bibliographer at the University of Michigan in the United States (1960–1964) I travelled to the Middle East to buy printed books for the University Library and, at the same time, acquired a few manuscripts for myself. Later the University of Toronto in Canada appointed me Professor of Turkish (1964), and I made a series of research trips to Turkey. Every working day at five o'clock the manuscript libraries in Istanbul, such as the Süleymaniye and Bāyazīd, expelled all the researchers, myself included. I would then visit the traditional *ṣaḥḥāflar* nearby. Several of them stocked some manuscripts, in addition to printed books. Over a period of some thirty years I bought many interesting

* This brief catalogue of Persian Manuscripts in the Birnbaum Collection, Toronto was first published in the *Journal of Islamic Manuscripts* 8 (2017) 144–217, edited by Jan Just Witkam of Leiden University.

© KONINKLIJKE BRILL NV, LEIDEN, 2019 | DOI:10.1163/9789004389670_017

manuscripts, one or two at a time, from the *ṣaḥḥāflar*, mostly Ottoman Turkish,[1] useful for my Turkish research, as well as much smaller numbers in Arabic and Persian, when I found them interesting.[2]

The present catalogue describes only my Persian manuscripts, numbering 34 works in 22 physical volumes. Some of these are bilingual (Persian-Turkish, Arabic-Persian), including several Persian texts with interlinear translation in Turkish, and Arabic texts with interlinear translation in Persian.

The Ottoman educated classes were generally expected to have some knowledge of Persian and to be able to use Persian constructions and Arabic and Persian loanwords, even when writing in Ottoman Turkish, attempting in this way to improve their literary style. To meet this need, Ottoman scholars composed a considerable number of Persian-Turkish dictionaries, vocabularies, etc., some of which are found in my collection.[3]

1 A Selection of Manuscripts of Special Interest[4]

1. Idrīs Bidlīsī, d. 926/1520, *Hasht bihisht*. A history of the Ottoman Empire, commissioned by the Ottoman Sultan Bāyezīd II (d. 1512). This manuscript was copied in the early 16th century.
3. Ṣā'ib (d. 1087/1676), *Dīvān*. The collected poems of a main initiator of the *sabk-i Hindī*, the intricate "Indian style" of Persian poetry. This manuscript was copied only six years after the poet's death.
4. Rashīd al-Dīn Vaṭvāṭ, d. 573/1177, *Ḥadā'iq al-siḥr fī daqā'iq al-shi'r*. "A much admired handbook of rhetorical figures", with many poetic examples, composed by a famous stylist. This manuscript, one of the oldest extant, was copied in the late 12th or early 13th century.
12. Mu'ammā'ī, Mīr Ḥusayn, d. 904/1499, [*Risāla-i mu'ammā*]. A very early manuscript of a famous rare treatise on the composition of riddles. It was

1 These are described in detail in Eleazar Birnbaum, *Ottoman Turkish and Çağatay Manuscripts in Canada: A Union Catalogue*. Leiden: Brill, 2015. I am grateful to Dr. Halil Şımşek for his computer expertise in the pre-production phase of that work and the present book.

2 The Islamic Persian ones appear in the present catalogue, while descriptions of those in Arabic will be found in the preceding (Arabic) section of the present volume. The small group of my Judeo-Persian manuscripts in Hebrew script is not included in the present catalogue, but may be the subject of a journal article in the future.

3 At some future date my Persian, Turkish and Arabic manuscripts will find a permanent new home in a major library.

4 The manuscript numbers refer to the running numbers, i.e. the sequence of the entries in the present work.

composed at the court of Sultan Ḥusayn Bayqarā at Herat, and dedicated to Mīr ʿAlī Shīr Navāʾī, the major patron of Turkish and Persian culture there. This copy is late 15th or early 16th century, shortly after the work was composed.

16. Qurʾān fragment with an interlinear translation into early modern Persian, ca. 12th–13th century.
19. [*Akhlāqnāma*]. An unidentified 13–14th-century work on ethics and Sufism, which frequently cites Khvāja Faqīh Zāhid (d. 702/1301). Copied ca. 14–15th century.
30. A previously unknown encyclopedic work on various subjects, including the virtues of learning, geography, astronomy and astrology, creation, nature of man, ethics, etc. Copied about the 13th century.
31. Kūshyār b. Labbān, fl. 4th/10th century, *Kitāb al-ikhtiyārāt*. An extremely rare unpublished astrological work by a famous mathematician and astronomer/astrologer. Copied about the 7/13th century.

2 Organization of This Catalogue

The description of each manuscript contains the following sequence of elements, where applicable:

1. Running number (i.e. sequence in this catalogue).
2. Between brackets the original accession group and number in the Birnbaum manuscript collections: P = Persian collection; T = Turkish collection; M = Mixed collection.
3. Author's name in both Persian and Latin scripts, with his death date, and folio number in the manuscript where his name appears.
4. Title of the work in both scripts, and alternative titles, if any.
5. Beginning and ending phrases of the MS (*incipit* and *explicit*).
6. Colophon with date of copy, if given, or as estimated.
7. Description of the subject and contents of the work, and basic information on its author.
8. Physical description of the manuscript, including the following details, if applicable:
    a. type of script (*naskh*; *nastaʿlīq*; Turkish *taʿlīq*; etc.);
    b. vocalization, if any;
    c. number of folios, or pages if paginated;
    d. dimensions in centimeters of the page and of its written area;
    e. number of lines per page;
    f. paper, with description of watermark (*filigrain*) designs in it. Water-

marks can be useful in confirming the copy date, and in providing an approximate date for undated manuscripts.

g. Decoration, such as *sarlavḥa* (ornamental headpiece), use of gold and colored inks, framing of written area, and use of rubrics.

h. Previous owners, as indicated by handwritten statements or seal impressions.

i. Other inscriptions added by previous owners or readers.

9. Binding: Material and ornamentation.

10. Other manuscripts: References to a few other MSS of the same work elsewhere, and to information in several library catalogues and/or standard reference works such as *Encyclopaedia Iranica*, *Encyclopaedia of Islam* (2nd ed.), and *Türk Diyanet Vakfı İslam Ansiklopedisi* (DİA).

3 Classification

The individual manuscripts cover a wide range of subjects, even within a single work. For convenience, in this catalogue I have grouped them somewhat arbitrarily under the following headings:

A. History
B. Literature
C. Islam; Religion
D. Ethics
E. Language, Lexicography, and Prosody
F. Encyclopedia
G. Astrology
H. Document
I. Majmūʿāt

The catalogue is followed by Author and Title Indexes, and a Concordance linking the the Collection Accession Number (P or T or M) with the corresponding Running Number. That is: their sequence in this catalogue.

A. History

[1] P1

Idrīs Bidlīsī, d. 926/1520 (f. 323ª)

ادریس بدلیسي

Hasht bihisht (f. 1ᵇ)

هشت بهشت

Begins (f. 1ᵇ):

ابتدآیی صار بسم الله الرحمن الرحیم * إذ مُرادی منها ذکرٌ له خُطَب عظیم

Original end of ***Hasht bihisht*** (f. 313ª):

همیشه کار شان فتح مبین باد

End of this *second* recension (f. 323ª):

بحمد الله طبیب خان سلیم است ... بحق النبی الکریم المصطفی * محمد و اله و اصحابه ایمه دین الهدی

وقع اختتام الارقام باقلام انامل اقل الانام * احقر الفقرا و افقر الوري مؤلف الکتاب ادریس بن حسام الدین البدلیسی * اصلح الله اعماله و حصل بالخیر و المعافیة آماله ...

Idrīs Bidlīsī was an important political and diplomatic personality at the court of Yaʿqūb Aq-Qoyunlu in Tabrīz towards the end of the 15th century. As the power of Shāh Ismāʿīl the Ṣafavid grew in the region, Idrīs fled, in 907/1501–1502, to the court of the Ottoman sultan Bāyazīd II. Although Turkish had already become the main language at the Ottoman court, Persian still remained an important language of culture there. In 908/1502–1503 Bāyazīd commissioned two scholars to enhance the prestige of the Ottomans by recording the history of the now powerful dynasty and empire: Kamāl Pashazāda (Ibn Kemāl Pāşā) to write in Turkish, and Idris Bidlīsī in Persian. With his history *Hasht*

© KONINKLIJKE BRILL NV, LEIDEN, 2019 | DOI:10.1163/9789004389670_018

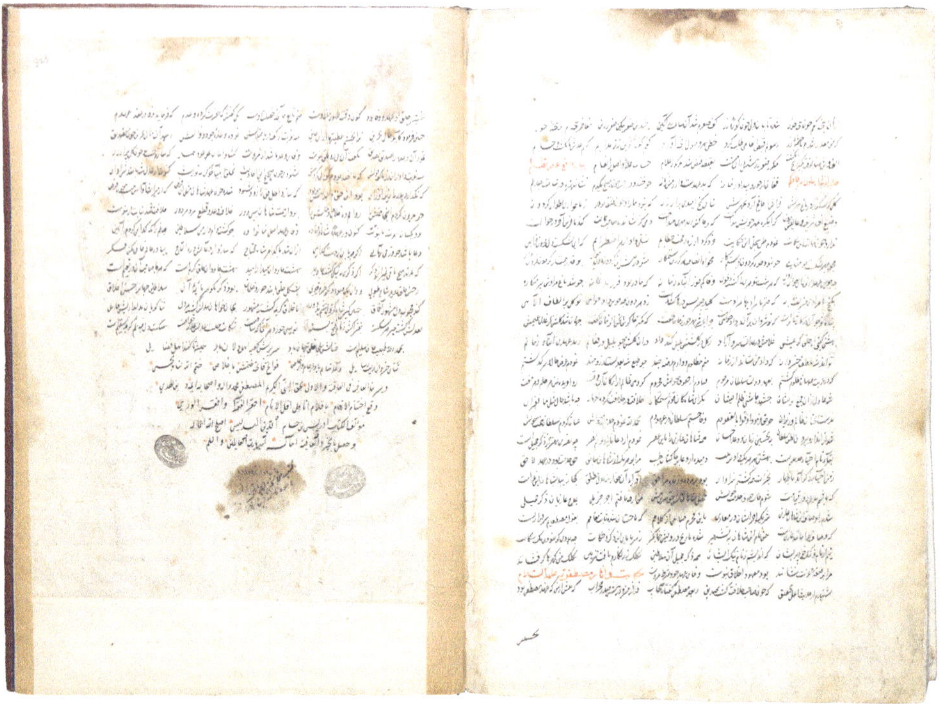

FIGURE 20 No. 1 (P1). Idrīs Bidlīsī, d. 926/1520. *Hasht Bihisht*, f. 322^{b}–323^{a}. Copied early 10/16th century

bihisht, Idrīs introduced the tradition of writing Ottoman history in a very elaborate Persian *inshā* prose style.

The "Eight Paradises" (*Hasht bihisht*) of the title are a laudatory reference to the eight Ottoman sultans from the founder of the dynasty, 'Us̱mān ('Os̱mān) Ghāzī to the reigning sultan Bāyazīd II. Each Sultan's reign is recorded in a separate long *katība* (chapter) detailing chronologically his achievements in prose, which is punctuated by much poetry, the latter also mostly composed by Idrīs himself.

Idrīs is reported to have presented his *Hasht bihisht* to the Sultan in 911 or 912/1506–1507. The author claims to have composed the complete work in the short span of "only thirty months". He may, however, have added to the original text a little later, as the last dated event in the main section of our manuscript took place in 913/1507; it concerns Iskandar Pasha, governor of Bosnia (f. 308^{b} and f. 312^{b}).

Idrīs presented his work at court, but did not receive from sultan Bāyazīd II the reward that he expected—perhaps because of a court intrigue. Some time after Bāyazīd's "abdication" in 918/1512 in favor of his son Salīm (Selīm), Idrīs produced what may be considered a "second editon", which is represented by the present manuscript. Added at the end of the original text is a long *khātima* (Conclusion, f. 313[a]–323[a]) consisting of 1250 *masnavī* verses in Persian, dedicated to, and in praise of, the new Sultan Salīm I, who reigned from 918–926/1512–1520.

The present MS, one of the oldest known, contains only *katība*s 6–8, covering the reigns of Sultans Murād II (824–885/1421–1451, ff. 1–69[b]); Muḥammad II the Conqueror/Meḥmed Fātiḥ (855–886/1451–1481, ff. 70[b]–204[a]); and Bāyazīd II (only the years 886–911/1481–1506, although, as noted above, an event of 913/1507 is recorded).

Turkish *taʿlīq*; ff. 1[b]–323[b]; 29 × 20.5 (20.5 × 14.5) cm; 25 lines.

European papers with at least six *different watermarks* in various quires, *all of them common in the first two decades of the 16th century*; they are in the following sequence (1) Oxhead with Horns, between which emerges a long Staff surmounted by a 3-leaved Maltese Cross; (2) Within a Circle, Mountains from which emerges a Staff surmounted by a 3-leaved Maltese Cross; (3) Gauntlet/Glove, it's middle finger surmounted by a 6-armed Star; (4) Oxhead with Horns; (5) Balance within a Circle topped by a Ring surmounted by a 6-armed Star; (6) Hat.

After the colophon on f. 323[a] an anonymous note in a different and later hand states that MS was copied "from the author's copy about 950"/1543: كتب من نسخة المؤلف فى حدود سنة خمسين وتسعمائة. This estimated date is certainly incorrect as the distinctive watermarks in the paper are those produced in papers manufactured considerably earlier in the 16th century.

Ownership: shown by ten different seals (five dated) and eleven handwritten notes, all on f. 1[a].

Dated seals: (1) round (diameter 2 cm) inscribed "… ʿAlī b. ʿAbd al-Raʾūf al-Ḥusaynī … 1028"/1629; (2) oval (diameter 2 cm) inscribed "… al-ḥaqq … Muḥammad Rafīʿ al-… 1081"/1670–1671, beneath a handwritten note "Muḥammad Rafīʿ al-… (? al-Ḥusaynī?) 1085"/1674; (3) oval (diameter 1.8 cm) with an inscription dated 1085/1674, which is difficult to read, under a handwritten "Muḥammad

Riżā Muḥammad [—] al-Sīrī (?) al-Ṭūsī …"; (4) oval (diameter 1.8 cm) inscribed "ʿAbdullāh b. Muḥammad 1283"/1866, the same seal again after colophon, f. 323ª; (5) oval (diameter 1.6 cm) inscribed "ʿAbdullāh 1295"/1878.

Undated seals: (6) round (diameter 2.2 cm), including "… sulṭān"; (7–8) round: defaced and illegible; (9–10) square: illegible.

Ownership: written statements on f. 1ª: Above seal (1) "min niʿam Allāh ʿalā ʿabdih … ʿAlī b. ʿAbd al-Raʾūf"; above seal (2): "min kutub … Muḥammad Rafīʿ … (al-Ḥusaynī?)"; above seal (3): see above dated seal (3); (10): "min kutub Muḥammad Shafīʿ …" (note dated Jumāẕī II 1299/1882).

Twentieth-century ownerships: "A.G. Ellis", (f. 1ª). He served as a librarian and manuscript cataloguer in London, first at the British Museum [now British Library] from 1883–1909, and afterwards at the India Office Library in London. He died on March 17, 1942, aged 84. After his death his collection of manuscripts and printed books was sold by his heirs to the London bookseller Luzac.[1] They were described briefly in Luzac's sale catalogue in 1943 by Arthur J. Arberry, who had been a librarian at the India Office Library in London, and was later professor of Persian at the University of London (1944–1947), and of Arabic at Cambridge (1947–1949). Arberry's brief description of this MS is written in his own hand on a slip of paper pasted on to the inner doublure of the MS. A note written in Ellis' distinctive hand on f. 1ª records that this MS was previously offered for sale at an auction at Sotheby's in London, held on June 13–16, 1938, was bought by Luzac on June 16, 1938 and from Luzac by Ellis on the same day. On his death, this MS was again acquired by Luzac, who sold it to E. Birnbaum in April 1958.

Binding: Very fine red morocco leather binding with dark brown leather inserts, in the front and back covers, of medallions, pendants and cornerpieces (*shamsa, sālbak, gūshāband*) in dark brown leather. In the opinion of Glyn Meredith-Owens, a specialist in Islamic manuscripts and Islamic art, formerly at the British Museum and the University of Toronto, the present binding is a combination of two parts: the older is the dark brown leather, probably dating from the 16th century. Pieces were cut out of it and reset into the present red morocco rebinding, perhaps in the 19th century to form the present handsome volume, which has no trace of flap-binding.[2]

1 Luzac & Co, *A Catalogue of the Library of the late A.G. Ellis, M.A.*, part III. London 1945, p. 17, M 187.

2 Personal letter from Glyn Meredith-Owens to E. Birnbaum, April 19, 1978.

Other MSS and references: Many manuscripts are extant. The fullest references, listing manuscripts from all over the world, until to about 1970, are in *Persidskaya literatura* by Yu. E. Bregel (Moskva, 1972), pt. 2, pp. 1255–1261, (the translation and expansion of Storey *PL*, vol. 1, pp. 412–416, and vol. 2, pt. 2, p. 1306). Four autographs appear to be known, including a fine gilded one in Istanbul: Nuru Osmaniye 3209, see *Türk Diyanet Vakfı İslam Ansiklopedisi*, art. İdrīs-i Bitlîsî, vol. 21, pp. 485–488, and *EI*², art. Bidlīsī, Idrīs, vol. 1, pp. 1207–1208; *Encyclopaedia Iranica*, art. Bedlīsī, vol. 4, pp. 75–76. Among the other manuscripts in Turkish libraries we may note also Nuru Osmaniye 3211; Millet Ali Emiri 800–807; Topkapı Sarayı Farsça Kat. Nos. 149–154; Süleymaniye, Esad 3197; Süleymaniye, Lala İsmail 979; Süleymaniye, Ayasofya 3541; Halis Ef. 3364; Rıza Paşa 888; Atıf Ef. 946; Bayezid 5161.

Of the many MSS in Iran we may note Tehran University, Dānishkada-i Adabiyāt, Tārīkh-i Īrān, no. 69B (see *Fihrist-i nuskhahā-yi ... muhdāt ... Asghar Mahdāvī*, p. 58); Tabrīz, Dānishkada-i Adabiyāt (cop. 968/1561, see M.T. Dānishpazhuh, *Nashrīya-i kitābkhāna-i markazī dar nuskhahā-yi khaṭṭī*, no. 4, 1344 sh/1965); Tabrīz, *Fihrist-i Kitābkhāna-i Davlatī-i Tarbiyat: kutub-i khaṭṭī*, Tabrīz 1329 sh/1950, MS no. (-?) (copied 1084/1673).

Still useful are the pioneer study by M. Şükrü, starting with his booklet *Osmanlı devletinin kuruluşu: Bitlisli İdrīs'in "Hešt Bihišt" adlı eserine göre ...*, Ankara 1934, and his article 'Das *Hešt Bihišt* ...' Tl. 1 in *Der Islam*, Bd. 19 (1931). See also Orhan Başaran, *İdris-i Bitlisi'nin Heşt Bihişti'nin Hatimesi*. Doktora tezi, Erzurum, Atatürk Universitesi, 2000.

In 1146/1733, 'Abdülbāḳī Sa'dī, (d. 1161/1748), prepared a translation into Ottoman Turkish (yet full of Persian and Arabic loan constructions!). A Latin alphabet transcription of a manuscript of Sa'dī's translation (Süleymaniye Hamidiye 928) was published in 2 volumes in Ankara by Mehmet Karabaş and others in 2008.

[2] P3

al-Shīrāzī, Sayyid Muḥammad b. Mīr Jalāl al-Dīn al-Ḥusaynī, fl. 1065/1655 (f. 1ª)

سید محمد بن میر جلال الدین الحسینی الشیرازی

Tarkhānnāma

ترخان نامه

Begins (f. 1ª, after the missing first page):

و اکناف عالم سایر است و ذکر سخاوت و شجاعت او مثل نیر اعظم در نصف النهار ظاهر وباهر

Ends (f. 64ᵇ):

عمر شریفش نود و پنج سال بود زهی توفیق که این همه عمر بطاعات الهی در امرائي العیش و عشرت و کامرانی گذرانیده و نام نامی خود را در چاردانك هندوستان به عدالت و شجاعت مشهور گردانیده است بتاریخ هفتم شهر شوال المکرم سنه ۱۰۹۷ هجري تمام شد

Mirzā Muḥammad Ṣāliḥ Tarkhān (f. 1ª), a mid-17th-century ruler of the Tarkhān dynasty of Sind, ordered Sayyid Muḥammad b. Mīr Jalāl al-Dīn al-Shīrāzī to find a manuscript of a history of that dynasty titled *Tarkhānnāma*. Being unable to find one, al-Shīrāzī compiled his own history under the same title. In a short introduction he noted among his sources "reliable works such as [*Tārīkh-i*] Ṭabarī; *Ravżat al-ṣafā*ʾ [= Mīrkhond]; *Ẓafarnāma-i Tīmūrī*; *Tārīkh-i Humāyūn*; *Akbarnāma*; *Nigāristān*; *Tārīkh-i Ṭāhir*; *Muntakhab-i bī badal-i Yūsufī*; *Tārīkh-i Guzīda*; *Majmaʿ al-ansāb*, and others". Storey[3] cites H.M. Elliot and J. Dawson who have shown[4] that in fact Shīrāzī compiled the *Tarkhānnāma* mainly from M[uḥammad] Maʿṣūm's *Tārīkh-i Sind*, since then printed in Poona in 1938. In his introduction Shīrāzī mentions some of the Tarkhān dynasty's Mongol

3 *PL*, vol. 1, p. 655.

4 In their *History of India*, London, 1865, vol. 1, p. 301, followed by a long extract in English translation, pp. 303–326.

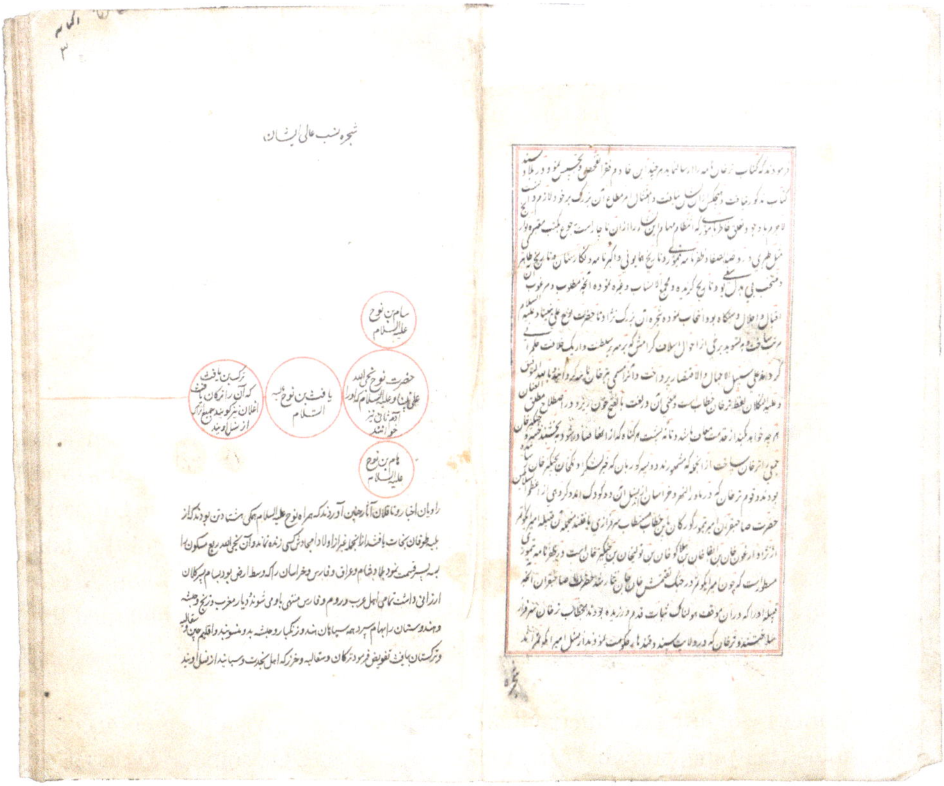

FIGURE 21 No. 2 (P3). Shīrāzī, Sayyid Muḥammad, d. 1065/1655. *Tarkhānnāma*. f. 1[b]–2[a]. Copied 1097/1686

and Turkish ancestors, including Chingiz Khān, Tīmūr, Arghūn Khān b. Abāqā Khān b. Hulāgū Khān, among others. The work is remarkable for presenting 24 genealogical charts: (ff. 2[a]–14[b]) from Nūḥ (Noah) through his son Yāfiṣ (Japhet) and "Turk b. Yāfiṣ", leading from there finally to "*Navvāb-i nāmdār gardūn-i iqtidār Mīrzā Muḥammad Ṣāliḥ Tarkhān b. Mīrzā ʿĪsā Tarkhān*", who had commissioned the work. The arrangement of the genealogical charts follows the classic Islamic model: the names are written within red ink circles which are linked by straight lines, with each ruler's children in their own smaller circles nearby. Some pages of the charts have brief historical notes by the author at the side, in the same copyist's hand, e.g. "At the present time, which is 1065 hijrī [1655], Turkistān is under the Chaghatāy dynasty" (f. 9[a]). From f. 15[a] to the end (f. 64[b]) the author's text is entirely narrative, beginning with a rubric "*Bayān-i aḥvāl-i Khānān-i Turkistān va khurūj-i Chingiz Khān va ḥukūmat-i avlād-i nāmdārash dar Īrān*". In this narrative text, the author sometimes mentions a specific source (e.g. f. 15[a] *Tārīkh-i Ravżat-i ṣafā'-i Khvāndamīr*.)

The last date mentioned in the text is Muḥarram 1071/November 1660 (f. 64[b]) when Muḥammad Ṣāliḥ succeeded his late father. This MS copy was completed nearly 26 years later, on 9 Shavvāl 1097/30 August 1686 (f. 64[b]). Our MS is one of the oldest known of this rare work.

Indian *nastaʿlīq*; ff. 1[a]–64[b]; 24.5×14.5 (16×9) cm; 17 lines.

Paper is "oriental" without chain lines or laid lines.

Decoration: Each page in triple frames: two in red ink, within outer frame in blue; headings and name of rulers in red.

Ownership: (1) Anonymous English owner (18th century?) wrote in pencil in the margins a summary in English of the contents of each page, starting from f. 23[b] ("*Ẕikr-i khurūj-i Chingiz Khān*"); (2) Luzac [Oriental bookseller in London], f. 64[b], in the hand of (3) A.G. Ellis, who signed his own name and the date 17. 6. [18]96 on f. 1[a]. For Ellis's brief biography see the ownership note to our manuscript 1/P1 (above); (4) After his death in 1942, Luzac again obtained the MS and sold it to E. Birnbaum in August 1958.[5]

Binding: Light brown mottled Indian leather binding with gilding around edges and on the spine; probably early to mid-19th century. On some pages, e.g. f. 2[a] and 14[b], small sections of the marginal notes trimmed off when the MS was bound or rebound.

Other MSS and references: Storey *PL* vol. 1, pt. 1, p. 655 knew of only four manuscripts (all 19th century): one in the India Office Library (MS 3871), and three in the British [Museum] Library; *Catalogue of Persian MSS in the British Museum*, vol. III, nos 950a, b, c; Dushanbe, *Katalog vostochnyikh rukopisei Akademii Nauk Tadzhikskoi SSR*, tom 1 (1960), no. 152, pp. 510–511, copied 1930 from a MS dated 1128/1716; Tashkent, *Sobranie vostochnyikh rukopisei Akademii Nauk Uzbekskoi SSR*, tom 1, pp. 103–104.

5 The manuscript does not seem to be mentioned in Luzac's sale catalogue of the Ellis collection of 1945.

[3] P14/I

Niʿmat Khān, ʿĀlī, d. 1122/1710 (f. 1[a]; f. 44[b])

نعمت خان، عالی

Rūznāmcha-i ayyām-i muḥāṣara-i dār al-jihād Ḥaydarābād (f. 1[b])

روزنامچه ایام محاصره دار الجهاد حیدراباد و تاریخ سیزدهم رجب سنه ۳۰ جلوس

Also known as ***Vaqāʾiʿ-i Niʿmat Khān*** (f. 1[b]) and ***Vaqāʾiʿ-i Ḥaydarābād.***

Begins (f. 1[b]):

دمی که مدرّس کشاف صبح در صفه صدق و صفا

Ends (f. 49[b]):

متوطن شهر کهنه اهالی صدر جهانی ستر الله ... بتاریخ بیستم شهر ذی الحجه سنه یکهزار و دو صد و جهل و پنج هجری ...

A satirical description, in prose mingled with verse, about the siege of Ḥaydarābād conducted by Avrangzīb in 1097/1686. The author, born in India to a Persian family, attained high offices under that ruler. Niʿmat Khān was notable both for the complexity of his satirical style and the simplicity of his *ghazal*s and a *masnavī, Ḥusn u ʿIshq* (see copy below MS 14, P14/II).

Indian *nastaʿlīq*; ff. 1[b]–49[b]; 24 × 14.5 (17.5 × 8) cm; 15 lines; copyist Aḥmad Shaykh al-Islām, completed 20 Ẕīʾl-Ḥijja 1245/1830 (f. 49[b]). Immediately following the same author's *Munākaḥa-i Ḥusn u ʿishq* (ff. 50[b]–56[a]; see MS 14, P14/II) in the hand of the same copyist, who completed it less than two months later, in Lucknow on 16 Muḥarrem 1246/1830.

Paper: Thin Indian paper, not watermarked; margins badly wormed, but the text is legible; headings and overlines in red ink; interlinear and marginal notes throughout the manuscript, many of them explaining uncommon Persian words in the text.

Ownership: Same as MS 17, P12.

Binding: Rebound in paper-covered cardboard, with cloth spine, mid-20th century.

Other MSS and references: Many copies in India and in western libraries; many 19th century Indian lithograph editions. See Storey *PL*, pt. 1, 589–592; Storey/Bregel, PL vol. 1, p. 152; *Encyclopaedia Iranica*, art. ʿĀlī, Neʿmatkhān.

B. Literature

[4] M4/III

Rashīd al-Dīn Vaṭvāṭ, d. 573 or 578/1177–1178 or 1182–1183 (f. 1a; 1b)

رشيد الدين وطواط

Ḥadāʾiq al-siḥr fī daqāʾiq al-shiʿr (f. 1a, 2a) [in Persian]

حدائق السحر فی دقائق الشعر

Begins (f. 1b):

الحمد لله على ما افاض علينا من نعمه المترعه الحياض ... جنين كويد مؤلّف اين كتاب محمد بن محمد بن عبد الجليل العُمَری المعروف بالرشيد كي روزی من بنده را خداوند ولی النعم ملك عالم عادل مويّد مظفر منصور خوارزمشاهْ علآء الملّة [sic] الدين ابو المظفّر اتسز بن محمد معينٔ [sic] امير المومنين اعزّ الله انصاره

Ends abruptly (at f. 56b, because the original last folio is lost):

زهی مخالفت ملك تو خطاء خطا * زهی موافقت صدر تو صواب صواب ارتجال

Followed by 2 faded lines of text difficult to read, as well as marginal notes in an old but later hand. Both this text and these marginal notes are on the now detached bottom of the last extant page of this MS. The final leaf (f. 56b) corresponds approximately with the text of the Paris MS completed 7 Shaʿbān 668/March 1270, edited by ʿAbbās Iqbāl (see below, 'Other MSS').

Rashīd al-Dīn Vaṭvāṭ, the chief secretary and panegyrist to the Khvārazmshāh Atsız at Gurganj, was famous as a literary stylist in prose and poetry, both in Arabic and in Persian. This work in Persian is a detailed and "much admired handbook of rhetorical figures" (F.C. Blois in *EI*², art. Rashīd al-Dīn Vaṭvāṭ, vol. 8, p. 444b), with many illustrative examples, some composed by the author himself. The main text of this MS seems to have fewer illustrative poetic citations than the Paris MS. Our MS, perhaps the oldest or second oldest known

© KONINKLIJKE BRILL NV, LEIDEN, 2019 | DOI:10.1163/9789004389670_019

FIGURE 22 No. 4 (M4/III). Rashīd al-Dīn Vaṭvāṭ, d. 573 or 578/1177–1182. *Ḥadāʾiq al-siḥr fī daqāʾiq al-shiʿr*. f. 1^b–2^a. Copied late 6th or 7th/12–13th century

copy this MS of this work, was probably copied in the late 12th or the 13th century, after the author's death (which occurred in 1178 or 1183), since citations of his verses are followed by *raḥimahu'llāh*.

Old fashioned *naskh* in two different but certainly contemporary main hands, since one follows the other on the same paper and bifold quire (f. 19^b and 20^a respectively). The first hand wrote f. 1^b–19^b; the second continued on the same paper on f. 20^a–52^b. This second hand is modified *naskh*, showing the beginnings of the development of *nastaʿliq* script. A supply paper bifold (f. 44–45 with a Scissors watermark, perhaps 17th century), was inserted later. Its margins and those of f. 40–52 contain many marginal additions of verses in *nastaʿliq* script, headed by the names of their authors in red ink; 20.5 × 13 (17 × 9.5) cm; 19 lines.

As the end of the MS is lost, there is no dated colophon; paleographically, it would appear to be not later than the 13th century. Both the main hands of the

MS use old fashioned orthographic conventions, such as *z̲āl* for later *dāl* (e.g. كويذ ; بوذه; ديذم); *bā* for *pā* (e.g. بارسى); *hamzah* as an alternative to *yā* (e.g. كوئذ and كويذ and كوىذ *yā* without dots or *hamza*); and often omit diacritic dots on frequently used words, (e.g. no dots with *jīm* and *yā* in *tajnīs*, nor with *tā*, *zā* and *yā* in *Tāzī*, nor with *chīm*, *yā* and *zā* in *chīzī*).

Paper: Thick "oriental" paper, except for the much later supply leaves, f. 44–45, which have a Scissors watermark. Some pages near the end are brittle, and have cracks or holes, perhaps due to drying after water damage, which is evident on some pages.

Ownership: Bought by E. Birnbaum in Istanbul, 1987.

Binding: The first ("original") binding is lost: when this work was later rebound, it was preceded by two works in Ottoman Turkish, probably in the 17th century, in a brown leather Ottoman binding, which is now loose. For further details, see our *Turkish and Çağatay Manuscripts in Canada: A Union Catalogue*, Nos. 44, M4/I and 91, M4/II.

Other features: The Paris MS (Blochet) IV, 2137, dated 668/1270, was edited and annotated by ʿAbbās Iqbāl (Tehrān, 1308sh/1929) and the editions dependent on that MS [see below] introduce citations of Vaṭvāṭ's own verses with the formulas *man gūyam* or *mis̲ālash marāʾst* whereas our MS usually writes *muʾallif gūyad raḥimahuʾllāh*.

A much later owner wrote on f. 1ª "*Yā Allāh, yā ḥafīẓ yā Kabīkaj*"; the latter being an invocation, to the king or shaykh in charge of bookworms, not to harm the MS.[1]

Other MSS and references: *Encyclopaedia Iranica*, articles Waṭwāṭ, Rashīd al-Dīn; and Atsiz Garčaʾī; *PL* Storey, vol. III pt. 1, pp. 176–178; *EI*², vol. 8, pp. 444–445; editions by ʿAbbās Iqbāl 1308sh/1929; ed. Saʿīd Nafīsī in his edition of Rashīd al-Dīn's *Dīvān*. Tehran, 1339sh/1960; ed. and tr. into Russian by N. Khalisova as *Sady volshebstva v ton'kostyakh poezii*: *Ḥadāʾiḳ as-siḥr* ... Moskva 1985.

1 Adam Gacek, 'The use of "kabikaj" in Arabic manuscripts', in *Manuscripts of the Middle East* 1 (1986), pp. 49–53. See also F. Steingass, *A Comprehensive Persian-English Dictionary* [...] London⁵, 1963, p. 1013.

[5] P10/I

Saʿdī, (f. 3^b), d. 691/1292

سعدی

Gulistān (f. 7^b)

کلستان

Begins (f. 1^b):

منّت خدایرا عز و جل که طاعتش موجت قربتست

Ends (f. 136^a):

یا ناظرا فیه سل لله مرحمة * علی المنصف (sic) [= المصنّف] و استغفر لصاحبه و اطلب
لنفسك من خیر ترید بها [sic] * من بعد ذلك غفرانا لکاتبه تمت بعون الله الملك المعین

Saʿdī's literary works, both in prose and in poetry, have been major influences on the development of Persian literature from the 13th century until the present time. His *Gulistān*, a charming work consisting mainly of short stories (*ḥikāyāt*) and anecdotes (some allegedly autobiographical), is written in beautiful, relatively simple clear prose. It is enlivened by his own verses, aphorisms, and advice on how to survive and prosper in an uncertain world.

The *Gulistān* served for many centuries not only as enjoyable reading but also as a text book for young Persians in Iran and neighboring Persian speaking lands, and also became a resource to teach Persian to the speakers of other languages, especially in the Ottoman Empire (mainly though not exclusively Turkish), India, and Central Asia. It was composed in 656/1258 (f. 10^a) and dedicated to the "*Atābeg* Abū Bakr b. Saʿd b. Zangī" (f. 3^b), the local ruler of Shīrāz, where Saʿdī was born and to which he returned after many years of travel. The *Gulistān* has been enthusiastically described (by Franklin Lewis, *Encyclopaedia Iranica*, art. Golestan-e Saʿdī) as "probably the most influential work of prose in the Persian tradition".

The present manuscript volume contains Saʿdī's two most famous works, *Gulistān* in prose, written at the centre of the page (ff. 1ᵇ–136ᵃ), and the *Būstān* in verse, occupying the margins from ff. 1ᵇ–136ᵃ, and then both centre and margins from ff. 136ᵃ to 145ᵃ. (For fuller details of the *Būstān* see the entry below, No. 8, P10/II).

It is evident that this two-part-manuscript was copied and used in a Turkish speaking environment because interlinear glosses explain in Turkish some of the less familiar Persian and Arabic words. These glosses are found only on ff. 1ᵇ–13ᵃ, at which point the early Turkish owner apparently abandoned his study of the *Gulistān*!

Turkish (not Persian) form of *taʿlīq* script; ff. 1ᵇ–136ᵃ (in a MS of 148 folios); fol. 1ᵇ is a supply leaf (ca. 18th century).

Paper: The MS is undated, but some of the paper's watermarks are the same as those found in European papers of the late 16th and early 17th centuries: Crossbow within Circle, surmounted by a Trefoil; small Crown surmounted by a 6-armed Star, topped by a recumbent Crescent; 3 short daggers; wine decanter with letters of LP within a square at its widest point.

Decoration: Fairly good *sarlavḥa* (headpiece) in gold, blue and red on supply leaf (fol. 1ᵇ), enclosed in multiple gold frames; in the rest of the MS, headings in red ink.

Ownership: f. 1ᵃ (supply leaf): Aḥmad Qāḍīzāda (Aḥmed Ḳāḍīzāde); bought by E. Birnbaum, Istanbul, August 1991.

Binding: Original binding absent; rebound in a recycled old brown leather binding, which must have come from a smaller MS, as the bottom and side edges of the present pages protrude up to half a centimeter beyond the present covers. Both covers bear the same blind-stamped scalloped floral medallion and are enclosed within four frames.

Other MSS and references: Thanks to its immense popularity, there are thousands of MSS in libraries worldwide, and several important critical editions. As the bibliography on Saʿdī and his works is immense, I note only a few general references: *Encyclopaedia Iranica*, art. Saʿdī; *İslam Ansiklopedisi*, art. Saʿdi Şīrāzī, cilt 10, pp. 36–40; *EI*², art. Saʿdī, vol. 8, pp. 718–723; *Türk Diyanet Vakfi İslam Ansiklopedisi*, art. Gülistan, cilt 14, pp. 240–241.

[6] T106

Saʿdī, d. 691/1292

سعدی

Gulistān va bihi muʿīd (f. 1ᵇ)

کلستان و به معید

Begins (f. 1ᵇ):[2]

خدایرا عزّ و جلّ که طاعتش موجب قربتست
منت تکریا عز و جل اولسون که انوك طاعتی یقنلوغی موجبدر

Last line with interlinear Turkish translation (f. 162, line. 9–10):

و الصلاة و السلام علی اکرم الرسل و هادی السبل محمد
رحمتی دخی اسنلك رسوللروك اکرم اوزرنه سبیللروك هادی سی اوزرنه محمد

Ends (f. 163ᵃ):

و اطلب لنفسك من خیر ترید به من بعد ذلك غفراناً لکاتبه

The title at the head of the text, meaning "The *Gulistān* with Tutor included", aptly describes this MS. Here the "Tutor" (*muʿīd*, who "repeats" the lesson with the student after the original lesson) is the interlinear Turkish translation, enabling the student to study on his own. It might be freely translated as "Teach Yourself the *Gulistān*." This Persian classic was widely used throughout the Islamic world as a text book of Persian language.

Many different Turkish translations of the *Gulistān* exist, but this particular one, expressly designated for self-teaching, seems to be a unique manuscript.

2 In the manuscript, the Turkish text elements are written exactly underneath the Persian words to which they correspond. Unfortunately, for technical reasons the typesetter could not emulate this in a consistent way for the description of bilingual works in the present catalogue.

It contains the complete text of the *Gulistān* except about one page of the *dībāja* (prologue) between f. 9 and 10, which probably fell out centuries ago. The text includes a Turkish translation [twice] of Saʿdī's original dedication to the Salghurid ruler of Fars, the *Atabeg* Abū Bakr b. Saʿd b. Zangī (reigned 623–658/1226–1260, f. 4[a]; f. 9[a]).

Persian text in clear Turkish *taʿlīq*; interlinear Turkish translation in very small more cursive *taʿlīq*, verging on *dīvānī*; headings and Arabic quotations in naskh fully vocalized in red ink; f. 1[b]–163[a] (f. 163[b]–164[a] and f. 167[b]–168[b] blank); 20×14.5 (17×10) cm; 18 lines (9 Persian, 9 interlinear Turkish); the MS is undated but paleographically probably 16th century.

Paper: Watermark: Anchor suspended from a Ring within a Circle, surmounted by a 6-armed Star.

Ownership: (1) Seal, oblong hexagonal, 1.5 cm diameter; inscription is illegible (defaced by later owner); (2) seal, rounded octagonal, 1.4 cm across, defaced and illegible; (3) bought by E. Birnbaum in Istanbul in July 1991.

Binding: Of the original black leather binding only the flap and backstrip remain. The V-angle of the flap is decorated with a triangle of 3 small identical hexagonal blind stamps, each containing a 6-pointed "Star of David" with a 6-point Asterisk (or flower) in the middle. The flap is framed in a double *jadval*. Many centuries ago, the original leather of the front and back covers, which are made of papers glued together, were covered with paper which is now very worn.

Other features: Many individual verses of Turkish *dīvān* poetry have been added in a later hand to the originally blank ff. 164[b]–167[a].

Other MSS and references: No other copies of this translation seem to be known. For a fuller description and discussion of this and other Turkish translations of the *Gulistān* see E. Birnbaum, "Interlinear translation and the case of the Turkish dictionaries" in *Journal of Turkish Studies* 26/I (2002), p. 70, and especially notes 20 and 21, and facsimile of a page from this MS on p. 77.

[7] T17/V

Lughat-i Kitāb-i Gulistān-i Shaykh Saʿdī (f. 66b)

لغت كتاب كلستان شيخ سعدي

Begins (f. 66b):

منّت طاعت موجب قربت
شكر عبادت كردن سبب يقين لق

End of Persian/Arabic-Turkish vocabulary (f. 78a):

فَرْسْ بَغَلْ حمار ظبى هرّه شاة
ات قتر اشك كِيكْ كدى قويون

Beginning of Arabic citations with interlinear Turkish translation (f. 78a):

الاية اعملوا آل داود شكر
عمل اعلاى [sic] يا داود اوغلانلرى شكر يوزندن

End of Arabic citations with interlinear Turkish translation (ff. 83a–b):

و نهرٌ الى نهرٍ اذا جَمَعَت بحرٌ
ارماق ارماغه چقن جمع اولسه دريا اولور

Colophon (f. 83b):

يا ناظر فيه سلِ بالله مرحمةً على المصنّف واستغفر لصاحبه و اطلب لنفسك من خير تريد بها
من بعد ذلك غفراناً لكاتبه والسلام على من اتّبع الهدى و لم يتخذ الّهاً من الهدى ... تم فى اواسط
شوال فى وقت عيشا [sic] سنه ٩٩٣

This manuscript is an anonymous interlinear Persian-Turkish select vocabulary consisting of some 1100 Persian words from the *Gulistān* with their translations interlinearly into Turkish. The Persian (or Arabic) words are not arranged in alphabetical order, but in the sequence in which these "difficult" Persian or Arabic words occur in the *Gulistān*, chapter by chapter. The "Turkish" translations are sometimes not words of Turkish origin but are other loanwords from Arabic or Persian which have entered common Turkish usage, e.g. *minnat*, T *şükür*; *khaṭā*, T *cürm*; *mavsim*, T *vaḳit*. Occasionally the Turkish translation includes Persian auxiliary verbal derivatives, such as *kardan, kunanda*: e.g., *tatimma*, T *tamam künende*; *ṭāʿat*, T *ʿibādet kerden*; *karīm*, T *kerem künende*. This feature would suggest that this kind of Turkish-Persian vocabulary was adapted from a Persian-Persian vocabulary (or "pony") of the *Gulistān*, which explained some of Saʿdī's more elite Persian expressions in simpler Persian. The chapters are numbered in Arabic words *al-bāb al-avval, al-bāb al-s̱ānī*, etc. They are: [*Dībāja*] f. 66ᵇ; *1* f. 68ᵇ; *2* f. 70ᵃ; *3* f. 71ᵇ; *4* f. 72ᵇ; *5* f. 73ᵃ; followed at f. 74ᵃ by *al-bāb al-panjum* [sic!, in fact *bāb* 6]; 6 f. 74ᵇ; 7 f. 76ᵃ ending at 78ᵃ (The three final chapters are here wrongly numbered and represent *bāb* 6–8 of the original *Gulistān*). While this vocabulary and that of Saʿdī's *Būstān* (No. 9, T17/II) are in the same copyist's hand, they are arranged quite differently: the *Būstān*'s lists the words in a single alphabetical sequence, while this *Gulistān*'s are listed chapter by chapter. This basic difference in method would indicate that these two compilations were originally composed by different anonymous authors.

In the *dībāja* (prologue) to the Persian original, Saʿdī dedicates the *Gulistān* to the Salghur ruler of Fars, the Atābeg "Abū Bakr b. Saʿd b. Zangī" (reigned 623–658/1226–1260), whom Saʿdī mentions with extravagant titles of praise *in Arabic*. They are cited twice in this MS (f. 79ᵃ; 79ᵇ), with interlinear translation into Turkish. In the present Persian-Turkish vocabulary of the *Gulistān*, its 8 *bāb*s are followed by a listing of Arabic quotations from the Qurʾan, *ḥadīs̱* and poetic verses and proverbs, in the order in which they occur in the *Dībāja* of the Persian original of the *Gulistān*. Beneath each Arabic quotation is an interlinear Turkish translation.

Fully vocalized *naskh* for Persian (and Arabic) headwords and citations; interlinear Turkish translations in *dīvānī*, occasionally in red ink, which is also used at times for chapter headings; ff. 66ᵇ–83ᵃ. Some leaves of this MS have been lost: between ff. 79 and 80, the leaves which would have contained the headings for *bāb* 2, 3 and 7. The following headings remain: *bāb* 1 (f. 79ᵇ); *bāb* 4 and 5 (f. 80ᵃ); *bāb* 6 (f. 81ᵇ); *bāb* 8 (f. 83ᵃ); 20×14 (17×10.5) cm; 16 lines (8 Persian, 8 Turkish interlinear translation).

Paper: Watermarked with an Anchor in a Circle, surmounted by a diamond-shaped Quatrefoil; MS completed in the middle of Shavvāl 993/November 1583 (f. 83ᵇ; same paper as No. 9, T17/II).

Ownership: (1) [f. 1[a]] Khvāja—?—? Ibrāhīm Ḥilmī, above round seal (diameter 1.4 cm), defaced and difficult to read; (2) [f. 66[b]; 78[a]] a different round seal, crowded with finely written text, (diam. 1.4 cm); (3) [f. 83[b]] octagonal seal (twice, 1.4 cm) below written ownership note dated Ṣafar 1158; (4) [f. 83[b]] round seal (1.3 cm) beneath written note of ownership of "Muḥammad Sīrazūlī (?) [= Sīrūzlī?] Ṣufalī (?)", presently *maṣda(rī)ya amīni* of Galata [1]197; (5) bought by E. Birnbaum in Istanbul, April 1973.

Binding: Light brown soft leather covers framed in faded gold paint; probably rebound in the 18th or early 19th century, when four other works were combined into this volume and the edges trimmed, cutting off parts of the words in some margins. Of the five works between the covers of this manuscript volume, three are Persian-Turkish vocabularies: the present work, No. 7, *Lughat-i Kitāb-i Gulistān*; No. 9, *Lughat-i Kitāb-i Būstān*, described below, which preceded it in this volume, and is in the hand of the same copyist; and No. 28, *Mushkilāt-i Shāhnāma* in another contemporary hand.

Other MSS and references: E. Birnbaum, "Interlinear translation: the case of the Turkish dictionaries", *Journal of Turkish Studies*, vol. 26/I (2002) = *Essays in honour of Barbara Flemming*, I, pp. 61–80, especially p. 71 and illustration p. 80. Many Ottoman Turkish translations of and commentaries on the *Gulistān*; i.e. commentataries on the *Gulistān* have been made from the 15th through the 20th century. See DİA, cilt 14, art. Gulistān, pp. 240–241 and references there; *Encyclopedia Iranica*, art. Golestan, vol. 4 (1990) pp. 573–574.

[8] P10/II

Saʿdī, d. 691/1292 (f. 4[b] and 6[b], margins; 143[b]; *passim*)

سعدی

Būstān (f. 1[b], margin)

بوستان

Begins (f. 1[b], margin):

بنام خداوند جان آفرین * حکیم سخن در زبان آفرین

Ends (f. 143[b], margin):

تضاعت نیاوردم الّا امید * خدایا زعفوم مکن نا امید

In 655/1257, one year before Saʿdī composed his *Gulistān* in prose, he completed his *Būstān* (f. 5[b]) in poetic couplets (*maṡnavī*). This entertaining moralistic work dispenses practical advice for achieving well-being and happiness, usually ethically, but sometimes even unethically when circumstances are difficult. Among the virtues promoted are justice, generosity, and contentment. The great variety of illustrative anecdotes, tales, epigrams, and verses make such pleasant reading that the *Būstān*'s popularity for the past seven centuries among Persians, and also non-Iranians studying Persian, is exceeded only by Saʿdī's *Gulistān*. Both are dedicated to the same patron, the *Atabeg* "Bū Bakr b. Saʿd" (f. 6[a]).

The present single physical manuscript volume contains the texts of both the *Gulistān* (in the centre of the page [see above No. 5, P10/I]) and of the *Būstān* (in the margins until f. 136[a], and from then onwards in both the centre of the page and the margin successively on each page from f. 136[a] to the end of the *Būstān* on f. 143[b]).

Immediately following (on ff. 144[a]–145[b]), and in the same hand is a 30 verse *munājāt* in *maṡnavī* in the same *mutaqārib* meter as the *Būstān*. It begins: خدایا توقع همین دارم از کردکار که در رستخیزم: and ends: چو امید دارم بتو بر آور امیدم که دارم بتو کنی رستکار

Turkish style of *taʿlīq* script in margins (ff. 1[b]–60[b]), followed by a gradual shift for some folios to *naskh*; and from ff. 63[a] to 147[a] (end of MS text) entirely in Turkish *naskh*. The same copyist wrote the marginal and the center-of-the-page texts of both the *Būstān* and *Gulistān* in this MS volume.

Paper: Although the MS is not dated, papers with similar watermarks were used in MSS of the late 16th and early 17th century. For details, see the *Gulistān* MS No. 5, P10/I, above.

For decoration, ownership, binding, and details of some of the many other MSS, see references in No. 5, P10/I; and catalogues of major libraries, including Ahmed Ateş, *İstanbul Kütüphanelerinde Farsça manẓūm eserler*, cilt 1.

[9] T17/II

Lughat-i Kitāb-ı Būstān (f. 47^b)

لغت كتاب بوستان

Begins (f. 47^b):

آلا آديم اَلسَّخَايَا اصل اهينمت
كيزلو نعمت و عظمت بريوي و ضتحيان جمع كوك قلج چكمك

Ends (f. 64^b):

يُوزْ يغُشِى النهار يَثْرِب
پارس كندوزين اقپلار مدينه

Saʿdī's *Būstān* was another Persian classic used as a text book by Turkish students. This MS is an anonymous Persian-Turkish select vocabulary compiled to help Turks learn Persian by studying the *Būstān*. The words are listed alphabetically from *alif* to *yā* by the first vowel in the sequence *a*; *i*; *u* (*maftūḥa*, *maqṣūra*, *mażmūma*). The MS contains approximately 1100 Persian words, each explained in one or more Turkish words. Some of the words, both Persian and Turkish, are evidently miscopied, perhaps misread from an imperfect *Vorlage*.

Naskh, fully vocalized for Persian words and Arabic loanwords in Persian; the interlinear Turkish in *dīvānī* script, occasionally in *naskh*, and sometimes partly vocalized; headings in red ink; ff. 47^b–64^b (lower part of f. 47^b torn off and lost); 20×14 (17×10.5) cm; 12 lines (6 Persian, 6 interlinear Turkish at 45-degree angle beneath the corresponding Persian word).

Paper watermarked: Anchor within Circle, surmounted by angular (diamond-shaped) Quatrefoil; copied shortly before the middle of Shavvāl 993/November 1585, which is the copy date of the Persian-Turkish vocabulary of Saʿdī's *Gulistān* (No. 7 above, f. 83^b) which is in the same hand and immediately follows it.

Ownership and binding: see No. 7/T17/V, above.

Other MSS and references: E. Birnbaum, "Interlinear translation: the case of the Turkish dictionaries" in *JTS*, 26/I = *Essays in honour of Barbara Flemming*, I (2002), pp. 61–80, especially p. 71.

[10] **P2**

Ḥāfiẓ, d. ca. 792/1390

حافظ

Dīvān

ديوان

Begins (f. 1b):

الا يا ايها الساقى ادر كأساً و ناولها * كه عشق آسان نمود اول ولى افتاد مشكلها

Ends (f. 181a):

بازآي كه بى روى تو ايشمع رو ديده * سيلاب سرشك از عقب نامه روانست

Colophon (f. 181a):

ختم شد ديوان شعر شيرين كلام * بر سر طاوس قدى اتشيان نخر ايام
هژدهم ماه ربيع الاخر اندر چاشتكاه * بدسه شنبه روز هجرت صاد و زال [sic = دال؟] و
واو و لام

Ḥāfiẓ is widely regarded as the greatest lyrical poet in Persian: for more than six centuries he has been probably the best known and the most widely quoted. Most of his poems are in the *ghazal* form. Thousands of manuscripts of his *Dīvān* are to be found not only in libraries worldwide in Iran, Central Asia, the Indian Subcontinent, the land of the former Ottoman Empire, as well as in major libraries in Europe and North America, and also in many private collections. Manuscripts titled *Dīvān-i Ḥāfiẓ* vary greatly in content and length. Although Ḥāfiẓ was a prolific poet, many *ghazal*s attributed to him are not his own, but the work of admirers and imitators. The sequence of poems in the

Dīvān varies greatly in the manuscripts. The *Dīvān* was used for centuries also as a *fāl-nāma*, as a means of divination of future events.

The present manuscript is a respectable sample of one of the recensions of the text current in India, probably in the early eighteenth century. The year given in the dated colophon on f. 181ª is problematic: "18 Rabīʿ II of the year *ṣād u ẕāl* [misspelled زال] *u vāv u lām*," i.e. 90 + 600 + 6 + 30, totaling 726 Hijrī/1324 is obviously impossible, whether we read the word as *ẕāl* or *za*.

The manuscript begins with the same *ghazal* as in the critical edition *Jāmiʿ-i nusakh-i Ḥāfiẓ*, ed. Masʿūd Farzād, Shīrāz, 1347 AHS/1968, and ends (on f. 181ª) with *qiṭʿa* 5, p. 628 in Farzād's edition.

Good Indian *nastaʿlīq*; ff. 1ᵇ–182ª; 19.5×10 (13×6.5) cm; 13 lines.

Paper has laid lines but no watermark designs.

Decoration: First opening (ff. 1ᵇ–2ª) has a multicolored *sarlavḥa* (headpiece) in gold, blue, red and green, and gold clouds float between lines; corner decorations; the text throughout is surrounded by multiple frames of gold, blue, black and red; vertical lines in red ink separate the two halves of each verse into two columns.

Ownership: (1) Inside back cover an engraved European Ex Libris label (18th or early 19th century) has been pasted in. It depicts an Eagle rampant holding an Arrow in the left leg; it is surmounted by the Latin motto "Non Praedâ sed Victoriâ." Beneath the Eagle the words "*Ligentia di*" [remainder of text cut off]; (2) "A/S 1904, Hafiz Diwan" penciled onto the bookplate noted above; (3) A.G. Ellis [See his biography and details of his books and manuscripts printed after his death in 1942 in Luzac's sale catalogue of 1945, noted in the entry for Idrīs Bidlīsī's *Hasht bihisht* (no. 1, P1 above). The present MS was briefly described by Arberry in the catalogue on p. 13, under item M1283; (4) Bought by E. Birnbaum from Luzac in London, August 1958.

Binding: Dark brown leather, Indian style; both covers have blind-stamped scalloped medallion with floral motif and pendants, all within outer blind-stamped frame; ca. 18th century.

Other MSS and references: *Encyclopaedia Iranica*, art. Ḥāfez contains a good summary of the current state of Ḥāfiẓ studies, and notes a selection of important MSS and printed editions.

[11] P15

Jāmī, d. 898/1492

جامی

Yūsuf u Zulaykhā

یوسف و زلیخا

Begins (f. 1[a]):

تو خورشیدي جوماهت کاستن جیست * زوال جاشتکاهت خواستن چیست

Ends (f. 1[b]):

ذکر کفتا که او خوبیست ناراست * جرا باید بهر ناراست جان کاست

This is a single leaf fragment which was originally part of a MS of *Yūsuf u Zulaykhā*, a long *maṡnavī*, one of a cycle of seven which constitute Jāmī's *Haft Avrang*. A major scholar, theologian, mystic, and author of many works on a variety of subjects, Jāmī is generally considered the last of the great classical poets in Persian.

This leaf comes from an early manuscript of this much admired work. It is paleographically probably from the 16th century. The text corresponds to lines 752–757 in the edition of Aʿlā Khān Afṣaḥzād and Ḥusayn-Aḥmad Tarbīyat, *Maṡnavī-i Haft Avrang*, jild 2, *Yūsuf u Zulaykhā* (Tehran, 1378 AHS/1999, pp. 55–56) in the section headed: *Az mushāhada-i taghyīr-i ḥāl-i Zulaykhā*. This leaf was found loose between the pages of a rare *fiqh* manuscript in Turkish: *Hediyet ül-mü'min* [sic] *ül-kirām fī beyān şerā'iṭ il-islām*, by Ḥācibzāde Meḥmed (d. 1100/1688) in a copy dated 1187/1773: see E. Birnbaum, *Ottoman Turkish Manuscripts in Canada: A Union Catalogue*, no. 118, T37/I.

Fine small *nastaʿlīq*; 18×12.5 (11.5×7) cm; 13 lines; watermarked paper without designs; letter *jīm* used for *chīm*.

Other references: See *Encyclopaedia Iranica*, art. Jāmī.

[12] P4

Muʿammāʾī, Mīr Ḥusayn al-Ḥusaynī, d. 904/1499

معمّای، میر حسین الحسینی

[*Risāla-i muʿammā*]

رسالهٔ معمّا

Begins (f. 1[b]):

بنام آنکه از تألیف و ترکیب * معمای جهانرا داد ترتیب ... اما بعد معروض آنکه فقیر حقیر
حسین بن محمد الحسنی [sic] را جند معمای بودکه ذرّه

Ends (f. 39[a]):

بیار است اول از ان نام خواست که باشد برو نیز ختم کلام ۰ انتهی الکلام تمت الکتاب

A treatise on the art of logogriphs, i.e. riddles or enigmas in verse (*muʿammā*), describing their structure and conventions (with numerous examples), consisting of a series of clues embedded in a *bayt*, hinting at a person's name. This work is the major classic of that genre. It was composed at the suggestion of, and dedicated to, Mīr ʿAlī Shīr Navāʾī (d. 906/1501, f. 1[b]–2[a]; 39[a]), the chief patron of culture at the court of Sultan Ḥusayn Bayqarā at Herat. Although Navāʾī was famous as the greatest master of Chaġatay Turkish literature in all its forms, he was also a poet in Persian (using the *takhalluṣ* "Fānī"), composing not only *ghazal*s, but also *muʿammā*s. He enthusiastically patronized the practitioners of this ingenious genre, as well as of other literary works, both in Persian and in Chaġatay.[3] This work in Persian by Ḥusayn Muʿammāʾī served as an inspiration to the subsequent composers of riddles in rhyme, not only in Persian but also in Ottoman Turkish. Surūrī completed a Turkish commentary on Ḥusayn Muʿammāʾī's work in 965/1558.

3 See Maria Eva Subtelny, 'A taste for the intricate: The Persian poetry of the late Timurid period', *ZDMG*, 136 (1986), pp. 56–79, especially p. 77 ff.

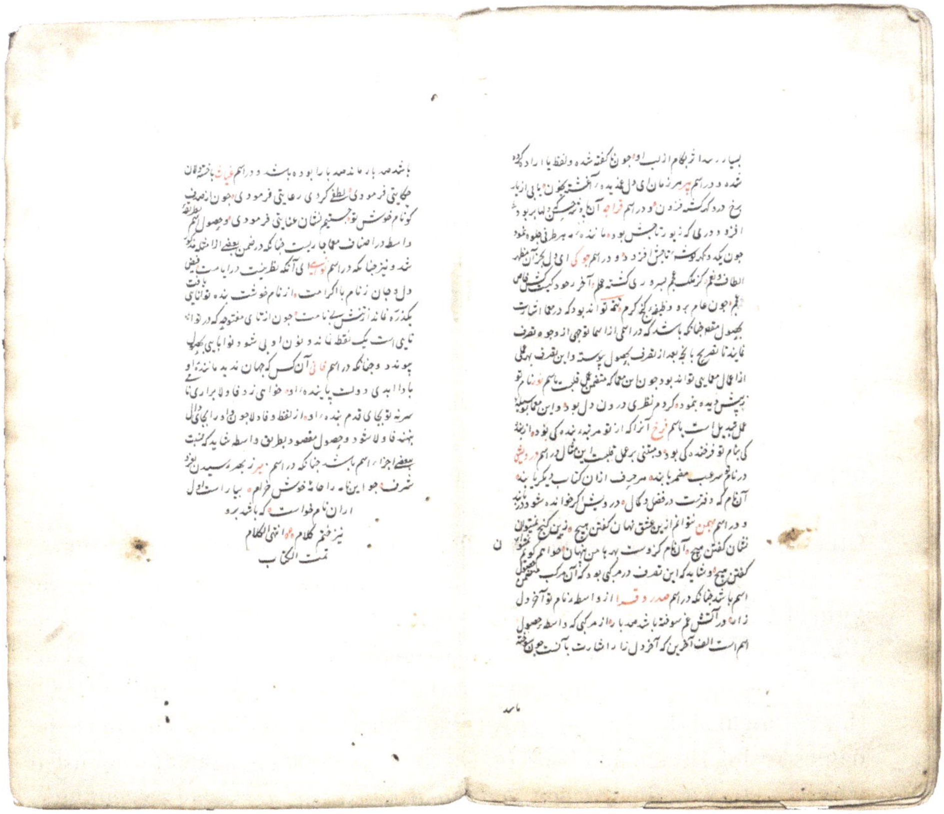

FIGURE 23 No. 12 (P4). Muʿammāʾī, Mīr Ḥusayn, d. 904/1499. *Risāla-i muʿammā*. f. 38^{b}–39^{a}. Copied ca. 905/1500

Manuscripts of this work are rare and this is one of the earliest. While the colophon is not dated, the paper on which the MS is written bears a form of the Oxhead watermark design typical of, and generally limited to, manuscripts of the period between the last years of the 15th century and the first decade and a half of the 16th century.[4] Paleographically its script is also typical of that period. Ḥusayn Muʿammāʾī died in 904/1499 and his patron Navāʾī some two years later. As the copyist of our manuscript did not append the formula *raḥimahu'llāh* to Navāʾī's name, it is possible that this manuscript was copied before his death in 906/1501.

4 See Gerhard Piccard, *Die Ochsenkopf-Wasserzeichen*. Stuttgart: Kohlhammer, 1966 = *Veröffentlichungen der Staatlichen Archivverwaltung Baden-Württemberg*. Sonderreihe, *Die Wasserzeichenkartei Piccard im Hauptstaatsarchiv Stuttgart*. Findbuch 2.

Small clear *nastaʿlīq*; ff. 1ᵇ–39ᵃ; 21.5×12.5 (13×6) cm; 21 lines.

Paper: Watermarked, Oxhead surmounted by a long Staff, around which a Snake rises, the Staff being topped by a three-sided Maltese Cross.

Ownership: (1) 2 oval seals (2×1.4cm diameter), deliberately obliterated; (2) scalloped oval seal (1.5cm × 1.2cm) flanked by an inscription of an [Ottoman Turkish] owner "Muḥammad *al-shahīr* bi-Salāmīzāda [Meḥmed eş-şehīr bi-Selāmīzāde] …"; (3) on paper-covered front cover, an ownership note in formulaic Arabic: "I bought this book from the *taraka* (estate) of the deceased Khalīl Beg for a price known [only] to me," followed by the puchaser's name "al-Sayyid Aḥmad Ḥusayn (?), known as al-Qarūlīzāda …" Between these two inscriptions the date 274 (= 1274/1857–1858) has been written in a very different hand; (4) bought by E. Birnbaum, Istanbul, August 1980.

Other ink inscriptions: (a) On the front doublure the outlines have been drawn of the classic diagram of the *ʿarūż* (prosody) metres of Islamic poetry, in the form of 5 concentric circles [see *EI²*, vol. 1, art. ʿArūḍ, or *Türkiye Diyanet İslam Ansiklopedisi*, art. Aruz, vol. 3, p. 428]. In our MS the diagram remains incomplete, since the names of the metres were not inserted; (b) On the last folio (f. 40ᵇ), originally blank, a later owner has added three riddles in Persian on the names Kāshif, Ḥusām and Badr; (c) On the back doublure a later owner listed 15 spices, etc. with their weight in *dirhams*, e.g. … *afyūn* 38; *filfil* 20; *qaranfil* 4 …; (d) On f. 1ᵃ, "*Yā Kabīkaj*", the traditional Islamic appeal to the chief or king of bookworms to spare this MS. It was quite successful, for the very few wormholes do not affect the text!

Binding: Leather used only for backstrip and edges of paperboard covers, which bear a remnant of an original binding flap; leather also retained as a sunken oval scalloped floral medallion in the middle of front and back covers. The rest of the binding on both coverboards is very worn *abrī/ebru* paper.

Other MSS and references: Ethé, India Office, I, 724–726; 1134–1135; 2049; Ethé, Bodleian 1353–1355, BL-P (Rieu), II p. 650a [Surūrī's commentary]; Paris Bibliothèque nationale, *Catalogue des MSS persans* (Blochet), II nos. 1067–1071; *Topkapı Sarayı Müzesi Farsça Yazmaları Kataloğu*, haz. F.E. Karatay, nos. 859–860 (cop. 980); A. Ateş, *İstanbul Kütüphanelerinde Farsça manzum eserler*, Nos. 674–675; *İzmir Millî Kütüphanesi yazma eserler kataloğu*, cilt 2, p. 533, no. 3074 (cop. 932); Konya Koyunoğlu, no. 13806 (cop. 979), (a Turkish translation also in Koyunoğlu, no. 13804); see also *İslam Ansiklopedisi*, art. Muʿammā, vol. 8, pp. 435–438; *Türk Diyanet Vakfı İslam Ansiklopedisi*, art. Muammâ, cilt 30, p. 322; *EI*², art. Mīr ʿAlī Shīr Nawāʾī, vol. 7, pp. 90–93; Dihkhudā, *Lughatnāma*, XIII, nos 18704–18705.

[13] P5

Ṣāʾib Tabrīzī, d. 1087/1676

صایب تبریزی

Dīvān-i … Ṣāʾib Tabrīzī (f. 173ᵃ)

دیوان … صایب تبریزی

Begins (f. 1ᵇ):

اکر نه مد بسم الله بودی تاج عنوانها * نکشتی تا قیامت نو خط شیرازه دیوانها

The end of the section on *ghazal*s has been lost. In this MS the last one written, beginning … یکروز کل has as its last written line on f. 171ᵇ a verse beginning چو بصورت دیوار and the catchword to the next folio does not match the first of the quatrains which occupy ff. 172ᵃ–173ᵃ.

The MS now ends (f. 173ᵃ):

میتوان کرد اثنا با خاك [-] شت اسمان * صایب انی همت اکر اقبال فرماند کسی

Ṣāʾib, a very prolific major 17th century poet, was born in Tabrīz, but lived most of his life in Iṣfahān. As a young man, however, he spent about seven years at Moghul courts in India, where the rulers generously patronized Persian poets and scholars. Ṣāʾib became famous as one of the initiators of the intricate Indian style of Persian (*Sabk-i Hindī*), which some have compared to the "baroque" of Europe. For many years he was the chief poet (*malik al-shuʿarā*) at the court of Shāh ʿAbbās II in Iṣfahān. His poetry was widely read and admired not only in Iran, but also in India and the Ottoman Empire. Libraries contain many MSS of his *Dīvān* of varying content. Our MS is an early one, completed only six years after the poet's death. Ṣāʾib also wrote some Turkish poetry. The copyist, Ibn (?) ʿAlī Taqī Malik ʿAlī Qummī, completed this MS on 20 Jumāẕī II 1092/July 1681 (colophon, f. 173ᵃ).

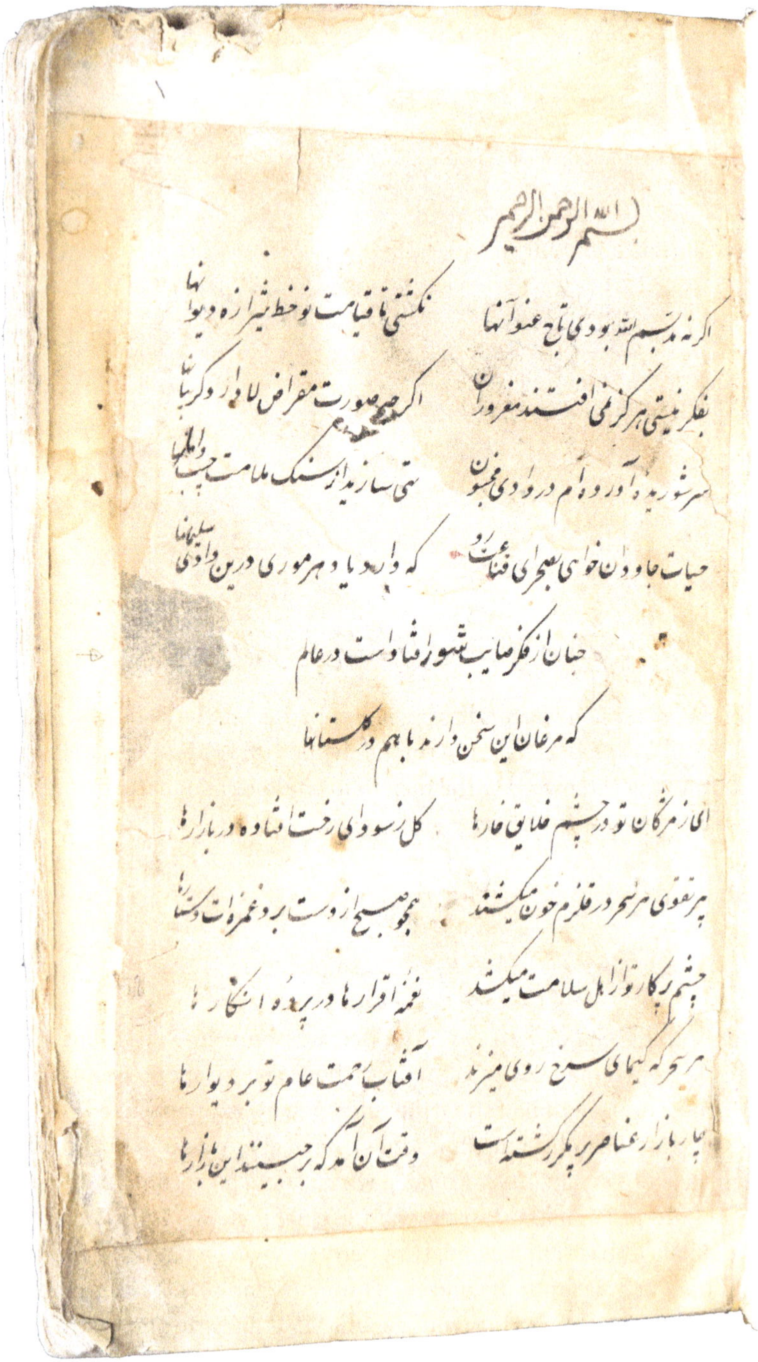

FIGURE 24 No. 13 (P5). Ṣā'ib Tabrīzī, d. 1087/1676. *Dīvān*. f. 1ª. Copied 1092/1681

Persian *nastaʿlīq*, with some omission of the diacritics which distinguish similar letters; ff. 1^{b}–173^{a}; 19×11 (13×8) cm; 14 lines.

Paper: Faint watermark design on f. 2 (Crown?).

Ownership: (1) Oval seal (f. 10^{a} and partly on f. 8^{a}), 1.7×1.3 cm diameter inscribed in *nastaʿlīq "Yā ilāhī bi-ḥaqq u qadīm ki bi-bakhshī gunāh hamah Ibrāhīm 1170"*/ 1757; (2) Bought by E. Birnbaum in Istanbul, June 1981.

Binding: Tightly rebound ca. 20th century in a refurbished 18/19th century leather binding with blind-stamped *zanjīrak* frame around front and back covers. Doublures of Turkish *abrī/ebru*, probably 19th century.

Other features: The verso of the last folio (f. 173^{b}), originally blank, is now covered with Persian verses written diagonally in a small clear 18th century hand.

Other MSS and references: The length, contents and sequence of poems in both MSS and printed editions vary widely. There is a valuable survey of many MSS and printed editions in the edition of the *Dīvān* by Muḥammad Qahramān, 6 volumes, Tehran, 1985–1991; see also printed *Kulliyāt-i Ṣāʾib-i Tabrīzī*, [ed.] Amīrī Fīrūzkūhī, [2nd ed.], Tehran 1336/1957; Manuscripts: Ahmed Ateş, *İstanbul Kütüphanelerinde Farsça manzum eserler, I.* (Istanbul, 1968), pp. 513–522 (14 MSS), plus references to other MSS, including to a facsimile edition of an autograph MS by Ṣāʾib, published in the series *İntishārāt-i Anjuman-i Āṣār-i Millī*, no. 52, in Tehran 1345 AHS/1966, and to some of the better editions elsewhere. MSS of varied content are recorded, scattered in many volumes of the printed catalogues of Iranian libraries, particularly those of the Kitābkhāna-i Millī, Tehran, and Tehran University. Among the numerous other MSS elsewhere are those in the British Museum: Rieu's *Catalogue of Persian MSS*, vol. 2, pp. 693–695; Ethé, India Office nos 1607–1611; also catalogues of Vienna, Uppsala, St. Petersburg and Munich. Less known are MSS in Dushanbe, *Kat. Vostochnye rukopisei Akad. Nauk Tadzhikskoi SSR*, tom 3, nos 1019–1025; *İzmir Millî Kütüphanesi Yazma Eserleri Kataloğu*, 3096; Sarajevo, *Katalog rukopisa Orientalnog Instituta*, ed. S. Trako, L. Gazić (Sarajevo, 1997), no. 473, p. 230; See also the valuable articles Ṣaʾeb Tabrīzī in *Encyclopaedia Iranica*; Ṣāʾib and Sabk-i Hindī in *Encyclopaedia of Islām*, 2nd ed., vol. 8, pp. 851–852; *Türk Diyanet Vakfi İslam Ansiklopedisi*, art. Sâib, cilt 10, pp. 75–77.

[14] **P14/II**

Niʿmat Khān, ʿĀlī (d. 1122/1710, f. 56)

نعمت خان، عالی

Munākaḥat-i Ḥusn u ʿIshq (f. 50[b])

مناكحة حسن و عشق

Also known as *Ḥusn u ʿIshq* (f. 50[b]) حسن و عشق

Begins (f. 50[b]):

حدیث عشق شد زیب [——] شمع افتاد آتش

Ends (f. 56[a]):

متوطن شهر کهنه اهالی صدر جهانی بمقام لکهنو در سنه ۱۲٤٦ هجری ششم محرم الحرام تحریر یافت ...

This allegorical love story in prose is an imitation of the famous *Ḥusn u Dil* of the Persian poet Fattāḥī (fl. ca. 852/1448). Our manuscript is copied by the same hand as the work which precedes it in this catalogue (No. 3, P14/I), Niʿmat Khān's *Vaqāʾiʿ* or *Rūznāmcha* (ff. 1[a]–49[b]). On f. 56[b] (the reverse of the last leaf) is a full-page biographical note headed "Niʿmat Khān ʿĀlī Mīrzā Muḥammad Saʿīd."

Indian *nastaʿlīq*; f. 50[b]–56[b]; same dimensions, lines and layout as No. 3, P14/I; copy completed 16 Muḥarram 1246/July 1830.

Paper and binding: Same as No. 3, P14/I; also badly wormed.

Ownership: Same as No. 17, P12.

Other MSS and references: Several MSS in India Office Library; lithographs, Cawnpore, 1259/1843, and others.

[15] T108

Faṣīḥ, Aḥmad d. 1111/1699, compiler

فصیح، احمد

[*Majmūʿa-i munshaʾāt-i Faṣīḥ va Nargīsī va Vaysī*]

[مجموعهٔ منشآت فصیح و نرگسی و ویسی]

Faṣīḥ, a Mavlavī *shaykh* in Istanbul, was famous as a composer of *inshāʾ* in Turkish, Persian and Arabic. This manuscript, entirely in Faṣīḥ's own hand, contains many elegant pieces in all three languages, composed by himself and others. He composed, selected and copied them over a period of nearly eight years, taking them from various sources: they bear his own copy dates between 1079/1668 (f. 1ᵃ) and 1087/1677 (f. 138ᵇ).

Faṣīḥ was a great admirer of Persian literature in particular, and composed both prose and poetry in that language. This MS includes, among his own *inshā* compositions, his *Munāẓarāt-i Gul u Mul* (ff. 133ᵇ–135ᵃ) in Persian; it combines religious, mystical and moral themes.

Persian Poetry: Scattered throughout the manuscript are Persian verses by a very large number of poets. I mention only a few here: f. 1ᵃ, Qāfzāda Fāʾiżī, Niẓāmī Ganjavī, Abū ʿAlī Sīnā [Ibn Sīnā], Abū Saʿīd b. Abī ʾl-Khayr; Jamāl al-Dīn Qazvīnī; Ghazālī; f. 10ᵇ–12ᵃ, Azraqī Afżal al-Dīn Haravī, Naṣīr-i Ṭūsī, Rafīʿ Qazvīnī, Ḥaydar Nasafī, ʿUmar Khayyām, Ḥusayn Bayātī, Maḥvī Ardabīlī, Malik Qummī, Murshid, Janūnī Qandahārī, Sulṭān Maḥmūd Mīrzā, Shifāʾī, ʿUrfī Shīrāzī, Luṭfī Shīrāzī, Ṭālib Āmūlī, Ghazālī Mashhadī, Rukn al-Dīn Masʿūd, Mīr Ḥusayn, Amīr Aḥmad, Qudsī, Fayżī Bayburdī, Ḥusayn Mutakallim, Āhī Sabzavārī, Ibn Ghiyās, Żāmirī, Ṭālib Ummī.

Large numbers of verses by many different poets are found especially on ff. 44ᵃ–73ᵇ, 76ᵇ–92ᵃ. Sometimes Faṣīḥ transcribed portions of classic *masnavīs*, e.g. f. 66ᵃ: *Intikhāb-i Haft Paykar-i Mollā Jāmī* …; ff. 66ᵇ–67ᵃ: *Intikhāb-i Mihr u Muḥabbat-i … Shifāʾī.*

Persian Prose: e.g. f. 63ᵇ: Two letters from Jāmī to the Ottoman Sulṭān Muḥammad II [Meḥmed Fātiḥ], the first thanking him for the gift of "500 *sikka-i ḥasana*", and the second a "confirmation of friendship"; f. 64ª: Text in rhymed prose by Ṣā'ib Tabrīzī in praise of تنباكو (tobacco).

Nasta'līq, varying from fine and clear to very fluid, and often lacking diacritical marks; written at different times with pens of varying width, but almost all in Faṣīḥ's distinctive hand; ff. 1ª–138ᵇ (last folio loose, now inserted between ff. 136 and 137); 28.5×17.5 cm; written surface irregular, and margins of varying width; number of lines varies; headings in red ink.

Paper: Several different watermark designs, difficult to decipher, because of the density of the writing on the pages.

Ownership: Several different seals of Faṣīḥ himself, some including the words "Aḥmad", "banda-i kamtar Faṣīḥ" and "Faṣīḥ Aḥmad"; bought by E. Birnbaum, Istanbul, 1987.

References: *Fasih Divanı*, [ed.] Mustafa Çıpan. Ankara, 2001.

C. Islam; Religion

[16] P9

[Qur'ān (fragment) with interlinear translation in Persian]

[قران]

Begins (f. 1[a]) [Sūra 9: 100–101]:

يُرَدّون الى عذاب عظيم وآخرون
بار [—] ند ايشان را بعذابى بزرك و ديكران

Ends (f. 2[b]) [Sūra 10: 2]:

ان اوحينا الى رجل منهم ان انذر الناس وبشر الذين
كى وحى كرديم بمردى از ايشان كه بيم كن مردمان را مردكان ده آنكس هارا

Fragment of an elegant quarto size manuscript of the Qur'ān in Arabic, with a word-by-word interlinear translation in medieval Persian in small script, angled downwards at 45 degrees.

This fragment is a single bifold sheet: ff. 1[a–b] contain Sūra 9: 101–110; and on ff. 2[a–b] Sūra 9: 124-Sūra 10: 2. Between the end of Sūra 9 and the beginning of Sūra 10, a conventional account in Arabic in small *naskh* script of the circumstances of revelation of Sūra 10, and a tally of the numbers of words and letters in it, and, finally, the reward awaiting those who recite it.

In addition to this bifold, I obtained photocopies of the two adjacent bifolds of the original manuscript, so that the Quranic text with this medieval Persian translation covering Sūra 9: 34–40; 64–69, 101–129 [end of Sūra 9] and Sūra 10: 1–2 is available for study here. These photocopies are kept with the manuscript. The margins of this illuminated MS contain letters and signs (mostly in gold ink) for *tajvīd*, pauses and subdivisions of various kinds. The recension of this translation remains to be identified.[1]

1 The Istanbul *ṣaḥḥāf* from whom I bought the present fragment was selling this disbound

© KONINKLIJKE BRILL NV, LEIDEN, 2019 | DOI:10.1163/9789004389670_020

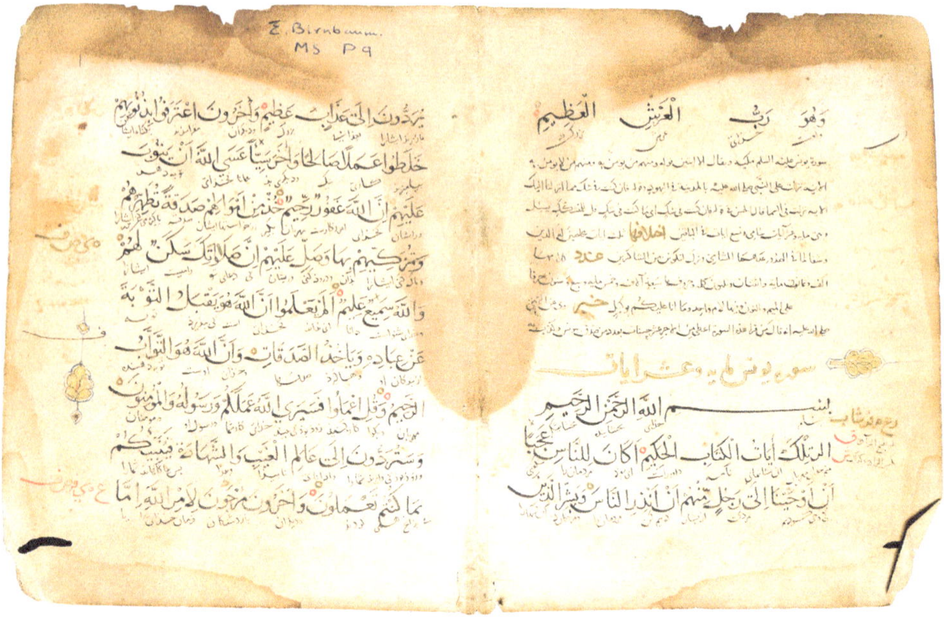

FIGURE 25 No. 16 (P9). Qur'ān with interlinear Persian translation, parts of Sūras 9 and 10. f. 1^a. Copied ca. 6–7/12–13th century

The MS is not dated, but paleographically would probably be 6th to 7th/12th to 13th century. The translation contains much fewer Arabic loanwords than later interlinear translations. In the Persian, the letter ذ (*ẕāl*) is widely used rather than د (*dāl*), e.g. خذای; دهذ; کویذ; etc.

Excellent old *naskh* for the Qur'ān text; small clear old naskh for interlinear translation; 19×15.5 (14×10.5) cm; 18 lines (9 Arabic, 9 interlinear Persian).

Paper: Buff colored "oriental"; not watermarked.

Decoration: Marginal decorations in gold and blue on all pages, and in a "wheel" on f. 1^b, bearing the "voluntary pause" sign قلی at its center. Title of Sūra 10 (*Yūnus*) outlined in blue ink and filled in gold (f. 2^b). Large water stain at top and inner margin does not affect legibility.

Qur'an with interlinear Persian translation piecemeal, bifold by bifold. When I tried (unsuccessfully) to persuade him not to break up the MS, he replied: "You speak as a professor, but I am a businessman, and I make much more money selling it page by page than as a single volume!"

Ownership: Bought by E. Birnbaum in Istanbul, July 1991.

References: E. Birnbaum, "Interlinear translation: the case of the Turkish dictionaries" in *Journal of Turkish Studies*, vol. 26/I = *Essays in honour of Barbara Flemming*, I. (2002), pp. 61–62, and 75 (illustration A). For some dated MSS (not Qur'āns) of similar period, see St. Petersburg, Akad. Nauk, C 652 (of 549/1154–1155 in *Arabskie rukopisi, Inst. Vostok. Akad. Nauk SSSR, Kratkie Katal.* II, 1986, p. 249); St. Petersburg [etc.], B 865 (dated 570/1164), D 345 (dated 595/1199); Paris, Bibl. Nat. Suppl. persan no. 1314 (of 635/1238); Strasbourg, Bibl. Nat. et Univ. 4256 (of 641/1245).

[17] P12

Ghazālī, Muḥammad b. Muḥammad, 450–505/1058–1111 (f. 103[b])

غزالی، محمد بن محمد

Kīmiyā-yi saʿādat (f. 1[b]; 104[a])

کیمیای سعادت

Begins (f. 1[b]):

فصل در توبه و فضیلت و ثواب و حقیقت آن

First ending (f. 103[b]):

ارحم عبدك من الخطر العظيم والمسلمين كلهم اجمعون [sic] واجعلنا مع الاحياء المرزوقين الذى [sic] انعمت عليهم من النبيين والصديقين والصالحين امين و [sic = يا] رب العالمين

Second ending (ff. 103[b]–104[a]):

فنقول في خاتمة الكتاب اللهم انّا نعوذ بعفوك من عقابك ... انت كما اثنيت على نفسك

تمت تمام كرد ... كاتب فقير ... سيد مير محى الدين قلندر ... شيخ محمد جعفر كورى در قصبه كوهانه در ايام ... مرزا محمد سعيد طال الله عمره ... در عهد پادشاه ... محمد اورنك زيب

غازی عالمکیر خلد الله ... ملکه ... بتاریخ سلخ شهر شوال ... سنه ۳۸ جلوس والا مطابق
هجری سنه ۱۱۰۵ ...

A summary in Persian by Ghazālī himself of his major Arabic work *Iḥyā ʿulūm al-dīn*. It tries to show how a Sufi can also base his life on observing the *sharīʿa*. The work is enlivened by illustrative anecdotes. *Kīmiyā-yi saʿādat* consists of four sections (*rukn*), of which the present MS contains only the fourth, consisting of *aṣl* 1–10: the first *aṣl* is on repentence and the tenth and the last on remembering one's mortality.

Indian *nastaʿlīq*; f. 1^b–104^a; 30×19 (23×12) cm; 21 lines.

Paper: Thin Indian paper, not watermarked; many wormholes in the margins, but the text is perfectly legible.

Copyist and copy date: Muḥammad Jaʿfar کروری in کوهانه in Shavvāl 1105/1694. The copyist's lamentable ignorance of even elementary Arabic is well displayed in the first colophon (f. 103^b), cited above.

Decoration: Pages double framed in red, within a blue outer frame. Headings in red ink.

Ownership: A Mr. Farooqi, a Pakistani pilot employed by Saudi-Arabian Airlines left this MS and No. 3, P14/I; No. 14, P14/II; and No. 18, P13 with Professor Glyn Meredith-Owens of the University of Toronto about 1972 for identification but never returned to retrieve it. On Meredith-Owens' retirement in 1989, he gave these MSS to E. Birnbaum.

Binding: Cardboard covered by marbled paper, with torn leather bookstrip, probably 19th century.

Other MSS and references: *Encyclopaedia Iranica*, art. Ġazālī, Abū Ḥāmed Muḥammad, II–III, vol. X, pp. 363–369.

D. Ethics

[18] P13

Naṣīr al-Dīn Ṭūsī, d. 673/1274

نصیر الدین طوسی

Akhlāq-i Nāṣirī (f. 2[a])

اخلاق ناصری

Begins (f. 1[b]):

حمد بیحد و مدح بیعد لایق حضرت عزت مالك الملکی باشد

End missing; last heading (f. 136[b]):

فصل هفتم در کیفیت معاشرت با اصناف خلق

Last words (f. 138[b]):

قومی باشند که به نصیحت همه کس تبرع نمایند ...//

Naṣīr al-Dīn Ṭūsī was a very prolific polymath, author of a host of important works on many different subjects, including philosophy, ethics, theology, politics, mathematics, astronomy, and astrology. The present work was largely inspired by a famous ethical work in Arabic, *Tahdhīb al-akhlāq* by Miskawayh (d. 421/1030). Ṭūsī titled his work in honor of his patron, Nāṣir al-Dīn ʿAbd al-Raḥīm (f. 2[b]), the Ismāʿīlī governor of Kūhistān.

Indian *nastaʿlīq*; f. 1–138; 25×14 (19×8) cm; 19 lines; marginal notes (mostly explanations of "difficult" terms in simpler words).

Paper: Thin Indian paper without watermarks.

Ownership: Same as No. 17, P12.

© KONINKLIJKE BRILL NV, LEIDEN, 2019 | DOI:10.1163/9789004389670_021

Binding: Rebound in paper-covered cardboard with cloth spine, mid-20th century.

[19] P11

[*Akhlāqnāma*] (title supplied)

اخلاقنامه

Beginning lost; now begins (f. 1[a]):

ده اورا زده بیرون کردند و در صحرا بند آختند و در کور و نکردند از گناهکاری

Ends (f. 59[a]):

من بعدی ابی بکر و عمر و عثمان و دوستی اینها ایمان و دشمنی اشان کفرت نقلت در عنوان دین

An unidentified old compendium of moral and religious advice (*akhlāq*) divided into rather short unnumbered chapters, many headed *bāb* alone, sometimes followed by a statement of subject. Within the *bāb* are illustrative examples (often subheaded *ḥikāyat, rivāyat,* or *faṣl*) attributed to various authorities, many of them Sufis, followed by the words *guft* or *gūyad*. The most frequent of these is "*Khvāja Faqīh Zāhid guft/gūyad, raḥmat Allāh ʿalayhi.*" He is probably Shaykh Zāhid Gīlānī (ca. 615–700/1218–1301) who was the spiritual guide (*murshid*) and later father-in-law of Shaykh Ṣafī al-Dīn al-Ardabīlī (650–735/1252–1334), the founder of the Zāhidīya, later the Ṣafavīya Sufi order [cf. *EI*[2], vol. 8, art. Ṣafī al-Dīn al-Ardabīlī].

Unfortunately, the beginning of the MS is lacking. The first section extant starts in the middle of a section on repentence (*tavba*, f. 1[a]). Many sections are headed *bāb*, but without a statement of contents. Those that do have a contents heading after the word *bāb* are listed below, in the hope of facilitating the identification of this work.

Bāb f. 4[a], *gursnagī va fażl dāshtan*; f. 7[b], *namāz*; f. 12[a], *nigāh dāshtan-i zabān az ghaybat*; f. 17[b], *tars az khudāy*; f. 21[b], *ummīd*; f. 25[b], *al-yaqīn*; f. 28[a], *tavakkul*; f. 31[a], *shinākhtan-i dunyā*; f. 34[b], *shinākhtan va mukhallafāt-i ān*; f. 39[a], *ʿajab dar*

FIGURE 26 No. 19 (P11). [*Akhlāqnāma*]. An unidentified old compendium of moral and religious advice. f. 30ᵇ–31ᵃ. Copied ca. 8–9/14–15th century

ṭāʿat; f. 42ᵃ, *shinākhtan-i dīv va ʿadāvat-i ū*; f. 45ᵇ, *pandkārī bī-qażā*; f. 49ᵃ, *naṣīḥat va nikūhāsh-i ḥasad*; f. 51ᵃ, *tavāżuʿ va nikūhāsh va ḥasad*; f. 53ᵇ, *ḥilm va farū khurdan-i chashm*.

Stories and quotations are attributed to many authorities, mainly scholars, sufis, etc., some of them several times: Ḥasan Baṣrī; Yaḥyā b. Maʿād; Suhaylī b. ʿAbdullāh; Ibrāhīm b. Adham; Suhayl b. Tushtarī; Kaʿb [b.] Aḥbār; Anṭākī; Azhar b. Mughīṣ; Aḥmad b. Ḥarb; Sufyān b. ʿAbdullāh; Vahb b. Munabbih; Sulaymān Dārānī; "Sharḥ-i Abī Bakr Varrāq"; ʿUmar b. ʿAbd al-ʿAzīz; Zayd b. Aslam; Bū ʿAlī Rūdbārī; Fatḥ Mavṣilī; Yaḥyā b. Abī Bakr; Khātim; Sahl b. ʿAbdullāh; ʿAbdullāh b. Mubārak; Bāyazīd; "Sufyān-i Ṣavrī dar *Tafsīr* guft"; ʿAbdullāh b. Masʿūd; Talḥa b. ʿAbdullāh; Zubayr b. ʿAvvām; Saʿd b. Abī Vaqqās; Saʿd b. Zayd; ʿAbd al-Raḥmān b. ʿAvn; Abū ʿUbayda b. al-Jarrāḥ; ʿAbdullāh b. Masʿūd; "va dar *Tafsīr-i Tāj al-Qurrā* …" (f. 59ᵃ).

From complimentary references to the four caliphs Abī Bakr, ʿUmar, ʿUṣmān, and ʿAlī (f. 57ᵃ–59ᵃ), it is clear that this is not a Shiʿa work.

Other features:

Orthography: Many archaisms:

- ج usually represents *chīm* in Persian words: جُهارم *chuhāram*; جنانکه *chu-nānki*; انج and انجه *anchi*; جنین *chunīn*; جون *chūn* (occasionally also چون).
- پ triple dotted below or one dot at the left and a small vertical line on the right under بـ /p/; rarely represented as بـ with only one dot below and no vertical line to the right.
- ش *shīn*. Unlike most MSS, this copyist usually writes ∵ i.e. 2 dots above and one dot below for *shīn*, or one dot at the left, and either two linked dots or a small line at the right.
- پس *sīn* sometimes has three dots underneath, an old fashioned device, to distinguish it from *shīn*, which has three dots above.

On ff. 59ᵇ–61ᵇ (originally blank), the following old inscriptions are written in various hands:

1. f. 59ᵇ: *"Dar taḥayyāt: shash chīz farīżah ast"*. (List of 6 requirements for praise of God).
2. f. 59ᵇ: List of 16 groups of people who will be consigned to hell (*dūzakh*) on the Day of Resurrection.
3. f. 60ᵃ–61ᵃ: Instructions for dyeing paper (*kāghazrā rang*) in various colors.
4. f. 61ᵃ: A poem in Āẕarī (?) Turkish, consisting of eight couplets:
   Begins:
   ینه سویله که ایمان ارکك میدرسن * دیشی میدر دیکل اشدیم من
   Ends:
   دیکل اولادی طاعت اولدی خیرات * بو دریادا ایلدوك ای اهل خیرات
5. f. 61ᵇ: Heading in Arabic: *Bāb Aḥkām al-ʿuqūd al-nikāḥ* [sic] followed by a one page discussion in Persian on the subject.

Mostly old *naskh*, sometimes with affinities to early *nastaʿlīq*. The MS is not dated, but seems paleographically about 8–9th/14–15th century, or possibly earlier; ff. 1–59 (one or more folios lost between 48/49 and 55/56); ff. 59–61, originally blank, now include items noted under the heading "Other features" (above); 18 × 13 (12.5 × 9) cm; 13 lines.

Paper: Several different buff colored "oriental" papers, none of them water-marked.

Ownership: Bought by E. Birnbaum, Istanbul, August 1991.

Binding: Disbound, but roughly resewn much later.

E. Language, Lexicography, and Prosody

[20] P7/I

Farāhī, Abū Naṣr [**Masʿūd b. Abī Bakr**], d. 640/1242–1243

ابو نصر فراهی

Niṣāb-i ṣibyān (f. 1b)

نصاب صبیان

Begins (f. 1b):

الحمد لله رب العالمین ... چنین کوید ابو نصر فراهی حُسِدَ حَافِدُه و حُفِدَ حاسده ما حرّکت الشِمال

Ends (f. 24a):

مهلاً آهسته باش و واها خوش * قلّما اَنْدَکَاوُیَخ نِیکَا تمت هذه المنظومه بعون الله الملك الوهاب

An Arabic-Persian glossary in about 200 verses, prepared to teach Arabic to Persian speaking boys (the *ṣibyān* of the title). Its 40 sections (*qiṭʿa*) are composed in nine different poetic meters, with the aim of imparting both Arabic vocabulary and the classic meters at the same time. This was achieved by making the students learn to recite the whole text by heart.

This work remained a standard textbook until the early 20th century. Little is known about the author, a scholar from Farāh in Sistān. The work begins with a brief introduction in Persian. Throughout the manuscript a large number of marginal and interlinear glosses have been added by several generations of readers, explaining in simpler Persian or in Turkish the meaning of some of the words of the original text (sometimes using Turkish *taʿlīq* script for the explanation rather than *naskh*). Many of the additions are citations from standard dictionaries, which are cited as "*sharḥ*"; "*Mirqāt al-lughāt*"; "*Akhtarī*"; "*Firishta*"; "*al-Vānī*", etc.

© KONINKLIJKE BRILL NV, LEIDEN, 2019 | DOI:10.1163/9789004389670_022

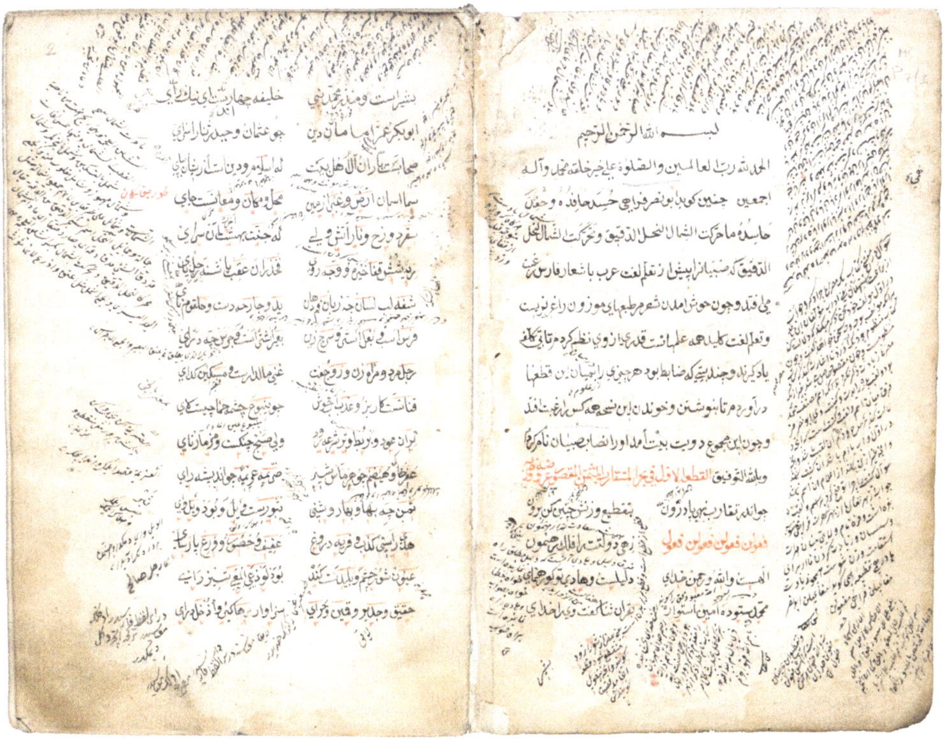

FIGURE 27 No. 20 (P7/I). Farāhī, d. 640/1242–1243. *Niṣāb al-ṣibyān*. f. 1ᵇ–2ᵃ. Copied ca. 10/16th century

Immediately following *Niṣāb al-ṣibyān*, on the verso of its last page and in the same copyist's hand, is a somewhat similar text book, *ʿUqūd al-jawāhir*, composed some two centuries later by Aḥmad-i Dāʿī (see below MS No. 21/P7/II).

Naskh; f. 1–24ᵃ (in a volume of 60 fol.); the whole original text (both Arabic and Persian) is fully vocalized (but not the marginal and interlinear additions); 20×13.5 (14×8) cm; 15 lines.

Paper: Watermarked with Anchor suspended from a Ring, within a Circle; on some folios the Circle is topped by a stylized "Clover Leaf" in the shape of 4 diamonds. This watermark was used in 16th century papers.

Ownership: (1) (f. 1ᵃ; f. 13ᵃ) Muḥammad ʿAlī b. Riżā Efendi الارکری al-Argari (?); (2) (f. 24ᵃ) an anonymous late 19th century note in Ottoman Turkish about a lithograph edition printed at the *Taqvīm al-vaqāʾiʿ* lithograph press [Istanbul] in 1269/[1852] of Shākir Efendi's book *Qavāʿid-i Fārsīya*; (3) an anonymous early

20th century owner who correctly identified the two works bound together in this volume; (4) bought by E. Birnbaum in Istanbul, June 1981.

Binding: Brown leather backstrip and edges on paperboard front and back covers; old *ṭaraqli abrī/ebru* paper pasted on front cover, and yellow paper on the back, on which is written in Ottoman Turkish "*mütenevvi' Farsī luġat. Ḳīmet* 200 *ḳurūş*", in a 19th century hand.

Other MSS and references: Storey *PL*, vol. III, pt. 1, A: Lexicography, no. 123, pp. 88–90, citing many MSS all over the world. Other MSS include İzmir ... ktp. 3/18; Sarajevo-P (ed. Trako) no. 86; Leningrad, Akad. Nauk SSSR, Inst. Vostokov, Persidsk., vyp. 5 (ed. Baevskii) nos 61–76; see also *Encyclopaedia Iranica*, art. Farāhī, Abū Naṣr. For commentaries on *Niṣāb-i ṣibyān*, see also Storey, op. cit., p. 89 ff. and printed editions.

[21] P7/II

Aḥmad-i Dā'ī (f. 25[b]), d. after 824/1421

احمد داعی

'Uqūd al-jawāhir (f. 25[b]; 26[a])

عقود الجواهر

Begins (f. 25[b]):

الحمد لله مبدع البدايع و منشئ الصنايع ... و بعد چنين کويد مؤلف ساعی احمدِ داعی اصلح الله شانه ... مختصری که موسوم است

Ends (f. 51[b]) [last fifth of the MS lost]:

القطعة التاسعة و الثلثون فی بحر المضارع الاخرب
مقضي گُزارْده چو مُؤدِّی ادا شده * مَبروز چون نجيز چه حاجت روا شده //

An Arabic-Persian glossary and manual of poetical meters, entirely in Persian verse. It has a Persian prose introduction (f. 25[b]–26[a]). The author says that it consists of 650 verses (*bayt*), arranged in 51 sections (*qiṭʿa*), each section composed in one of the classical poetic meters. He describes his work as an abridged metrical adaptation of the Arabic-Persian glossary in verse *Ḥamd u s̱anā*, attributed to Rashīd al-Dīn Vaṭvāṭ (d. 571/1182–1183). The title *Ḥamd u s̱anā* comes from the first words of the introduction (*dībāja*). It was a tradition to use the opening words of a dictionary as a substitute title, often even when the work had a formal title.[1] Aḥmad-i Dāʿī notes that there was a manuscript of *Ḥamd u s̱anā* in the library of the Ottoman prince Murād: "*Khizāna-i maʿmūra-i sulṭānzāda ... Murād Chalabī*" (f. 26^{a}).

Aḥmad-i Dāʿī was a learned Turkish scholar who wrote in both Turkish and Persian, including adaptations and translations from Arabic and Persian. As prince Murād's tutor, he dedicated his *ʿUqūd al-jawāhir* to his royal student. The date of composition is not stated, but it must have been before the prince's accession as Sultan Murad II in 824/1421, as the dedication addressed him as "prince" Murād. The work aimed to teach the traditional system of Arabic and Persian prosody at the same time as selected vocabulary of those two languages. The student was expected to learn the text by heart. (This traditional educational technique long predated Aḥmad-i Dāʿī's work and continued until at least the beginning of the 20th century, as proved by the range of copy dates of many MSS and printed editions).

Of this MS's original 51 sections, the leaves containing the last 12 sections (40–51) as well as most of section 39 have fallen out and are lost. This copy was diligently used by generations of students. The marginal and interlinear notes in many different hands, some in *naskh* and other in various form of Turkish *taʿlīq*, and the many translations of the Persian and Arabic words into Ottoman Turkish, attest to the variety and number of students who used this MS. Some of these notes include citations from standard Arabic dictionaries, such as the *Ṣiḥāḥ*.

Naskh, fully vocalized in both Arabic and Persian, copied in the same hand as Farāhī's *Niṣāb-i ṣibyān* (No. 20/P7/I), a shorter work of similar character, which precedes it in this volume; headings, meter statements and scansion signs in red ink; f. 25^{b}–51^{b}; 20 × 13.5 (14 × 8) cm; 15 lines.

1 See E. Birnbaum, 'Interlinear translations: the case of the Turkish dictionaries' in *Essays in honour of Barbara Flemming, I = Journal of Turkish Studies*, I (2002), p. 66, note 9.

Paper: Watermarked: Anchor, in a form typical in the 16th century. (For details, see No. 20/P7/I).

Ownership: Bought by E. Birnbaum, Istanbul, June 1981.

Other MSS and references: Storey *PL* vol. III, pt. 1, pp. 85–87 listing MSS in Calcutta (Ivanow), British Library, Cambridge (Browne), Oxford (Bodleian), India Office (now part of British Library), Bombay (Rehatsek), Mashhad, Uppsala, etc. Also see the important study in Turkish by İsmail Hikmet Ertaylan, *Ahmed-i Dâ'î, hayatı ve eserleri*, Istanbul, 1952, pp. 108–116, including an 8-page facsimile of part of a MS dated 957/1550, with many Turkish interlinear glosses [probably the MS which once belonged to Raif Yelkenci]. Gönül Alpay [Tekin]'s edition of Ahmed-i Dāʿī's *Çengnāme* (Harvard University, 1992) includes an informative section on *ʿUqūd al-javāhir*, and notes three MSS in the Süleymaniye library: Bağdatlı Vehbī 1949; H. Hüsnü Paşa 1102/3; and Murad Buharī 321/6. DİA, art. Ahmed-i Dâî, vol. 2, p. 56 mentions that there are 4 MSS in the Süleymaniye, of which one (Muğla 624) has interlinear Turkish glosses.

See also *Encyclopaedia Iranica*, art. Dāʿī; *Aḥvāl va āṣār va taḥlīl-i ashʿār-i Dīvān-i Fārsī-i Aḥmad Dāʿī*, [ed.] F. Tolga Ocak.

A later addition to this MS: A quire (f. 52–59) on much younger paper (f. 52; watermarked IMC) has been sewn into the end of this MS. It consists of two parts, each in a different hand: (1) In late Ottoman *ruqʿa* script, penciled notes in Turkish headed *"Iʿtiqādīyāt"*, on the Sunnī *maẕhab*s, taken from the book *Ṭarīq-i hudā* (f. 52^a); and (f. 52^b) a reference to an article by Ahmed Ağaoğlu in the newspaper *Cumhuriyet*, criticizing as despotism (*istibdād*) the firing of naval canons as a salute to the President of the [Turkish] Republic; (2) Notes (in red ink) in Arabic, on Persian history and culture (f. 53^b–59^b), beginning قال سيد على زاده فى شرح كلستان الذى الّفه بلسان العرب

[22] **T16**

Ḥalīmī, Luṭfullāh b. Abī Yūsuf (d. 896?/1490?)

حليمى، لطف الله بن ابى يوسف

Lughat-i Ḥalīmī

لغت حلیمی

Originally titled: ***Baḥr al-gharāʾib*** بحر الغرائب

Later revised as ***Qāsimīye*** قاسمیه

[First 2 leaves (3 pages) of original lost. First words now are the end of a Persian verse citation explaining the definition of the (missing) Persian word: ابدندان]

Daftar 1 begins (f. 1[a]):

در دهان حاسدان * لیك همچون علك دومی بوی خوش اید زمن * اب روغن اشوك ازرینه کلن

[Corresponding to No. 24/T119 f. 3 line 4, and No. 23/T107 f. 4 line 5].

Daftar 1 ends (f. 144[b]) with last head word:

یهیدن یِقْمق و بوزمق لطیفی اکرچه خانهٔ عمرم یهیده کرد بجور * اساس عمری وی اندر امان حق بادا

Copyist's colophon to *Daftar* 1 (f. 144[b]), headed: "*li-kātibih Murīdī*", is in the form of 3 Turkish couplets, including the date of the copy, 960/1553:

طقوز یوز التمشه ارمشدی تاریخ * کتابت اولیجق اشبو کتابت
مریدینك مرادی بو ایدی کم * ایدیجك انی بر عارف تلاوت
دعادن یاد ایده روح روانن * بولا تا کلشن رَوْح ایچره راحت

Daftar 2 begins (f. 145[b]):

بسم الله الرحمن الرحیم و بلطف الله العلیم الحکیم دفتر دوم عبارات غیر ظاهره و قواعد معتبره از اول کتاب تا اخر و الله المعین الناصر باسمك اللهم بشلرم سنك آدوکله اي بزم مولامز فتاح القلوب ای کوکللر اچجی تکری

Daftar 2 ends (f. 178[b]):

قصور قصرك جمعيدر يعنى كوشك لره درلر والله اعلم بالصواب واليه المرجع والماب

Daftar 2, which is in the same hand as *Daftar* 1, does not name the copyist, but gives the date of completion in 960 (corresponding to June 13, 1553):

فى غرة رجب المرجّب ... فى يوم الاثنين من شهور سنه ستين و تسعمايه ...

Since all educated Ottomans were expected to be well acquainted with Persian and Arabic, which would also allow them to enrich their Turkish literary style with loanwords from those classical languages of Islam, bilingual dictionaries were prepared to assist them. *Lughat-i Ḥalīmī* is such a work. It consists of two *daftar*s. The first is a Persian-Turkish dictionary in standard *alif* to *yā* alphabetical order. Ḥalīmī follows each Persian word with its translation into Turkish and often adds an illustrative verse in Persian showing its use by a classical Persian poet such as Kamāl Iṣfahānī, Shams-i Fakhrī, Bahrāmī, Farrūkhī, Rūdakī, ʿUnṣurī, Firdavsī, to mention just some of those cited in the first few pages of the present MS. It has a wholly Persian introduction to *daftar* 1 (f. 2[b]). Ḥalīmī notes that he had previously composed a book in verse on the subject, titled *Baḥr ul-gharāʾib*, but readers found it difficult and he therefore composed the present work as a kind of explanatory commentary (*sharḥ*).

Ḥalīmī was a learned Ottoman *qāḍī* and a specialist in Persian, who found favor and patronage with Maḥmūd Pasha, the powerful Grand Vezir of the Ottoman Sultan Muḥammad II ("the Conqueror").

Fairly soon after this work was composed, many manuscripts of the dictionary portion only (i.e. *daftar* 1) began to be copied, mostly titled *Lughat-i Ḥalīmī*, if not at the head of the text, then on a flyleaf, or at the bottom or the fore-edge of the MS, as in the two other MSS in the Birnbaum collection (23, T107 and 24, T119). *Daftar* 2, which is less than one fifth the length of *daftar* 1, is devoted to "expressions that are not obvious and valuable rules" (f. 145[b]). As most extant MSS do not include *daftar* 2, it is little known, and therefore some details of its contents are given here. Ḥalīmī notes that it contains 8 sections (*bāb*), corresponding to the number, and in honor, of the first eight Ottoman sultans from ʿOs̱mān to his own contemporary, the reigning Bāyazīd II, referring to them as "*sekiz ata … yaʿnī Bāyezīd* [II] *b. Meḥemmed* [II] *b. Murād* [II] *b. Meḥemmed* [I] *b. Bāyezīd* [I] *b. Murād* [I] *b. Ōrḫān b. ʿOs̱mān b. Erṭuġrūl*" (f. 146[a]) and corresponding also to the eight gates of Paradise (*Jannat*). He mentions a considerable number of works in Persian and Arabic, and their authors (ff. 146[b]–147[a]), including 'Abd al-Ḥamīd Sīvāsī's *Lahjat al-'Ajam*, Shams-i Fakhrī's *Mi'yār-i javāhir*, *tafsīr Miftāḥ al-adab*, and the *tafsīr* of Ḥakīm Qaṭrūn Urmavī, *Ṣiḥāḥ al-Furs* by Hindūşāh Nakhjavānī, *Muntakhab al-Furs* by Abū al-Fatḥ Bundār b. Abī Naṣr Khāṭırī, the *Shavāhid* of Asad Ṭūsī, *Miftāḥ ul-adab* by Muṭahhir Lādīqī, and works by "Jārullāh" [i.e., Zamakhsharī], Sāmī and Maydānī.

Among other subjects, Ḥalīmī devotes some pages to the literary device: *laff u nashr* (ff. 146–147[a]); metres (ff. 147[a]–149[b]); the Byzantine (solar) calendar from *Tishrīn-i avval* to *Aylūl* (f. 150[a]); the Persian Jalālī solar calendar (ff. 150[a–b]); the names of each of the Persian months (f. 151[a]); and the names of the 7 planets in Arabic, Persian and Turkish: he notes that he has put these into a rhymed form for easy memorization "in my book *Qāsimīye*" (f. 151[a–b]); the orbit of the sun as it progresses through the months, from Āẕār to Shubāṭ (f. 152[a]); a listing of the *Ayyām-i maḥẕūr-i Mūsā*, days which are not propitious for beginning tasks or travel, month by month from Āẕār to Shubāṭ (ff. 152[b]–153[a]); rules for setting the *ghurra* (first day) of the month (f. 153[a]); on the art of *tajnīs* (puns/wordplay), describing seven different kinds (ff. 153[b]–155[a]); on *tashbīh* (similes, ff. 155[a–b]); on *majāz* (metaphor) and *tasmīya* ("naming", ff. 155[b]–156[b]). Most of the remainder of the *daftar* deals with the art of *ta'miya/mu'ammā* (riddles) with many examples of riddles on personal names, including some sultans and notables, such as (among others) Luṭfullāh, Sulaymān, the reigning Sultan Bāyazīd (three times), Muḥammad Khān, 'Alī Beg, Shāh Valī, Sāmī, Uruj Beg, Qayā, Salmān Tājī Beg, Ḥajji Ibrāhīm, Muḥammad Pasha, Sulṭān Muḥammad, Mavlānā Sayyidī Aḥmad, Sulṭān Muṣṭafā, Mavlānā Sayyidī Ḥusayn, Kayqubād, Pīr Aḥmad Beg, Shaykh 'Alī, Yūsufī, (f. 156[b]–166[b]); also numbers and letters (f. 166[b]–170[b]); "Beginning of Part 2" on various poetic metres and miscellaneous observations (f. 171[a]–178[b]). (Ḥalīmī later returned to the subjects of *daftar* 2 in two treatises in Turkish, *Risāla fī Bayān ḳavā'id al-mu'ammā*, on Persian riddles, and *Risāla fī Tajnīsāt va al-tashbīhāt va al-majāzāt* on similes, metaphors, etc.).

This MS is one of the minority which contain *daftar* 2. Why do most MSS (including **23**, **T107** and **24**, **T119** in the Birnbaum collection) omit that *daftar*? Perhaps the answer is to be found in the nature of the Ottoman book trade. The market for dictionaries was largely generated by *madrasa* students who, by definition, were usually rather poor. They might well find a dictionary an important resource for their studies, but would generally regard the variety of interesting information in defter 2 as an inessential "frill", which most of them could not afford to pay for. The copyists would obviously produce MS copies in accord with the demands of their student clientele.

Niʿmatullāh b. Aḥmad (d. 969), the author of *Lughat-i Niʿmatullāh* refers to Ḥalīmī's work as *Qāsimīye*, and it is cited as *Qāʾime* in the great bibliography *Kashf al-ẓunūn* by the great Turkish polymath Kātib Çelebi (d. 1067).

Clear professional *naskh*; Persian headwords, headings and verse citations in red ink and occasionally vocalized; *Daftar* 1 f. 1–144^{b}, *Daftar* 2 f. 145^{b}–178^{b}; 18.5×13.5 (15×19) cm; 19 lines.

Paper: Beige, with watermark: Anchor suspended on a ring within a Circle surmounted by a 6-armed Star, common in the 16th century; each page is framed in double rules, the outer one blue, the inner one red.

Ownership: (1) A 19th century owner has written a partly obliterated note in Turkish in the margin of the last page (f. 178^{b}), beginning *"Dördüncü Ordu-yı Hümāyūn dāʾirelerine ..."*; (2) an early 20th century reader has written in pencil on the inside of the front cover eight Persian words (seven beginning with *alif*) and their Turkish translations; (3) E. Birnbaum bought this MS in April 1973 from an Istanbul *saḥḥāf* who said it had come from the stock of the famous Istanbul *saḥḥāf* Rāʾif Yelkenci. It still bears his stock number label T83 on the spine.

Binding: The current flap binding, now loose, is a late 19th century rebind: it is cardboard covered with green cloth, with brown leather spine; inner side of flap is lined with *abrī/ebru* paper. The rebinder, apparently trying to hide the fact that the original first two folios of *daftar* 1 were lost, moved the whole of *daftar* 2 (34 leaves, which I have renumbered ff. 145–178) to the front of the MS, and also carelessly misplaced certain quires; some quires are still missing. I have restored most of the MS to its original sequence. At present the 2 folios originally preceding the present fol. 1 are missing; ff. 2–7 still in some disorder, and gaps still remain: e.g. between f. 14 and f. 15, which contained most of the entries between *bā* and *jīm* (corresponding to MS **24, T119**, f. 90^{b}–101^{a}).

Other MSS and references: Birnbaum collection MSS **23, T107** and **24, T119**; both have only *daftar* 1; THSS Tl. 5, no. 198 and other collections listed there; Storey *PL* vol. III, pt. 1, pp. 63–64. The following are among the few which contain *both daftars*: Leiden 1, Or. 663 (cop. 942/1535–1536); TDKK-YEK 436+447 (a single MS copied 909/1503); Köprülü vol. 1, p. 199 no. 1567 (cop. 957); Süleymaniye,

Esad 3281; DK 3797; 3799; Blochet II, 1007 (cop. 911); Fluegel I, 122; 123; Oxford Ethé 1688; 1689; (and perhaps Aumer 302; Browne, Cambridge, Supp. 282; 1106); Sadberk Hanım Yaz. Kat. 141.

The following MSS seem to contain *daftar* 1 only (inadequate cataloguing may have failed to indicate that some of them may also contain *daftar* 2): Flügel I, no. 124 (cop. 1509); TDKK-YEK 437 (cop. 917); 438 (cop. 938); 439 (cop. 944); 440–442; TKS-T 2039 (cop. 882); 2040; 2041; 2042 (cop. 922); 2043–2044; THSS Tl. 5, no. 198; Köprülü II, p. 563 nos. 316; 317; TUYATOK Süleymaniye, Esad 3281; Yeni Bağışlar 4286 (cop. 949); Nafız Paşa 1448/I; 34/I; Süleymaniye A.N. Tarlan, 142; Leiden 1, no. 181 (cop. 942); 664; 823; DK 3796; 3798; 3800–3804; İzmir 3822; Budapest no. 745; Burnt Books (Oriental Institute Sarajevo) 158; Mevlana Müz. Yaz. Kat. III, p. 432 (incomplete); 140; BM-T (Rieu) p. 137; Escurial 609; Dorn 496 (cop. 930); Uppsala, p. 17 nos. 23 (cop. 933); 24; 25; Kraft 21; Maʿarif I, 168; Majles (Tehran) II, 86; Sarajevo, Oriental Institute, *Katalog perzijskih rukopisa*, [comp.] Salih Trako, nos 101–106; Yusuf Öz, "Anadolu sahasında yazılmış Farsça-Türkçe sözlükler", in *Türk Dili Araştırmaları Yıllığı Belleten*, 1999/I–III, s. 177–187.

For a useful biography of Ḥalīmī and details of eleven of his works on variety of subjects, see DİA, art. Halîmî, Lutfullah, cilt 15, pp. 341–343.

[23] T107

Ḥalīmī, Luṭfullāh b. Abī Yūsuf d. 896?/1490? (f. 2ᵇ)

حلیمی، لطف الله بن ابی یوسف

Lughat-i Ḥalīmī (f. 2ª in an owner's hand)

لغت حلیمی

Begins (f. 2ᵇ):

حمد بلیغ و ثناء بی دریغ خدایرا جل جلاله و عمّ نواله که شرح کننده صدوراست ... و بعد
چنین می کوید ضعیف و شکسته بال ... لطف الله بن [sic] یوسف الحلیمی

Ends (f. 190[a]):

یهیدن یقمق و بوزمق لطیفی اگرچه خانه عمرم یهیده کرده بجور * اساس عمروی اندر امان حق بادا

An early copy of *daftar* 1 of this standard Persian-Turkish dictionary, which was widely used in the Ottoman Empire from the 15th through the 19th century. For the descriptions of two other copies in the Birnbaum collection, see above, No. 22, T16, which contains *daftar* 1 and 2, and No. 24, T119 which like the present MS contains only *daftar* 1. Both the one-*daftar* and the two-*daftar* versions circulated simultaneously from at least the 16th century.

At least two professional copyists co-operated to produce this MS: ff. 1–86[b] in good small *naskh*; another copyist continued in mid-quire from f. 87[a] to 190[a] (the end of the MS), in a larger *naskh*; 21×13 (14 ×. 7.5) cm; 21 lines; lemmata and headings in red ink, which is also used to frame all pages; Persian words occasionally vocalized, but Turkish only rarely.

Paper: Several different papers used, all with rather early watermark designs: (1) from the beginning to about f. 58, the letter H but with two horizontal bars in the middle, within a Circle which is surmounted by a 6-armed Star; (2) from f. 75 onwards an Oxhead with a Staff between the horns, topped by a 5-leafed clover; (3) from f. 86 to the end of the MS, an Oxhead with a Staff between the horns, topped by a triangular Trefoil. This MS is undated but these designs were common in the earlier 16th century (cf. MS **24, T119** copied in 934/1527); (4) Countermark letters P and A flanking a vertical line.

Ownership: [1] (f. 2[a]) inscription deliberately defaced by a later owner and mostly illegible, but one can still decipher "Muḥammad b. ʿAlī (?) *al-shahīr bi*-Surūrī", together with an illegible oval seal, diameter 1.2×1.1 cm; [2] (f. 1[a]) inscription "Ḥammāmji ʿAlī Chalabi—?—? *al-shahīr* el-Marmūr? (or *mazbūr*?)", followed by an illegible oval seal, diameter 1.6×1.3 cm; [3] (f. 2[a]) "*Lughat-i Ḥalīmī az Furs* ... Ḥāj Ḥāfiẓ Muḥammad al-Āsumānī"; [4] Bought by E. Birnbaum in Istanbul, August 1991.

Notes in various hands: On f. 1[a]: the word for God in 9 languages, expressed in Arabic script; Arabic (*Allāh*); Persian (*Ḫudā*); Greek (ابنوش); Indian (کریاد); "Khvārizmī" (تمانداك); "Turkish" (بیاد); "Bulgarian" (*Tañri*); Syriac (ایده); 2 *bayt* in Turkish by Necātī and one by Aḥmed Paşa; on f. 1[b]: a *bayt* in Persian; a prayer in Arabic seeking Muḥammad's intercession with God (اشفع لنا عند الله یا رسول الله).

Binding: The front cover is made up of papers stuck together. The upper one on the inside, which acts as a doublure, is recycled from a page of a 13–14th century Arabic MS. The outside of this cover is bound in brown leather with an oval medallion adorned with a floral motif, framed in quadruple rules. It is in bad condition, marred by four wormholes; it may have been recycled from another MS. The back cover is missing and is replaced by a piece of 20th century cardboard, attached to the front cover by a crude paper backstrip. The sewing of the quires is loose when not totally detached.

Other MSS and references: See No. 22 (T16), above.

[24] T119

Ḥalīmī, Luṭfullāh b. Abī Yūsuf, d. 896?/1490? (f. 2^b^)

حلیمی، لطف الله بن ابی یوسف

Lughat-i Ḥalīmī (on bottom edge)

لغت حلیمی

Begins (f. 1^b^):

حمد بلیغ و ثنای دریغ خدایرا جل جلاله و عم نواله که شرح کنندۂ صدوراست ... و بعد
چنین میکوید ضعیف شکسته بال و نحیف برکشته حال المتوسل الی ما ینال باللطف الالهی
والعون العلیمی لطف الله بن ابی یوسف الحلیمی

Ends (f. 201^b^):

یهیدن یخمق و بوزمق. لطیفی اکرچه خانه عمرم یهیده کرد بجور اشاس [sic] عمروی حق بادا
تمت الکتاب ...

Another early copy of *daftar* 1 of this standard Persian-Turkish dictionary. For more details, see No. 22, T16 in this collection which contains both *daftar*s, and No. 23, T107. This copy was completed by Nūrullāh b. Uvays al-Ṣamṣūnī on Sunday at noon *avāsiṭ-i Rabīʿ I 934*/December 1527 (f. 201^b^).

Coarse scholars' Turkish *taʿlīq*, sometimes verging on *naskh*, the work of more than one copyist; headings in red ink, which is also used to overline the names of Persian poets whose verses are cited as examples of the usage of the head-words; ff. 1–203 (last two folios blank); 17.5×13 (13×9.5) cm; 9 lines.

Paper: Cream colored, but a minority dyed yellow (with no change of copyist); 2 groups of watermarks: (a) Oxhead with a Staff between the horns topped by a 5-leafed clover; (b) Anchor within Circle.

Ownership: [1] (f. 1[a]) "*al-sayyid* Saʿd al-Dīn ʿAbd al-Karīm *al-madʿū bi*-Mudarris-zāda"; [2] Bought by E. Birnbaum in Istanbul, August 1991.

Binding: Flap binding, worn brown leather backstrip and cover edges; yellow paper pasted onto cardboard covers; faded, except still bright on flap.

Other MSS and references: See **22, T16.**

[25] **T21/I**

Shāhidī, Ibrāhīm, d. 957/1550 (f. 18[a])

شاهدی، ابراهیم

Tuḥfa-i Shāhidī

تحفهٔ شاهدی

Begins (f. 1[b]):

بنام خالق وحی و توانا قدیم و قادر و بینا و دانا

The main text ends in Turkish (f. 18[a]):

شاهدیه هر کم ایدرسه دعا ایده محشرده شفاعتْ مصطفی

This rhymed Persian-Turkish vocabulary was designed to enrich Turcophone students' knowledge of literary Persian and by extension their understanding of literary Ottoman Turkish. It contains more than 1350 Persian equivalents to some 1200 Turkish words. Its enormous popularity as a text book may be gauged from the fact that between the time it was completed in 930 or 931/1524 or 1525 and the end of the 19th century hundreds of copies were made. MSS are found in most Ottoman Turkish manuscript libraries and in major collections of Oriental MSS in Europe. Immediately following the last *bayt* are the Persian words for numerals from 1 to 1000, and (ff. 18^{b}–19^{a}) a selection of Persian verbal forms with interlinear Turkish translations at an angle of 45 degrees. The first verbs are *dānis-*, *shinākh-*, *khvun-*, *navis-*, *farmā-*, translated by *bil-*, *añla-*, *oḳı-*, *buyur-*. We may see here the influence of one of the most popular Persian-Turkish dictionaries, widely used in *madrasa*s throughout the Ottoman Empire for centuries: *Tuḥfat al-hādiya* by Muḥammad Ḥāj Ilyās of Zile; its first entries are *dānistan/bilmek*; *shinākhtan/añlamak*. Most MSS of the *Tuḥfat al-hādiya* omit its *dībāja* and start with these two verbs, so the work is often called *Lughat-i Dānistan*. (See E. Birnbaum, "Interlinear translation: the case of the interlinear Turkish dictionaries", *JTS* 26/1 (2002), pp. 66–67). Shāhidī records in his introduction that his work is in imitation of the *Tuḥfa-i Ḥusāmī* (by Ḥusām b. Ḥasan Qonavī, which was composed in 802/1399).

Professional scribal *naskh*, fully vocalized (occasional confusion between Persian *iżāfat* and conjunction *vāv* with *żamma*); headings in red ink, and Persian words overlined in red; ff. 1^{b}–19^{a}; 20.5×14 (14.5×8.5) cm; 17 lines; paper watermarked: Crown above a bunch of Grapes.

The MS is undated, but ca. late 17th or early 18th century.

Decoration: Text arranged in two columns between red ink rules, each page also framed in red rules; on f. 1^{b} a space left for a *sarlavḥa* was filled in wrongly with the words *Dīvān-i Fużūlī* in purple indelible pencil (about the beginning of the 20th century).

This *Tuḥfa-i Shāhidī* is the first of 3 separate MSS later bound together. (The second MS is described in my catalogue, *Turkish and Çaġatay MSS in Canada*, No. No. 42, T21/II. There it is the Turkish *Dīvān* of Fużūlī, copied in 1131/1719; the third work in that collection is No. 156, T21/III, *Akhlāq-i Sulaymānī* in Turkish by Favrī).

Binding: Turkish brown leather with small diamond-shaped motif incised in the middle of both covers, themselves in blind-stamped *zanjīrak*, ca. 18th century; later backstrip of leather is an old repair.

Ownership: Bought by E. Birnbaum, Istanbul, June 1974.

Other MSS and references: The fullest listing of MSS (some 57 in European and 19 in Turkish libraries) is given on pp. 82–87 of A.C. Verburg, "The *Tuḥfe-i Şâhidî* ..." in *Archivum Ottomanicum*, vol. 17 (1999) which includes a photocopy of Leiden MS Or. 148, with a Latin script transcription based on that MS, with English translation and index of the words; 19 more MSS in libraries in the former Yugoslavia, the majority in Sarajevo (OIS) and Zagreb (OZJA). Those in the Archives of Bosnia and Herzegovina in Mostar are noted in Ždralović, II index p. 423; those in OIS, destroyed by fire in the 1992 civil war in Yugoslavia, are noted in "Burnt Books", no. 163 (OIS 3478, 3903, and 67 other MSS).

THSS Tl. 4 nos 480–483; Tl. 5 no. 199 (both THSS volumes include references to other MSS); Leiden vol. 1, Or. 148 (listing MSS elsewhere); Leiden vol. 2 nos. 1582, 1583, 5808, 6965, 6967, 8330; 11.117/II; 11.575/I; Leiden vol. 3, nos. 12.428, 25.760/III; Oxford, Kut 273–276, Ethé 2231; Kayseri, Raşid 594; Smitskamp 218 (listing several MSS); Brill, *Catalogue* no. 214 (Leiden 1981) no. 127/2; Khalidiya 69, 71; Köprülü vol. III nos. 678, 679; Sadberk Hanım Müz. HKYK 518–521; Kıbrıs İsl. Yaz. Kat. 55 (5 MSS); Yapı Kredi Sermet no. 176/2; Dublin, Chester Beatty, Supp. Handlist (by G. Meredith-Owens, typescript, no. 39, (cop. 1158)); Wien, Mixt. 1538, 1331, 748, 1245, 1782, 838 (Balić, Bd. 5, Nos. 2783–2786); Izmir Milli Ktp. Yazma Eserler Kat., no. 3827–3829.

See also: Storey *PL* III, pp. 66–67; Ahmet Hilmi İmāmoğlu, *Farsça-Türkçe manzum sözlükler ve Şâhidî'nin sözlüğü*. İnceleme, metin, doktora tezi, Atatürk Üniv. 1993; Adnan Kardić, "Originality in and outside the lexicographic tradition: a comparison of the dictionaries of Uskufī and İbrahīm Şâhidî" [in Bosnian], *Prilozi za Orijentalnu Filologija*, Sarajevo, vol. 52–53 (2002), pp. 73–90.

Note: The final leaf (f. 18ᵇ) contains: (1) a letter in Turkish headed *Ḥāmevī 'Ali Efendi'nüñ Yedekçi Meḥmed Aġa'ya irsāl eyledügi mektūbuñ ṣūreti*; and (2), (in a different hand) the Arabic text of several short *ḥadīs̱*.

[26] T57/I

Riyāżī, Muḥammad b. Muṣṭafā, d. 1054/1644 (f. 1ᵃ, 3ᵇ)

رياضى، محمد بن مصطفى

Dustūr al-ʿamal (f. 4[a])

دستور العمل

Begins (f. 4[a]):

سپاس فراوان اول متکلم بی زبانه ارزانی در که ایفای …

Ends (f. 46[b]):

کر آید که پیش تو کویم دروغ * دروغ اندر آرد سر من بیوغ

A vocabulary of Persian words and expressions explained in Turkish, with many illustrative citations of their use in verses by classical Persian poets. On fol. 4[a] alone, verses by the following are cited: Kamāl Iṣfahānī, Khusrav, Jāmī, Salmān, Anvarī, Khāqānī. Riyāżī is best known for his important Turkish biographical dictionary of Ottoman poets, *Riyāż üş-şuʿarā*. Many marginal notes give further examples, some with informative comments (e.g. *az nuskha-i Mīrzāda* [f. 33[b]]; Surūrī [f. 16[b]; 25[a]]). (This *Dustūr al-ʿamal* must not be confused with a work in Turkish of the same title by his contemporary Kātib Çelebi [d. 1067/1657] on reforms needed in the Ottoman Empire).

Small professional Turkish *taʿlīq*; f. 1–46 (f. 1–3 originally blank, now full of notes—see below); copyist's colophon (f. 46[b]) *"darvīsh ʿAbdullāh al-Mavlavī al-Adranavī/Adirnavī, dar sana hasht u ṣad u hazār"* [= 1108/1696–1697]; 20×14 (15×7) cm; 23 lines.

Paper watermarked: Shield?; countermark VC.

Decoration: First opening of main text (f. 3[b]–4[a]) is framed in gold rules; all other pages framed in red ink; which is also used for headings, and to overline the names of poets cited.

Ownership: (1) Muṣṭafā Bijūqjī [?]-zāda (f. 1[a]); (2) al-ḥājj Ḥāfıẓ Muṣṭafā al-Islāmbūlī (f. 1[a]); (3) Bought by E. Birnbaum, Istanbul, June 1981.

Binding: Brown leather, with old *abrī* doublures.

Other features: (1) On *abrī* doublure facing f. 1[a]: exhortation addressed to the *shaykh* or king of the bookworms يا كبيكج احفظ مجموعتى ["O Kabīkaj, protect my collection!"]; (2) Many marginal citations giving further quotations from Persian poets (e.g. Mīrzā, Saʿdī, Niẓāmī Samarqandī, Mavlānā [Jalāl al-Dīn Rūmī], Sulṭān Valad, Khusrav), and Ottoman commentators on Persian classics (e.g. Surūrī) and dictionaries (e.g. Niʿmat Allāh); (3) This MS is followed immediately by MS 27, T57/II, a 6-page work of similar content.

Other MSS and references: THSS Tl. 4, no. 443–445 and references there; Leiden 1, MS Or. 752/1 and references there; Oxford, Kut Ethé 2225; Budapest no. 772 and references there; Brill cat. no. 514, p. 61, no. 154; Kayseri Raşid no. 377; TÜYATOK 34/I no. 137 (cop. 1073); 138; 34/IV no. 851; Beyazıt Devlet Ktp. Veliyüddin 3101 (cop. 1064); Sül. Reisülküttab 793 (cop. 1083); Yapı Kredi Bankası Sermet Çifter Ktp. 143; Sül. Reşid Ef. 737 (cop. 1154); Sül. Darülmesnevi 556 (cop. 1178); JNUL Ar. 9.9; Storey PL, vol. III, pt. 1, p. 72, no. 105.

[27] T57/II

Provisional title supplied:

[*Farhang-i Fārsī-Turkī*]

[فرهنك فارسی تركی]

[*Farsçadan Türkçeye luġat*]

[فارسجه دن تورکجه يه لغت]

Begins (f. 46[b]):

[بسمله] باب الالف المفتوحه بو مثل بى بدل بين الاعجام شول زمانده كنايه اولنوركه زبان تركيده بر كمسنه معرفتدن ...

First rubric heading (f. 46[b]):

آفتاب يتيم كش بويه كداز امثالدندر آفتاب يتيم كش شول ...

Last rubric heading (f. 48[b]):

باب الباء المفتوحة بر افتد شول زمانده مستعملدر كه زبان تركيده بر كمسنيه بد دعا ايتمك لازم

Ends (f. 49[b]):

مراد بالذات كامل و مكمّلم ديو اشعار ايدرلر

A fragment of an anonymous vocabulary explaining in Turkish the meaning and usage of some Persian poetic expressions. This is presumably the first part of a longer work: the present MS contains only a discussion of expressions beginning with *alif* and *bā*. The remainder of the page (f. 49[a]) is blank. The handwriting is identical to that of the work immediately preceding it, No. 26, T57/I: Riyāżī's *Dustūr al-ʿamal*, by the copyist *darvīsh ʿAbdullāh al-Mavlavī al-Adranavī* (f. 46[b]). He had finished copying the *Dustūr al-ʿamal* in 1108/1696–1697 and presumably copied this one immediately afterwards.

Small professional Turkish *taʿlīq*, with main headings in red ink; ff. 46[b]–49[a], followed by f. 49[b]–51[b], all blank except for a later owner's addition of a recipe for a medicinal paste (*maʿjūn*) to treat sexual impotence; 20×14 (15×7) cm; 23 lines.

Paper, ownership and binding: Same as No. 26, T57/I Riyāżī, *Dustūr al-ʿamal*.

[28] T17/I

Mushkilāt-i Shahnāme (f. 1[a]; 3[a])

مشكلات شهنامه

Begins (f. 2[b]):

شُكْر و سپاس بر ان قادريرا كه بيك نظر رحمت

منت دخی سباس اول قادر اوزرنه كه بر رحمت نظريله

(f. 3^{a}, line 9):

... و این کتابرا مشکلات شه نامه نام نهادم

... دخی بو کتاب مشکلات شاه نامه دیو آد قودم

Beginning of Persian and Turkish headword definitions (f. 3^{b}):

اختن اخانیدن | آرامیدن

ارمك و كوز كورمك | طشره چكمك قلج چكمك و چالمق و بچق و اوق دولنمك و قرار

اتمك

Ends (f. 45^{b}):

یُوزْیُوزْدَاریُوهَه یون تمت

پارس پارسجی دلی طغان خور [?]

On *this last line* the red ink of the Turkish words written under the Persian is so faded that my readings are tentative.

The *dībāja* (introduction) states that the purpose of this work is to help students learning Persian. The Persian text (in black ink) was written first, and the Turkish interlinear translations were added later beneath each word, in red ink. The work is divided into 4 chapters: 1. (f. 3^{b}) *Maṣdar* (Infinitives). First entries: *akhtan irmek ve göz görmek* ...; 2. (f. 15^{a}) *Fī Qavāʿid amṣila al-fārisīya* (Rules of Persian paradigms). This chapter and chapter 3 remain mostly in Persian without Turkish translation; 3. (f. 19^{a}) *Fī al-amṣila* (examples, paradigms); 4. (f. 19^{a}) *Fī al-asmā* (Nouns) First entries: āb *ṣu*; av *miṣluhu*; ābdān *ṣūluḳ*; ābdān *mashraba*. Entries from *alif* to *yā*, ending on f. 45^{b}. The alphabetical order is maintained for the *first* letter of the word only. When the Persian word has been widely adopted in Turkish as a loan, the word is glossed as م (= *maʿlūm* or *maʿrūf*, "well-known"), or مثله (*miṣluhu*, "the same"), without Turkish translation, or left blank. A fairly large number of other Persian words remain without Turkish glosses, sometimes because their meaning can be easily deduced (e.g., causatives from a simple infinitive). Occasionally the "Turkish" glosses are loan words from Arabic widely used even by uneducated Turks.

Naskh; Persian headwords and untranslated narrative fully vocalized, but interlinear Turkish translations mostly unvocalized, or only occasional letters; ff. 2^b–45^a; 20×14 (17.5×10.5) cm; 22 lines (11 Persian; 11 interlinear Turkish).

Paper watermarked: Crown surmounted by a 6-armed Star, itself surmounted by a recumbent Crescent (often found in 17th-century MSS: this MS is undated).

Ownership and binding: see No. 7, T17/V

Other MSS and references: E. Birnbaum, "Interlinear translations: the case of the Turkish dictionaries" in *JTS*, vol. 26/1 = *Essays in honour of Barbara Flemming*, vol. I (2002), pp. 61–80 (especially p. 71 and 79), giving details of 3 MSS (in Cambridge University, the Vatican and St. Petersburg) which begin as our MS (See Storey *PL*, vol. 3, p. 76). Another copy titled *"Kitāb-i Mushkilāt-i Shahnāma"*, dated 949/1542, is in Istanbul, *Atatürk Kitapliği, Mu'allim Cevdet Yazmaları*, erroneously titled *Luġat-i Müşkilāt* ... in Nail Bayraktar's catalogue (no. 640; original number was K. 171). I examined this MS and found that, unlike our MS No. 7, T17/V, the Persian text of the introduction remained untranslated, but the Persian definitions were translated into Turkish interlinearly. Other quite different works may also bear similar titles, notably one by 'Abd al-Qādir Baghdādī (1030–1093/1620–1682) of which MSS in various libraries are noted in THSS Bd. 5, no. 202; and E. Birnbaum in *JTS*, vol. 26/1 p. 71 n. 24.

[29] T80/I

Vahbī, Sunbulzāda Muḥammad, d. 1224/1809

وهبى، سنبل زاده محمد

Tuḥfa-i Vahbī (f. 33^a)

تحفۀ وهبى

Begins (f. 1^b):

حمد بى حد او كرمفرمايه كه انك انعمتيدر بى غايه

Ends (f. 33[a]):

دی سرآمد اولسه بر نسنه تمام * تحفهٔ وهبی ده بتدی و السلام

Below this is a heading introducing a final chronogram:

بو تاریخیله ذیل تحفه مسکی الختام اولدی هزاران شکر ایدوب حقّه دیدم اتمام تاریخن بحمد
الله بو زیبا تحفهٔ وهبی تمام اولدی

A well-known Persian-Turkish vocabulary in 58 sections of rhymed verse, composed in 1196/1782 (f. 33[a]) for the author's son, and then widely used as a text book in Ottoman schools. It includes sections of Persian words, and (from f. 28[b] on) idiomatic expressions (*iṣṭilāḥāt*). Although not explicitly stated, it is modeled on a book of similar content, the *Tuḥfa-i Shāhidī*, composed nearly 3 centuries earlier by Ibrāhīm Shāhidī (d. 957/1550), of which there is a MS in this collection (No. 25, T21/I).

The copyist "*al-Sayyid* ḥāfiẓ ʿAlī al-Shukrī al-Isbārtavī, *min talāmīẕ* Ḥalvajīzāda," completed this MS on 9 R[abīʿ] II 1246/8 August 1830 (f. 33[a]).

Good professional naskh; ff. 1–33[a] [first part of a volume of 46 folios; the second part (T80/II) ff. 37[b]–44[a] contains a short treatise in Arabic on Persian grammar titled *Mafātīḥ al-durrīyah fī ithbāt al-qawānīn al-Darīyah* (f. 37[b]) by Muṣṭafā b. Abī Bakr al-Sīvāsī (f. 44[b])]; 21×14 (15.5×9) cm; 23 lines. The same copyist completed the copy of the treatise on Persian grammar on 30 Muḥarram 1246/21 July 1830.

Paper: Burnished, cream colored, with watermarks: (1) Crown above an Eagle with spread wings and letters EGA; (2) On other pages GFA below the Eagle; (3) Letters GFA below Crown and Shield.

Decoration: First opening (f. 1[b]–2[a]) *sarlavḥa*, multicolored floral motif, in gold, yellow, pink and blue. First opening framed in double gold rules, within double black rules, within red ink rules; remaining pages within red rules; all headings in red ink, within red ink frames. (The opening of the second work (ff. 37[b]–38[a]) has similar *sarlavḥa* and frames).

Ownership: (1) (f. 1[a]) round seal stamp (1.3 cm diameter) "Amīn …" (other words illegible); (2) on back flyleaf rubber stamp: "Professor Glyn M. Meredith-Owens", who presented it to (3) E. Birnbaum, May 2, 1986.

Binding: Good middle 19th century European type marbled paper on boards, except for red leather gold-decorated spine with gold-stamped title in Arabic script Turkish: "*Tuḥfe kitābı şerḥiyle berāber.*" Doublures are also European type marbled paper.

Other MSS and references: Leiden vol. 2, Or. 11.989; vol. 3, Or. 18.692/I and references there; Oxford, Kut, 278; Budapest, no. 755; TDKK-YEK, no. 577–579; 581; Sarajevo, Or. Inst. *Kat. Persijskih rukopisa,* [comp.] Salih Trako, 239–244 (MSS destroyed in 1992); many printed edd. in Arabic script, Istanbul, from 1213/1799 onwards. A modern Turkish edition: Sünbülzade Vehbi, *Tuhfe* [ed.] Numan Külekçi, Turgut Karabey, Erzurum, 1990.

F. Encyclopedia

[30] P8

An old encyclopedic work, original author and title not found. Penciled "title" inside front cover (early 20th century):

> ***Kitāb-i sukhanī-i Khudā'ī-i jahānnamā***

كتاب سخنئ خدائ جهان نما

Working title here supplied:

> [***Jahānnamā***]

[جهان نما]

Begins now (f. 1[a]; original beginning folio(s) now missing):

جمع است و ان مفید همه باشد بر سبیل استغراق بس لازم اند [= آیذ] که جملهٔ درجات قرب و ثواب داخل باشد بحسب اں [= این] لفظ والذن اوتوا العلم درجات

First heading (f. 1[a]):

دلیل فهم حق تعالی از سلیمان سغمبر [= پیغمبر] صلوات الله علیه حکایت می فرماند که او کفت هب لی مُلکاً لا ینبغی لاحدٍ من بعدی

Ends (f. 62[b]; original ending now missing):

نوع جهارم انست کی ملصق باشد وان همحان است [= همچنان است]//

An incomplete copy of an extremely rare encyclopedic work of miscellaneous contents by an anonymous author (f. 2[a], *īn żaʿīf*). The first section extant here expounds on the virtues of learning (f. 1[b], *bar fażīlat-i ʿilm*), citing multiple proofs from named sources, e.g. "*Torah*; *Injīl*; *ʿAlī*; *Qurʾān*; *ʿAbdullāh b. al-Zubayr*; *Ibn ʿAbbās*; *Kalīla va Dimna*; *Khalīl b. Aḥmad*" (ff. 1[b]–4[a]). Later portions of this book are devoted to geography, astronomy and astrology, followed by sections

© KONINKLIJKE BRILL NV, LEIDEN, 2019 | DOI:10.1163/9789004389670_023

FIGURE 28 No. 30 (P8). An unidentified old encyclopedic work, f. 17^{b}–18^{a}. Copied ca. 7/13th century

on the creation and properties of mankind (*āfarīnash-i insān*). Much of the work may also be described as *akhlāq*. There are plenty of citations from the Qurʾān. The book is divided into many numbered main sections, generally headed *faṣl*, followed by a definition of the subject. Each *faṣl* is subdivided into a rich multiplicity of variously titled short subsections and subdivisions of subsections using the following headings: *dalīl, navʿ, manfaʿat, ḥikmat, ḥujjat, mukhāl, vajh, ṭāʾifa, burhān, qism, qāʿida, munāẓara, maqām, masʾala, martaba, sukhanī, qavl, ṣifat, munāsabat.*

This manuscript seems to be unique. I have not found any manuscripts of this work in the printed catalogues available to me, and four eminent scholars whom I consulted[1] have never seen another copy. The first few folios are

1 The manuscript was shown to the four distinguished Persianists mentioned below. None of them could identify the book or its author, and all of them independently essentially corroborated my estimated dating of its composition and paleography: (1). The late Professor

lost, and one or more folios are missing between ff. 1 and 2, one folio between ff. 61 and 62, and all folios after f. 62 (which is the last fragment extant). A fairly recent [19th century (?)] reader paginated the top of each page in "oriental" Arabic numerals as follows [3]–4, 7–52; 69–146. Unfortunately, the copyists did not use catchwords, which would have made it easier to identify the loss of folios.

The linguistic form and the literary style are remarkably simple and date the composition of the work to approximately the 12th to 13th century. This manuscript was written by two different copyists: paleographically ff. 18–66 are probably about mid-13th century, while ff. 1–17 seem slightly more recent, perhaps late 13th or even 14th century. It is possible that, as sometimes happened, the task of copying this text from the same Vorlage manuscript was shared by two contemporary copyists, an old man and a young man, as all pages seem to be written on the same buff-colored unwatermarked "oriental" paper.

The main sections bear the following headings and are noted here in detail, in the hope that this may help in identifying any other extant MSS of this work.

f. 1ª [*faṣl* 1. Heading and preceding folios lost]

f. 4ª *Faṣl-i* 2. *dar ḥaqīqat-i ʿilm va kashf-i māhīyat-i ū.*

f. 5ª. *Faṣl-i* 3. *dar fażīlat-i ʿilm va kamāl-i daraja-i ū.*

f. 7ª. *Faṣl-i* 4. *dar sharḥ-i aqsām-i ʿulūm.*

f. 9ᵇ. *Faṣl-i* 5. *dar sharḥ-i fażīlat-i ʿilm-i uṣūl.*

f. 14ᵇ. *Faṣl-i* 6. *dar bayān-i ānki īmān bi-taqlīd durust na-bāshad.*

f. 15ª. *Faṣl-i* 7. *dar bayān-i faż[ī]lat-i ʿilm-i Qurʾān va tafsīr.*

(18ª–62, by a different copyist, who used a different sequence of numbering for each *faṣl*).

G.M. Wickens (University of Toronto, Sept. 1987): "Composed and copied 13th century"; (2) Dr. Živa Vesel (Université de la Sorbonne Nouvelle, Paris, October 1988): "12–13th century"; (3) Dr. Francis Richard (Bibliothèque nationale, Paris, February 1989): "ff. 18–62 copied perhaps 13th century; ff. 1–17, early 14th century"; (4) Prof. Gilbert Lazard (Université de la Sorbonne Nouvelle, Paris, May 1989): "Composed possibly 12th, more likely 13th century; ff. 18–62 copied 13th century; ff. 1–17 [a little] later".

f. 23^{b}. *Faṣl-i 4. dar tafẓīl-i dalālat-i aḥvāl-i zamīn.*

f. 26^{b}. *Faṣl-i 5. dar sharḥ-i dalālat-i āftāb bar qudrat-i Ḥaqq Taʿālā ...*

f. 31^{b}. *Faṣl-i 6. dar dalālat-i aḥvāl-i māh.*

f. 33^{a}. *Faṣl-i 7. dar dalālat-i shurūq va ghurūb.*

f. 35^{b}. *Faṣl-i 8. dar kayfīyat-i istidlāl kardash-i shab [u] rūz.*

f. 39^{a}. *Faṣl-i 9. dar istidrāk-i aḥvāl-i kayfīyat-i burūj.*

f. 42^{a}. *Faṣl-i 10. dar istidrāk-i aḥvāl-i dīgar-i sitāragān.*

f. 43^{a}. *Faṣl-i 11. bar istidrāk-i aḥval-i ajlāl.*

f. 43^{b}. *Maqālat-i siyam dar kayfīyat-i aḥvāl-i insān barhastī Āfarīdagān-i Qadīm Taʿalā.*

f. 48^{b}. *Faṣl-i 3. dar kayfīyat-i āfarīnash-i Ādam.*

f. 51^{b}. *Faṣl-i 4. dar kayfīyat-i āfarīnash-i insān.*

Some selected archaisms in letter shapes, diacritics, vocalization and orthography can be observed:

- *Kāf*: written as a *lām* surmounted by a small *kāf* touching the top of the upright (on f. 18–62 only).
- *Diacritics* are often omitted from frequently used words throughout, e.g. *yā* in *īn, nīst, dīgar*, etc.; *tā* in *ast, nīst, zā* in *az*, etc.

Orthographic archaisms by both copyists:

- ء *hamza* is used in mid-word as a vowel glide for *a* and to indicate passage from one vowel to an adjacent one without an intervening consonant, e.g. جئست *chiyast*, سيئم *siyam*.
- ب may represent either *b*, or *p*; both copyists are inconsistent: sometimes they express *p* with three subdots ∵
- بادشاه or پادشاه; بهتر or پهتر; بيذا or پيدا

The dots for *bā* and *tā* are written to the right of the spike (below the spike for *bā*, and above it for *tā*), not under the middle of the spike.

- ج can represent both *jīm* and *chīm* هيج، جهار، جون
- ذ and د are both used where later orthography uses only *dāl*. Each copyist writes both كويذ and كويد (though كويد is more common in ff. 1–17). باذشاه and پادشاه are both used.
- س is sometimes written with 3 dots below پيم، تپلپل، اپب، رپم
- ک *kaf*/*gaf* for كه or كى at the end of a word جنانک، آنک (on ff. 18–62 only).
- ن when *nūn* is in initial or final position the dot is always above the *right* spike.
- ي the dots on medial *yā* are often omitted on frequently used words, such as كوىذ *gūyad*, نىست *nīst*.

Vocalization of some ordinal numbers:

دُوَم ؛ سِيئُم، سِيُم، سِئُم، سِيَم ؛ جُهارم ؛ شُشُم ؛ دَهُّم، دَهُم ؛ يَازْدُهُمْ ؛ دُوازَدَهُم ؛
چُهَارْدَهُم، چَهاردَهُم ؛ هَجْدَهُم

Old naskh; ff. 1–62; 23×14.5 cm. (18.5×12); 17 lines; Persian text mostly unvocalized, except for occasional vowels on some letters; the dots which usually distinguish some letters (e.g. *bā, jīm, bā/yā, tā, khā, zā, shīn, nūn*) are sometimes omitted in frequently occurring words (e.g. *īn, ast, bāshad, būd, nīst, gūyad, chi, chūn, dīgar*, etc.).

Decoration: Each page is framed in double red rules; most headings are in larger letters, usually in red ink, or in larger black ink letters, overlined in red ink. Citations in Arabic are in red ink (mainly from the Qur'an), fully vocalized; numbered division headings are usually in large letters in black ink, and often vocalized. From f. 23[b] to 50[a], *faṣl* (chapter) headings are framed in double rules in red ink.

Ownership: Occasional short marginal annotations (not signed), perhaps 18th century; and a few early 20th century pencilled notes, the longest being a portion of a hymn in Turkish in an inexpert hand on f. 1[a]. No names of the previous owners are noted. Bought by E. Birnbaum in Istanbul, June 1987.

Binding: The present binding, though several centuries old, is a little too small for this MS and may have been recycled from another manuscript already several centuries old. It is in very bad condition: old, now tattered, paper boards made largely of fragments of pages of old manuscripts glued together (at least one being in Persian) and also some pages which had been used for calligraphy practice. The book now has an old coarse leather backstrip. The beginning words of a series of verses of a Persian poem in good, fairly old *nastaʿlīq* occupy the margins of f. 41^{b}. The volume must have been trimmed when rebound many centuries ago, since the beginnings of the verses were cut off.

G. Astrology

[31] P6

Kūshyār b. Labbān al-Jīlī (f. 2ª), fl. 4th/10th century

كوشيار بن لبّان الجيلى

Tuḥfat al-ikhtiyārāt (f. 2ª)

تحفة الاختيارات

Begins (f. 2ª):

جنين كويد ملك الحكما و المنجمين الفضلاء و المهندسين خواجه امام ابو الحسن كوشيار بن لبان الجيلى قدس الله روحه ... كه جماعتى از دوستان موافق از داعى التماس مختصرى كردند موخر و در باب اختيارات اين سطور قلمى شد و نامش تحفة الاختيارات كرده آمد بعون الملك القديم. المقدمة [sic] الكتاب. بدان و اكاه باش كه در هر كارى كه شروع خواهى كردن بايد كه اول را طالع نظر كنى و رب طالع را انكه ماه را و خداوندان خانه كه ماه دروست

(f. 22ᵇ) End [of *Bāb-i avval*]:

و عطارد بهر نظر كه ناظر باشد بكدخدا اكر مسعود بود بر عطيه بيفزايند و اكر منحوس بود از عطيه بكاهند و الله اعلم بالصواب و اليه المرجع و المآب

Beginning of *Bāb* 22 (f. 22ᵇ):

الباب الثايى و العشرون در امدى كانون ثانى در روزها هفته ار روز يكشنبه والله اعلم. باب اول در كسوف شمس در ماه ...

© KONINKLIJKE BRILL NV, LEIDEN, 2019 | DOI:10.1163/9789004389670_024

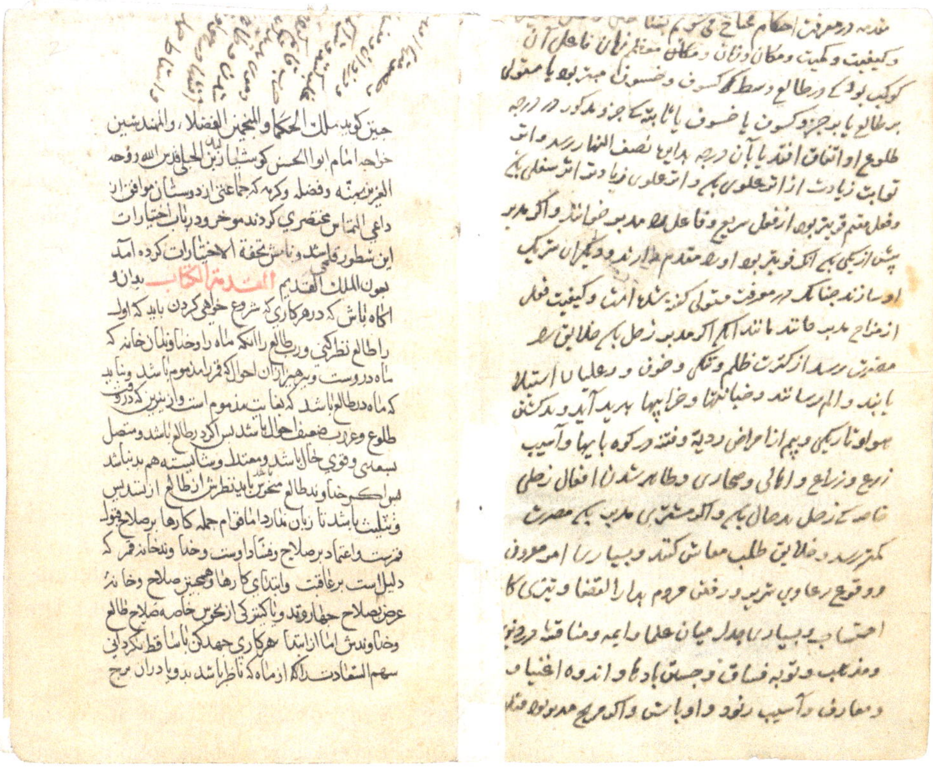

FIGURE 29 No. 31 (P6). Kūshyār b. Labbān, fl. 4/10th century. f. 2[a] [left page]. *Tuḥfat al-ikhtiyārāt*. Copied ca. 7/13th century

End of *Bāb* 22 and end of the work (f. 26[a]):

و علما و مشایخ را حال متردد بود در عقب این جمعیت و فراخی بدید اید والله اعلم بالصواب
و الیه المرجع و المآب

Kūshyār b. Labbān, a famous medieval Islamic astronomer, mathematician and astrologer, was a native of Gīlān in Iran, but spent much of his life in Baghdad. The present MS, titled *Tuḥfat al-ikhtiyārāt*, is about the "selection" (*ikhtiyār*) of astrologically auspicious days of the month for beginning various tasks. In contrast to most of his pioneering astronomical and mathematical works, which are written in Arabic, the classical Islamic language of science, this is one of the very few which he wrote in Persian. As was conventional amongst medieval Islamic authors, he makes the standard claim that he composed this work "at the request of a group of friends" (f. 2[a]).

The first part consists of more than 40 mostly numbered short sections (*faṣl*), the majority less than a page. One of them is headed *faṣl dar tārīkh-i Fārsīyān*, and begins with a list of the traditional Persian months starting with *Farvardīn* (f. 7[b]). The second part of the MS, headed *al-bāb al-s̱ānī va al-ʿishrūn … bāb-i avval* (f. 22[b]) is in the same hand, and this continues to the end of the MS. This treatise describes both "lucky" and "unfortunate" days, and cites such ancient classical "authorities" as Hermes, Ẕū al-Qarnayn [Alexander], Bilʿam and Baṭlamyūs (Ptolemy) (ff. 22[b]–23[a]).

Although MSS of Kūshyār b. Labbān's other works are found in many libraries, this *Tuḥfat al-ikhtiyārāt* is extremely rare, and apparently remains unpublished. This MS is undated, but is paleographically about the 13th century.

Clear old *naskh*; f. 1–23; 18.5×11.5 (14×7.5) cm; 18 lines. The copyist occasionally omitted the diacritical dots from frequently used words.

Remnants of an early foliation, using older "oriental" Arabic numerals intermittently on some pages, starting with 80 on f. 9[a] and ending with 107 on f. 26[a]. The folios originally numbered 90–99 seem to have been lost.

This MS was evidently once part of a larger MS, probably consisting of a series of separate short works (*risāla*), each one preceded by a blank folio or page. In the present MS, the originally blank f. 1[a] now contains in a different hand, a formula in Arabic for a prayer addressed to Allāh by "Fulān b. Fulān" for the love of "Fulān b. Fulāna" [sic]. On the reverse of this folio, yet another hand has filled the page with a long note in Persian about astrology.

Paper: "Oriental", without watermark designs.

Ownership: Bought by E. Birnbaum, Istanbul, June 1981.

Binding: None; apparently disbound from a volume which contained many more folios.

Other MSS and references: Sezgin, GAS, Bd. 7, p. 183 no. 47, cites an incomplete MS of *Kitāb al-Ikhtiyārāt* in Mashhad, Riżā 5529, pp. 20–21; also Bd. 8, p. 321; see also *Encyclopaedia Iranica*, art. Gūšyār Gīlānī.

H. Document

[32] P16

A document, perhaps a rental agreement or a bill of sale, mentioning a *bāgh* (garden) and noting that the property is free of defects.

This one page text is written in an extreme form of flowing Persian *nastaʿlīq*, lacking most essential diacritics, and is very difficult to read.[1] It is inscribed on a sheet of cardboard and has artistic pretensions. Each line is calligraphed within white red-edged "clouds", surrounded by gold paint. The written area is encased in multiple rectangular ruled parallel frames of gold, blue and red ink. The first 8 lines are in black ink; the ninth and last line is in red ink.

Date (line 9): "8 Rabīʿ I 1300"/January 17, 1883.

On thin buff cardboard: 32 × 21 (20 × 12) cm; 9 lines.

Ownership: Gift of Mr. Altman, manager of H.P. Kraus (dealer in rare books and MSS), New York, 1969 to E. Birnbaum.

1 I thank my colleague Professor Maria Subtelny for help in deciphering this document.

© KONINKLIJKE BRILL NV, LEIDEN, 2019 | DOI:10.1163/9789004389670_025

ADDENDUM

I. [*Majmūʿa*]*

[33–34] **M1**

Introductory note

This volume contains five separate treatises (*rasāʾil*)—two in Persian and three in Arabic—on various aspects of the art of prosody as used in Persian verse. Four of the treatises are here anonymous. Of the two in Persian, one mentions Jāmī as its author. However, the other one in Persian is also by Jāmī. The three remaining treatises are also about Persian poetry, but as they are composed in Arabic, they are described in my *Arabic* catalogue above, numbers: **67, 68, 69**. Although they are anonymous in this manuscript, their author is the Turkish polymath Shaykh al-Islām Ibn Kamāl Pasha (d. 940/1534).

All five *rasāʾil* were transcribed by a single anonymous copyist, probably within a short time, as they share the same Turkish style of *taʿlīq* script, and are written on paper bearing the same watermarks. The copyist provided a completion date only at the end of the first Arabic *risāla* (f. 19^{b}): *11 Rabīʿ I*, $^{1}{}_{8}{}^{0}$.

The position of the number 8 below the line is an anomaly: the date may be interpreted as [1]108/8 October 1696, or (less likely) 1008/2 October 1599.

Paper: European, at least two different watermarks: (1) Horn (e.g. f. 2–3; 54–55); (2) Crown and Grapes (e.g. f. 44^{a}); 55 folios; professional Turkish style *taʿlīq*; not vocalized; headings in red ink; 20.5×17.5 (14×7 cm); 17 lines; red ink also used for the Turkish translations of the Persian *maṣdar*s in no. **34 (M1/V)**.

Binding: Probably (re)bound in 19th century in cardboard covers, which are now overlaid with paper printed with a blue repeat pattern; sewing of quires is now loose; spine is light brown cloth, now worn and torn.

Ownership: Bought by E. Birnbaum in Istanbul, August 1980.

* This section is an addendum to the Persian catalogue as published in *JIM*.

© KONINKLIJKE BRILL NV, LEIDEN, 2019 | DOI:10.1163/9789004389670_026

[33] **M1/II**

[Jāmī ʿAbd al-Raḥmān, d. 898/1492]

[جامی ، عبد الرحمان]

[*Risāla-i ʿarūż*]

[رسالۀ عروض]

Begins (f. 20[b]):

سپاس وافر قادری را که حرکۀ سریع دوائر افلاک را سبب ...
اما بعد ، بدانکه ارباب صناعۀ عروض بناء أصول اوزان ...

Ends (f. 34[b]):

چنکم (sic) دل من برست * فعلن فعلن فعلن . مقطوع هر دم ایم سویت باشد بینم رویت *
فعلن فعلن فعلن فعلن . تم

An esteemed treatise in Persian on the art of prosody (*ʿarūż*) by the major poet, theologian and mystic Jāmī. The copyist did not mention Jāmī's name in this manuscript.

The section on quatrains (*rubāʿī*) includes examples (f. 28[b]–29[a]). A "wheel" (*dāʾira*) illustrating the poetic meters is drawn on f. 29[a].

For physical details of this MS see the immediately preceding entry, [**33–34/M1**].

Other MSS: A. Ateş, *İstanbul Kütüphanelerinde Farsça manzum eserler*, nos 586/19; 588/25; 591/17; 529/9; 594/17; *Topkapı Sarayı Müzesi Kütüphanesi Farsça yazmalar kataloğu*, hazırlayan F.E. Karatay: nos 322/II; 318 (wrongly described); 671/XIX; 679/X; 680/XXIII; Köprülü vol. 3, no. 1/436.

[34] **M1/IV**

Jāmī ʿAbd al-Raḥmān, d. 898/1492 (f. 39b)

جامی ، عبد الرحمان

مختصر وافی بقواعد علم قوافی

Mukhtaṣar-i Vāfī bi-qavāʿid ʿilm-i qavāfī (f. 35b, line 6)

or

Vāfī bi-qavāʿid ʿilm-i qavāfī

or

al-Qavāfī (f. 39b)

Begins (f. 35b):

بعد از تمین بموزون ترین کلامی را که قافیه ...

Ends (f. 39b):

و آن کوکشایدش دل حون (sic) کشته کاردست .
تمت القوافی من تصنیف مولانا عبد الرحمن الجامی . تم

A short treatise in Persian on the rules of rhyme (*qāfiya*, plural *qavāfī*) in poetry.

For physical details of this manuscript see **33–34/M1.**

Other MSS: *Topkapı Sarayı Kütüphanesi Farsça yazmalar kataloğu* ... nos 678, xxx; 680, xxii; 681 xxxviii.

Bibliography and Sigla

Akademiia Nauk SSSR. Institut Naradov Azii: *Opisanie persidskikh i tadzhikskikh rukopisei*, see Baevski.

Akademiia Nauk SSSR. Institut vostochnikh SSSR: *Kratkie Katalog* II. Stalinabad, 1986.

Akademiia Nauk Tadzhikskoi SSR: *Katalog vostichnikh rukopisei*, Tom I. Stalinabad [= Dushanbe], 1960.

Akademiia Nauk Uzbekskoi SSR: see Tashkent.

Ateş: *İstanbul Kütüphanelerinde Farsça manzum eserler*, [haz.] Ahmet Ateş. Cilt I. İstanbul, 1968.

Atsız: 'Kemalpaşa'nın oĝlu'nun eserleri', [ed. Nihal] Atsız. (*Şarkiyat mecmuası*, cilt 6 [1966], pp. 71–112; cilt 7 (1972), pp. 83–135).

Aumer: *Verzeichniss der orientalischen Handschriften der K. Hof- und Staatsbibliothek in München*, von Joseph Aumer, 1875.

Baevski: *Opisanie persidskikh i tadzhikskikh rukopisei Instituta Narodov Azii*, Vypusk 5: *Dvuiazychnye slovar.* [Ed.] S.I. Baevski. Moskva, 1968.

Balić, see Wien.

Bayazit/Beyazıt: Beyazıt Devlet Kütüphanesi, Istanbul.

Bibliothèque Nationale, Blochet: *Catalogue des manuscrits persans*, par E. Blochet. Tomes 1–4, Paris, 1905–1934.

Birnbaum, Burnt: see: "Burnt Books".

Birnbaum, Eleazar: 'On some Turkish interlinear translations of the Koran'. *Journal of Turkish Studies*, vol. 14, 1990, pp. 113–118.

Birnbaum, Eleazar: *Ottoman Turkish and Çaĝatay MSS in Canada*. Leiden, 2015.

Birnbaum, Interlinear: "Interlinear translations: the case of the Turkish dictionaries" in *JTS*, vol. 26/I, pp. 61–80.

BL/BM: British Library/British Museum, London.

BL-P/BM-P: [British Library, London]. *Catalogue of the Persian manuscripts in the British Museum* by Charles Rieu, 3 vols. London, 1879–1883.

BL-T/BM-T: [British Library, London]. *Catalogue of the Turkish manuscripts in the British Museum* by Charles Rieu. London, 1888.

BM: see BL.

Bodleian: see Oxford, Ethé and Oxford, Kut Ethé.

Brill, cat. 514: *Oriental manuscripts offered for sale by E.J. Brill*. Catalogue 514. Leiden, 1981.

Brockelmann: See GAL.

Browne: E.G. Browne, *A supplementary handlist of the Muḥammadan manuscripts ... preserved in the libraries of ... Cambridge*. Cambridge, 1922.

Budapest: İsmail Parlatır, *Macar Bilimler Akademisi Kütüphanesi'ndeki Türkçe elyazmaları kataloğu*. Ankara, 2007.

Burnt Books: "Burnt Books: a catalogue of some Turkish manuscripts destroyed in the 1992 war in Bosnia", by Eleazar Birnbaum, in *Şinasi Tekin anısına, II: Uygurlardan Osmanlıya*. Istanbul, 2005, pp. 171–256.

Cairo, Dār al-Kutub: see DK.

Chester Beatty Supp.: The Chester Beatty Library [Dublin]. *Supplementary handlist [of Islamic manuscripts], second draft*. By G.M. Meredith-Owens. [Typescript, ca. 1967].

Cyprus: *Kıbrıs İslâm yazmaları kataloğu/Catalogue of Islamic manuscripts in Cyprus*. By Ramazan Şeşen, Istanbul, 1995.

DİA: *Türk Dıyanet Vakfı İslam Ansiklopedisi*. İstanbul, 1988–2016.

Dihkhudā: Lughatnāma. Teheran, 1931–, 50 volumes, with continuation online in progress.

DK: Cairo. Dār al-Kutub al-Qawmīya. *Fihris al-makhṭūṭāt al-Turkīya*, Cairo, 1987–1992.

Dublin, Chester: see Chester Beatty.

Dushanbe: see Akademiia Nauk Tadzhikskoi SSR.

EI^2: *Encyclopaedia of Islam*. 2nd edition. London, 1954–2005.

EIr: *Encyclopaedia Iranica*. London, New York, vol. 1–, 1982-[In progress].

Emiri: See Millet, Ali Emirî.

Encyclopaedia Iranica: see EIr.

Ethé, Bodleian: see Oxford.

Ethé, India Office: see India Office.

Flügel: G. Flügel, *Die arabischen, persischen und turkischen Handschriften der K. K. Hofbibliothek zu Wien*. 3 Bde. Wien, 1865–1867. [See also Wien (below)].

Gacek, Adam, 'The use of "kabikaj" in Arabic manuscripts', in *Manuscripts of the Middle East* 1 (1986), pp. 49–53.

GAL: *Geschichte der arabischen Litteratur*, von C. Brockelmann, 2. Auflage. [= G I–II]. Leiden, 1946–1949; Supplement, Leiden [= S I–III], Leiden, 1937–1942.

GAS: See Sezgin.

Gazi Husrev Beg: *Katalog arabskih, turskih, perzijskih i bosanskih rukopisa Gazı Husrevbegova biblioteka u Sarajevu/Catalogue of the Arabic, Turkish, Persian and Bosnian manuscripts [in the] Ghazi Husrev-Beg Library in Sarajevo*. Tom 1–16. London, Sarajevo, 2000–2008.

Hoghughi: see Strasbourg.

India Office: *Catalogue of Persian manuscripts in the library of the India Office*, by C.F. Ethé. Vol. I. Oxford, 1903.

İst.: İstanbul.

İstanbul Kütüphanelerinde Farsça: see Ateş.

İstanbul Üniv. Ktp.: İstanbul Üniversitesi Kütüphanesi.

İzmir: *İzmir Milli Kütüphanesi yazma eserler kataloğu*. [Comp.] Ali Yardım, 4 vols. İzmir, 1992–1997.

JNUL: Jewish National and University Library, Jerusalem.

JTS: *Journal of Turkish Studies/Türklük Bilgisi Araştırmaları*. Cambridge, Mass., 1977–.

Kashf al-ẓunūn: [by] Kātib Chalabi [Ḥājjī Khalīfa], [ed.] S. Yaltkaya [wa Kilisli] Rifat Bilge. 2 vols. Istanbul, 1941–1943.

Kayseri: *Kayseri Râşid Efendi Kütüphanesi, Türkçe, Farsça, Arabça yazmalar kataloğu*. Hazırlayan Ali Rıza Karabulut. Kayseri, 1982; 2. bas. 2 cilt, 1995.

Khalidiya: *The Ottoman-Turkish MSS in al-Khalidiyyah Library, Jerusalem*. Prepared by B. Kellner-Heinkele, London. 2008.

Konya, Koyunoğlu: Koyunoğlu Kütüphanesi, Konya [Unpublished catalogue in that library in Konya].

Konya, Mevlânâ: *Konya Mevlânâ Müzesi yazmalar kataloğu*. Haz. ʿAbdülbaki Gölpınarlı. Cilt 1–4 Ankara, 1967–1994.

Köprülü: *Fihrist makhṭūṭāt maktabat Kūprīlī / Catalogue of manuscripts in the Köprülü Library*. [Ed.] Ramazan Şeşen, vols. 1–3. İstanbul, 1986.

Leiden: *Catalogue of Turkish manuscripts in the Library of Leiden University and other collections in the Netherlands*. Vol. 1–4, compiled by Jan Schmidt. Leiden, 2000–2012.

Mach: *Catalogue of Arabic manuscripts (Yahuda section) in the Garrett Collection, Princeton University Library*. By Rudolf Mach. Princeton, 1977.

Mashhad: Kitābkhāna-i Āstān-i Quds-i Rażavī.

Mevlana Müzesi: See Konya, Mevlânâ.

Millet, Ali Emiri: Millet, Ali Emiri Kütüphanesi, Istanbul.

Mostar: *Katalog arabskih, turskih i perzijskih rukopisa, (Arhiva Hercegovine, Mostar)*. [By] Hivzija Hasandedić, Mostar, 1977.

Nuruosmaniye: Nuruosmaniye Kütüphanesi, Istanbul.

OIS Sarajevo: see Sarajevo, Oriental Institute.

Oxford, Ethé; Oxford, Kut, Ethé: *Supplementary catalogue of Turkish manuscripts in the Bodleian Library*, with reprint of the 1930 catalogue by H. Ethé. By Günay Kut, Oxford, 2003.

OZJA (Zagreb): Orijentalna Zbirka Arhiva Jugoslavensko Akademija Znanosti ... u Zagrebu. [Manuscripts in the Oriental Section of the Archive in Croatia, previously a branch of the Yugoslav Academy of Sciences].

PL: See Storey.

Rado: Rado, Şevket. *Türk hattatları*. Istanbul, 1985.

Raif Yelkenci: See Yelkenci.

Rieu: See BL-P and BL-T.

Sadberk Hanım Müzesi: *Sadberk Hanım Müzesi Kütüphanesi Hüseyin Kocabaş yazmaları kataloğu*. [Haz.] İsmail Bakar. İstanbul, 2001.

Sarajevo, Gazi Husrev Begova Biblioteka: see Gazi Husrev Beg.

Sarajevo, Oriental Institute, Persian: *Katalog Perzijskih rukopisa Orientalnog Instituta u Sarajevo*. Obradio Salih Trako. Sarajevo, 1986.

Sarajevo, Oriental Institute, Trako-Gazić: *Katalog rukopisa Orijentalnog Instituta Ljepa Knjizevost.* [By] Salih Trako, Lejla Gazić. Sarajevo, 1997.

Sezgin GAS: Fuat Sezgin, *Geschichte der arabischen Schrifttums.* Bd. I–IX. Leiden, 1967–1984.

Smitskamp: *Islamic manuscripts: Catalogue 635*, compiled by Nico van den Boogert. [Offered for sale by] Smitskamp Oriental Antiquarium. Leiden, 2002. [All MSS were purchased by an undisclosed "private collector" in 2002].

F. Steingass, *A Comprehensive Persian-English Dictionary* [...] London⁵, 1963.

Storey/Bregel, PL: C.A. Storey, *Persidskaia literatura.* [Translated into Russian and expanded] by Yu.É. Bregel. Vols. 1–3. Moskva, 1972.

Storey, PL: C.A. Storey, *Persian Literature: a bio-bibliographical survey.* London, 1927–.

St. Petersburg. Akademiya Nauk SSSR. Institut Vostokovedeniya: *Kratkie katalog.* Tom 2. 1986.

Strasbourg: Strasbourg. Bibliothèque nationale et universitaire. *Catalogue critique des manuscrits persans*, par Asghar Hoghughi. Strasbourg, 1964.

Süleymaniye/Sül.: [This great library in Istanbul houses a large number of collections of manuscripts gathered from other locations, which still retain their original names and manuscript numbers, but are now preceded by the word "Süleymaniye", e.g. Fatih, Serez, Esad Ef.].

Strasbourg: Bibliotheque nationale et universitaire.

Tabrīz, Tarbiyat: *Fihrist-i kitābkhāna-i davlatī Tarbiyat: Kutub-i khaṭṭī.* Tabrīz, 1329sh/1950.

Tashkent: *Sobranie vostochnykh rukopisei Akademiia Nauk Uzbekskoi SSR.* [ed.] A.A. Semenov [and others]. Tom 1–. Tashkent, 1952–.

TDAYB: *Türk Dili Araştırmaları Yıllığı Belleten.* Ankara, 1953–.

TDED: İstanbul Üniverstiesi Edebiyat Fakültesi, *Türk Dili ve Edebiyatı Dergisi.* İstanbul, 1946–.

TDKK-YEK: *Türk Dil Kurumu Kütüphanesi Yazma Eserler Kataloğu.* Hazırlayanlar Müjgân Cunbur ... Ankara, 1999.

Tehran. Dānishkada-yi Adabīyāt: *Nashrīya-yi Kitābkhāna-yi Markazī dar nuskhahā-yi khaṭṭī*, no. 4. 1334sh/1965.

Tehran. Danishkada-yi Adabīyāt, Mahdavī: *Fihrist-i nuskhahā-yi khaṭṭī-i kitābkhāna-i Asghar Mahdavī.* Tehran, 1962.

THSS: *Türkische Handschriften.* Wiesbaden (Verzeichnis der orientalischen Handschriften in Deutschland, Bd. XIII, 1–5). Wiesbaden, 1968–1981.

TİEM: Türk ve İslam Eserleri Müzesi, İstanbul.

TKS-F: *Topkapı Sarayı Kütüphanesi Farsça yazmaları kataloğu.* [Compiler] F.E. Karatay. İstanbul, 1961.

TKS-P: *Topkapı Sarayı Kütüphanesi Farsça yazmalar kataloğu.* Hazırlayan F.E. Karatay İstanbul, 1961.

TKS-T: *Topkapı Sarayı Kütüphanesi Türkçe yazmalar kataloğu*. Hazırlayan F.E. Karatay. İstanbul, 2 vols. 1961.

Topaloğlu, Ahmed [ed.]: *XVI. yüzyıl başlarında yazılmış satır arası Kuran tercümesi*. İstanbul, 1976.

Topkapı Sarayı: see TKS-P.

Türk Diyanet Vakfı İA: see DİA.

TÜYATOK: *Türkiye yazmaları toplu kataloğu*. Ankara/İstanbul.

Vakıflar: *Vakıflar dergisi*. İstanbul. Cilt 13 (1981).

Wien: *Katalog der türkischen Handschriften der Östereichischen Nationalbibliothek* (Neuerwerburgen, 1864–1994). Bd. 5, von Smail Balić. Ankara 2006 (See also Flügel).

Yapı Kredi, Sermet: *Yapı Kredi Bankası Sermet Çifter araştırma kütüphanesi yazmalar kataloğu*. Hazırlayan Yücel Dağlı. İstanbul, 2001.

Yelkenci, Raif: [İstanbul bibliophile and bookseller, 1894–1974].

Zagreb OZJA: See OZJA (Zagreb).

ZDMG: *Zeitschrift der Deutschen Morgenländischen Gesellschaft*.

Arabic Manuscripts: Author Index

References are to the running numbers of the catalogue.

Abū ʿAmr, ʿUthmān b. Abī Bakr al-Mālikī 8
Abū Ḥanīfa, al-Nuʿmān b. Thābit 38
al-Anbārī, ʿAbd al-Raḥmān b. Muḥammad 2, 5
al-Bābilī, Aḥmad b. Muḥammad b. Aḥmad 50
al-Bākūhī, ʿAbd al-Rashīd b. Ṣāliḥ 1
al-Barmakī, Yaḥyā b. Abī Bakr b. Muḥammad 59
al-Bayḍāwī, ʿAbdullāh b. ʿUmar 31
al-Bisṭāmī, ʿAbd al-Raḥmān b. Muḥammad b. ʿAlī b. Aḥmad 43
al-Dawwānī, Jalāl al-Dīn 59
Faṣīḥ, Aḥmad Dede 24
al-Futūḥī, ʿUthmān 52
Ḥafīd al-Taftāzānī, Aḥmad b. Yaḥyā 18
al-Ḥarīrī, al-Qāsim b. ʿAlī 2, 4
Ḥasan Efendizāda, Yaḥyā b. Aḥmad al-Deñizlī 62
Ibn Kamāl Pāshā, Aḥmad b. Sulaymān 9, 14, 32, 60, 67, 68, 69
al-Isfarāʾīnī, Muḥammad b. Muḥammad 6
al-Īshī, Muḥammad b. al-Tīrawī 57
Jāmī, ʿAbd al-Raḥmān 19, 20, 59
al-Jazūlī, Muḥammad b. Sulaymān 54, 55
Khaṭībzāda, ʿUthmān al-Chūnkushī 61
al-Khiṭāʾī, ʿUthmān Mullāzāda 17
al-Kisāʾī, Muḥammad b. ʿAbdullāh, Abū Jaʿfar 47
al-Maʿlqarawī, Muḥammad Amīn b. Muḥammad 64
al-Mubarrad, Muḥammad 2, 3
al-Nasafī, Abu al-Barakāt ʿAbdullāh b. Aḥmad b. Maḥmūd 40
al-Nasafī, Najm al-Dīn ʿUmar b. Muḥammad 39
Niyāzī Miṣrī 21
al-Qoyulḥiṣāri/al-Ḳoyulḥiṣārī, Tāhir Ḥilmī b. Aḥmad 63
al-Ṣaghānī, al-Ḥasan Muḥammad b. al-Ḥasan 48
al-Suyūṭī, Jalāl al-Dīn 22
al-Taftāzānī, Saʿd al-Dīn Masʿūd b. ʿUmar 7
al-Ūshī, ʿAbdullāh b. ʿUthmān, Sirāj al-Dīn 33
al-Yaḥṣūbi, ʿIyāḍ b. al-Mūsā 49

Arabic Manuscripts: Title Index

References are to the running numbers of the catalogue.

Anwār al-tanzīl wa asrār al-ta'wīl 31
al-ʿAqīda al-Nasafīya 39, 40
Asrār al-ṭahāra 51
Badʾ al-amālī 33
Basṭ al-maqbūḍ fī ʿilm al-ʿarūḍ 5
Bushrā al-karīm al-amjad bi-ʿadm taʿdhīb man tusammā bi'sm nabīhi Aḥmad aw Muḥammad 52
Ḍabt al-muḍāriʿ min lisān al-ʿAjam 15, 68
Dalāʾil al-khayrāt 54, 55
al-Ḍawʾ [ʿalā al-Miṣbāḥ] 6
al-Fiqh al-akbar 38
Ḥāshiya ʿalā sharḥ Mukhtaṣar al-maʿānī 17, 18
Ḥawāshī ʿalā sharḥ Mukhtaṣar al-maʿānī Talkhīṣ Miftāḥ al-ʿulūm li-Khaṭīb Dimashq ʿalā Miftāḥ al-ʿulūm li'l-Sakkākī 16
Ijāza 61, 62, 63, 64
al-Jawāhir fī uṣūl al-dīn ʿalā madhhab al-Imām Abū Ḥanīfa 41
Kitab al-duʿāʾ 34, 53
Kitāb al-khayl 12
Kitāb al-malakūt 47
Majmūʿa fī al-fiqh al-Ḥanafī 37
Majmūʿa: 3 Kutub ʿan al-lugha al-ʿArabīya, wa al-iʿrāb wa al-ʿarūḍ 2
Majmūʿā munshaʾāt 24
Majmūʿa rasāʾil mutanawwiʿa 10
Maqāmāt 22
Masāʾil wa ajwiba ʿalā kitāb fī uṣūl al-fiqh al-Ḥanafī 36
Masāʾil wa ajwiba: ḥāshiya ʿalā kitāb majhūl fī uṣūl al-fiqh 35
Mashāriq al-anwār al-nabawīya min ṣiḥāḥ al-akhbār al-Muṣṭafawīya 48
Mulḥāt al-iʿrāb wa subḥat al-ādāb 4
Muqaddima fī al-basmala wa al-ḥamdala 50
Muqaddimatā al-taṣrīf wa al-khaṭṭ 8
Nawādir wa maḥāsin min shuʿarāʾ wa udabāʾ ahl al-Jibāl wa Fars … 23
al-Qawāʾid al-Fārisīya 9, 13, 14, 67
Qurʾān 25, 26, 27, 28, 29, 30
Rasāʾil fī al-lugha al-Fārisīya 13
Rasāʾil al-ḥikma 56
Rasāʾil Ibn Kamāl Pāshā 60
Rasāʾil Ikhwān al-ṣafāʾ 58
Rasāʾil al-Mubarrad wa ghayrihi 3
Rawḍat al-ʿulamāʾ 57
Risāla ʿalā al-qawāʿid al-Fārisīya 9, 14, 67
Risāla fī al-ʿarūḍ 19
Risāla fī ḍabṭ al-muḍāriʿ 15, 68
Risāla fī al-iʿjāz 12
Risāla fī al-kuḥl 12
Risāla fī al-maṣdar fī al-Fārisīya 69
Risāla fī al-qiyās 60
Risāla fī Yawm al-Qiyāma 42, 43
Sharḥ ʿalā kitāb Maṣābīḥ al-sunna li'l-Baghawī wa ghayrihi 46
Sharḥ al-Maṣābīh 44
al-Sharḥ al-Muṭawwal 7
[Sharḥ] al-Ṣiḥāḥ 45
Sharḥ Talkhīṣ al-Miftāḥ 7
al-Shifā bi-taʿrīf ḥuqūq al-Muṣṭafā 49
Sirāj al-ẓulma wa al-raḥma 59
Tafsīr al-Bayḍāwī 31
Tafsīr Kamāl Pāshāzāda 32
Talkhīṣ al-āthār jamīʿ mā waṣal ilayya min laṭāʾif ṣunʿ Allāh 1
Taʿrīfāt wa iṣṭilāḥāt 11
Tasbīʿ al-Qaṣīda al-Burda 21
al-ʿUmda fī ʿaqīdat ahl al-sunna wa al-jamāʿa 40
al-Wāfī bi-qawāʿid ʿilm al-qawāfī 20

Concordance of Arabic Manuscripts

References are to the running numbers of the catalogue.

Accession number	Catalogue number
A1	54
A2	58
A3	7
A4	56
A5	62
A6	26
A7	61
A8	64
A10 (I–XV)	10, 11, 12
A11	60
A12	55
A13	53
A14	30
A15	47
A16 (I–IV)	37, 38, 39, 40, 41
A17	52
A18	31
A19	57
A20	22
A21	8
A22	6
A23	48
A24 (I–II)	42, 43
A25 (I–II)	50, 23
A26	35
A27	36
A28	27
A29	39
A30	60
A31	32
A32	36
A33 (I–III)	2, 3, 4, 5
A34 (I–II)	16, 17, 18
A35	63
A36	1
A37 (I–II)	44, 45
A38	66
M1 (I–IV)	9, 13, 14, 15, 19, 20

(*cont.*)

Accession number	Catalogue number
M4/II	51
P9	25
T10	28
T15/I	21
T77(V)	59
T108(A)	24
T109 (I–II)	33, 34

Persian Manuscripts: Author Index

References are to the running numbers of the catalogue.

Aḥmad-i Dāʿī 21
Farāhī 20
Faṣīḥ, Aḥmad 15
al-Ghazālī 17
Ḥāfiẓ 10
Ḥalīmī 22, 23, 24
Idrīs Bidlīsī 1
Jāmī 11, 33, 34
Kūshyār b. Labbān 31
Muʿammāʾi, Ḥusayn 12
Naṣīr al-Dīn Ṭūsī 18
Niʿmat Khān, ʿĀlī 3, 14
Rashīd al-Dīn Vaṭvāṭ 4
Riyāżī 26
Saʿdī 5, 6, 7, 8, 9
Ṣāʾib Tabrīzī 13
Shāhidī 25
Shīrāzī 2
Vahbī 29

Persian Manuscripts: Title Index

References are to the running numbers of the catalogue.

Akhlāq-i Nāṣirī 18
Akhlāqnāma 19
Būstān 8
Dastūr al-ʿamal 26
Dīvān-i Ḥāfiẓ 10
Dīvān-i Ṣāʾib Tabrīzī 13
Document 32
Farhang-i Fārsī Turkī 27
Gulistān 5
Gulistān va bihi muʿīd 6
Ḥadāʾiq al-siḥr 4
Hasht bihisht 1
Ḥusn u ʿIshq 14
Jahānnumā 30
Kīmiyā-yi saʿādat 17
Kitāb-i sukhanī-i Khudāʾī 30
Lughat-i Bustān 9
Lughat-i Gulistān 7
Lughat-i Ḥalīmī 22, 23, 24
Majmūʿa-i munshaʾāt 15
Munākaḥa-i Ḥusn u ʿIshq 14
Mushkilāt-i Shāhnāma 28
Niṣāb-i ṣibyān 20
Qurʾān 16
Risāla-i muʿammā 12
Rūznāmcha 3
Tarkhānnāma 2
Tuḥfa-i Shāhidī 25
Tuḥfa-i Vahbī 29
Tuḥfat al-ikhtiyārāt 3
ʿUqūd al-jawāhir 21
Yūsuf u Zulaykhā 11

Concordance of Persian Manuscripts

References are to the running numbers of the catalogue.

Accession no.	Running no.	Author & title
P1	1	Idrīs Bidlīsī, *Hasht bihisht*
P2	10	Ḥāfiẓ, *Dīvān*
P3	2	al-Shīrāzī, *Tarkhānnāma*
P4	12	Muʿammāʾī, *Risāla-i muʿammā*
P5	13	Ṣāʾib Tabrīzī, *Dīvān*
P6	31	Kūshyār b. Labbān, *Tuḥfat al-ikhtiyārāt*
P7/I	20	Farāhī, *Niṣāb-i ṣibyān*
P7/II	21	Aḥmad-i Dāʿī, *ʿUqūd al-jawāhir*
P8	30	... *Jahānnumā*
P9	16	[*Tarjama-i*] *Qurʾān*
P10/I	5	Saʿdī, *Gulistān*
P10/II	8	Saʿdī, *Būstān*
P11	19	[*Akhlāqnāma*]
P12	17	Ghazālī, *Kīmiyā-yi saʿādat*
P13	18	Nāṣir al-Dīn Ṭūsī, *Akhlāq-i Nāṣirī*
P14/I	3	Niʿmat Khān, *Rūznāmcha-i ... Ḥaydarābād*
P14/II	14	Niʿmat Khān, *Ḥusn u ʿIshq*
P15	11	Jāmī, *Yūsuf u Zulaykhā*
P16	32	[Document about property]
M4/III	4	Rashīd al-Dīn Vaṭvāṭ, *Ḥadāʾiq al-siḥr*
T16	22	Ḥalīmī, *Lughat*
T17/I	28	*Mushkilāt-i Shahnāma*
T17/II	9	*Lughat-i ... Būstān*
T17/V	7	*Lughat-i ... Gulistān*
T21/I	25	Shāhidī, *Tuḥfa*
T57/I	26	Riyāżī, *Dustūr al-ʿamal*
T57/II	27	[*Farhang-i Fārsī-Turkī*]
T80/I	29	Vahbī, *Tuḥfa*
T106	6	Saʿdī, *Gulistān va bihi muʿīd*
T107	23	Ḥalīmī, *Lughat*
T108	15	Faṣīḥ, [... *Munshaʾāt* ...]
T119	24	Ḥalīmī, *Lughat*
Addenda		
M1/II	33	Jāmī, *Risāla-i ʿarūż*
M1/IV	34	Jāmī, *Mukhtaṣar-i vāfī bi-qavāʿid ʿilm-i qavāfī*

Printed in the United States
By Bookmasters